BENT

ON WRITING

BENT

ON WRITING

CONTEMPORARY QUEER TALES

edited by **ELIZABETH RUTH**

Bent on Writing: Contemporary Queer Tales | Edited by Elizabeth Ruth

The first paperback edition published in 2002 by
Women's Press | 180 Bloor Street West, Suite 1202 | Toronto, Ontario | M5S 2V6
www.womenspress.ca

"Monologue of the Mandible" by Anurima Banerji is reprinted courtesy of Sinha Dance.
"Nine New Undershirts" and "Storks of Kampala" by Maureen Hynes were previously
published by Brick Books in Harm's Way, by Maureen Hynes, 2001. Reprinted with
permission. "Alberta" by Karen Woodman was previously published in Pottersfield Portfolio,
Vol. 20, No. 3 (Summer 2000). Ten Good Seconds of Silence by Elizabeth Ruth, from which
an excerpt has been reprinted, was published by Dundurn Press, 2001. "UNCOMFORTED" by
Margaret Christakos was previously published by Coach House Books in Excessive Love
Prostheses, by Margaret Christakos, 2002. Reprinted with permission. "In the night, suddenly" by Sina Queyras was previously published by ECW Press in Slip, by Sina Queyras, 2001.
Reprinted with permission. "The Money Shot" by Zoe Whittall is reprinted from The Best
10 Minutes of Your Life, published by McGilligan Books (2001), all rights reserved.

Every reasonable effort has been made to identify copyright holders. Women's Press
would be pleased to have any errors or omissions brought to its attention.

Women's Press gratefully acknowledges financial assistance for our publishing activities
from the Ontario Arts Council, the Canada Council for the Arts, and the Government
of Canada through the Book Publishing Industry Development Program.

NATIONAL LIBRARY OF CANADA CATALOGUING IN PUBLICATION DATA

Main entry under title:

Bent on writing : contemporary queer tales / edited by Elizabeth Ruth.

Includes bibliographical references.
ISBN 0-88961-403-2

1. Lesbians' writings, Canadian (English) 2. Gays' writings, Canadian (English)
3. Lesbianism–Literary collections. 4. Homosexuality–Literary collections. 5. Canadian
literature (English)–Women authors. I. Ruth, Elizabeth

PS8235.L47B46 2002   C810.8'0353   C2002-901733-5
PR9194.5.L47B46 2002

COVER & BOOK DESIGN Zab Design & Typography

02 03 04 05 06 07 08   6 5 4 3 2 1

Printed and bound in Canada by Transcontinental

To Shannon Olliffe for her years of tireless work behind the scenes and in the sound booth.

CONTENTS

Acknowledgements

Thanks to Althea Prince, Jack Wayne and all at Canadian Scholars' Press/ Women's Press for supporting this project, and to Makeda Silvera for reading the manuscript and for offering feedback. I would also like to recognize the past and current management at the Red Spot for providing space for Clit Lit. Thanks to the women with whom I work at *Fireweed*, who have taught me much about editing. A special thank you goes out to gulzar raisa charania for her graffiti pages idea, and to Gretel and Isaac Meyer Odell for computer rescues. I'd like to acknowledge Karen X. Tulchinsky for her early vision with Dyke Words. The Clit Lit audience, a most loyal group, deserves acknowledgement, as does *Herizons* magazine for its 2001 feature on the reading series. And finally, I would like to recognize the more than four hundred individuals who have read and performed their work at Clit Lit between 1998 and 2002, and the hundreds yet to read.

Introduction

Bent On Writing is more than a collection of queer women's writing in the new millennium: it's a glimpse into the very intimate life of a shockingly beautiful and talent-filled reading series that continues on today. Here you will find work that is sublime and subtle, brilliantly structured and lyrical. Poetry that moves to fresh rhythms. You will find creative non-fiction that tackles personal experience alongside fiction born from fierce and untamed imaginations. *Bent On Writing* is sensuous, well-crafted, sometimes gritty verse.

Good writing breeds good writing. I believed that when I founded the Clit Lit reading series in the fall of 1998, and I believe it still. Writers find inspiration and motivation in community, not only in abject isolation. Good writing breeds good writing and the way to promote innovative, inspiring art is to draw an enthusiastic audience, introduce themes of interest, provide an energetic and encouraging host and above all, mix established and emerging writers at the same events. Let them learn from each other. Allow the established writer to remember what those early sparks of inspiration felt like, and expect her to raise the bar for the rest of us.

For four years and running, the first Monday of each month, Clit Lit has been Canada's only monthly queer literary series. *Bent On Writing* is meant as a permanent and lasting record of the energy and spark which ignited and continues to burn on a small literary stage. I hope it encourages others, in faraway communities perhaps, to begin their own word-based events.

From its inception, the setting for the series has been a restaurant/lounge called the Red Spot in the heart of the "gay ghetto" in Toronto, Canada. Inside, it is dark and lush, with dramatic deep red walls and black tables and floor. The stage sits at one end of the long space and is framed with floor-length red velvet curtains. On the stage I usually place two tall stools: one for the reader if need be, and the other for a glass of water. Flyers for the event are hand-delivered and floating about the room before we begin. Sometimes I pass around a donation jar with the words "Fund For Thought" taped on to help offset the cost of photocopying. Other than this, the event has always been free, and that is important to me. The evening begins with banter and humour at the microphone (which from time to time requires duct tape to remain operational). I introduce each author with a brief biography; after the first five or six readings, we take a break and return for the second half. The entire event runs from seven o'clock to about quarter to ten and each reader is allotted an equal amount of time. Most events are themed in order to encourage writers to write to a deadline on a particular topic. The themes presented within this collection, much like those presented live onstage, are contemporary, traditional, edgy, timely, taboo and whimsical.

Over the past two decades there have been other collections of women's writing in Canada, including lesbian and gay writing, writing about feminism, class consciousness, or the intersections of race, class and gender. More recently, because of their own tenacity, there is a greater public transexual presence in the arts. *Bent On Writing* emerges from this rich tradition and builds on the work of writers such as those found in Beth Brant's *A Gathering of Spirit*[2], *Dykewords*[3], Makeda Silvera's *Piece of My Heart*[4] and the 1998 innovation *Boys Like Her*[5] — set down by Anna Camilleri, Ivan E. Coyote, Zoe Eakle and Lyndell Montgomery. American writers Dorothy Allison, Joan Nestle, Kate Bornstein, Leslie Feinberg and Judith Halberstam are but a few who've consistently challenged and disrupted traditional notions of gender, sex and sexual identity through their writing. As such, they too have provided the context and departure point for this collection. *Bent On Writing* picks up their varied and overlapping conversations and sets them down in a fresh literary space where contemporary queers may further bend and stretch their senses of self and community and, of course, the page.

More than a traditional anthology, *Bent On Writing* springs from live performance and so brings together three-dimensional talent for the two-dimensional page. It features the writers as much as it does the writing — sharing with you their reflections on the reading series and it measures the socio-political and personal relevance of a decidedly queer literary space, as well as presenting original work. Having these writings contextualized by the authors themselves and showcased in the context of the series stays true to the workshop aspect of Clit Lit, and to the writing process that brought these authors to the point of publication.

Whatever their sexual and gender orientation, the writers here have joined in the creation of sexually transgressive art. Straight women read at the series and so are included. Gay men also. F to Ms. M to Fs. Lesbians.

Dykes. Bisexuals and, without a doubt, those who reject all labels. These writers have made the audience laugh and cry with tales never before told. They've put a fresh spin on an old formula. They've inspired silence so thick it was hard for the audience to breathe after they were done. Many who've graced the Clit Lit stage consider themselves to be professional artists and have gone on to achieve great success with their writing — being widely published, receiving grant money to continue long-term projects. Some, including Nalo Hopkinson, Margaret Christakos and Karen X. Tulchinsky, to name but three, have watched their novels take flight, earning nominations for and winning national and international literary awards. Some have been signed on by literary agents, have started their own writing groups, or have gone back to school for creative writing courses. Many have simply experienced the joy and exhilaration of reading their work in public and for the very first time. All of these are equally worthwhile experiences. Art is for everyone and a reading series is just one way to share it. This collection is another.

The Clit Lit audience, which monthly numbers in the hundreds, is comprised of both writers and non-writers. Spoken-word artists who want a place to gather not organized around the club scene. Queer and straight poets and playwrights and storytellers of all ages, along with those who just love a good show. The audience and the entertainers complete each other. They are the flip side of any wildly successful artistic endeavour and at Clit Lit, performance has always been emphasized. Writers at all levels need an audience. Now Bent On Writing brings some of them to you in print.

Here you will find a sample of the hundreds who contributed to the reading series over the course of its first four years. They are a reflection of the audience — varied in age, ethnicity, gender, political perspective and sexual orientation. They identify themselves to differing degrees as artists, queers, political beings. Some insist on the primacy of their writing selves while others identify themselves as workers, mothers, lawyers, professors, secretaries, construction workers and so on first. Here you will also find suggestions for writing exercises, graffiti pages to get you going on your own mad writing journey and hopefully, the inspiration to begin. The contributors' styles and subject matter are as varied as their backgrounds, but they always entertain and frequently challenge us to think in a different direction. (Agents scouting new clients and publishers looking for the real "cutting-edge" author would do well to pop by from time to time.)

This collection features writers who might say they "just happen to be queer" and "write fiction for a broader audience" as well as those who insist on the primacy of queerness in their work. The latter "queer-identified" writers see themselves as lesbian, bisexual, transgendered, transsexual or gay writers, and insist that queer themes *are* universal themes. All are vital to a thriving literary culture. All authors presented here write bent, challenging stories, either thematically or stylistically. Some write from a straight male perspective; some choose the third or first person narration. Some use the genres of sci-fi and mystery or the Gothic and film noir traditions in order to subvert the canon. Others are traditionalists through and through, and simply seek to hone their craft as authors of literary fiction while gaining public exposure. Some are spoken-word artists who prefer to share their work through live performance but who've agreed to share it here. Many are closeted novelists and poets who, like Dorothy Allison[6], spent years writing in secret or destroying their words before anyone had the oppor- tunity to hear them. (One woman from out of town was so moved by the first few readers one night that she approached me with a piece she'd just "had to" write in the washroom during the break. I squeezed her into the line-up for the second set and that night her impassioned words stole the show.) Some writers are born and some are made – just like queers.

Anyone who has done the literary circuit can attest to the fact that there is a certain insider, exclusionary feeling about showing up at a literary event. It seems to come with the territory. Writers all appear to know one another as far as the "younger" writer is concerned, and sometimes they do. They often feel they need to suck up to the host, whom they assume to be well-connected. And then there's the open-mic nights, which most writers usually find excruciating. Someone reads about her favourite childhood toy being kidnapped by the neighbours and the years of therapy that ensued, and then this is followed by a rabid diatribe aimed at some poor sop's ex-wife. You know what I mean. So Clit Lit has never been an open-mic event. Readers book their spots one or two months in advance. Works-in-progress have always been welcomed, including novel excerpts, with the caveat that the writer must be prepared for instantaneous feed- back from the audience.

But what about the fact that Clit Lit is a predominantly queer reading series? Am I contributing to the further marginalization of these writers by providing such a forum? I have been asked this question many times and I have asked it of myself. It first needs to be said that Clit Lit, like other arts-based cultural events, stands not in relation to anything else, but in relation to itself. It is not a reaction to an absence in the mainstream literary world — it's an addition. An opening. A creative endeavour that expands artistic possibilities. Everyone is welcome. Still, the question persists: "Does there really need to be a queer reading series?" Aren't we now in fact enjoying a label-free post-gay cultural evolution? Depends who you ask. Depends who's doing the asking. I say that *all* writers need to practice gaining confidence in their voices on stages where they know they are welcome before they decide to venture farther out. And all writers begin among their own communities, whatever those may be. With Clit Lit I was able to provide one starting point. But still, a queer literary series?

Imagine the possibilities for community-building and for the development of your own writing potential. Consider the voices you rarely hear on stages, even today. It has long been my belief — and here I speak only for myself — that writers are writers *first* and that, as British novelist Jeanette Winterson has already asserted, who we fuck should not be more important than what we write. I also think that queer material, in all its glorious and inglorious incarnations, will eventually make its way onto mainstream stages to be shared among all. The writers at Clit Lit are authentic and talented and may also choose to read at mainstream series if they wish. Many do. To my mind, art is not created for limited, censored consumption. It is exciting for me to run into writers whom I know began at Clit Lit, on other stages. To me it means there are fewer boundaries separating artists from their work and artists from their audiences. A queer series or collection doesn't detract from any of that. In fact, it adds.

As a novelist whose literary passions and subject matter do not exclusively or even primarily deal with sexuality, I attend and read at many literary events. I have never seen as devoted an audience as I have at Clit Lit and this tells me that there remains a need to be filled. Queer writers, poets and spoken-word artists are hungry for a place to gather. They are not turning up in droves to brave the open-mic nights at some of the more high-profile literary events. They are sitting at home, hunched over their desks with their material and I, always a snoop, am still terribly interested to read over their shoulders.

Clit Lit is both a literary and a community event and in this challenges some of our notions of what constitutes "real" art — real art still being rumoured to be neatly tucked away in a dark smoky room, disconnected from our material, socio-political realities. Okay, the Red Spot is also dark and sometimes very smoky, and a few writers there might define "true" art as apolitical, but the majority would likely reject the notion of any absolute, even the simple idea that any writing can be void of political content or context. The writers presented in this collection are sometimes also activists, visual artists, musicians and academics, engaged in changing the socio-political and economic structures within which we all live. This interests them. Many, by virtue of their active connection to the outside world (not just the inner workings of their creative processes), do not fit the traditional stereotype of the writer as a solitary isolationist, obsessively creating art *about* but not *of* the world. Most hold full-time day jobs unrelated to their writing. A few who've read at the series lived in shelters or, in one case, on the street. An even smaller few are fortunate enough to be able to make a living full-time from their writing.

Throughout the series I have always welcomed words not likely to make it onto mainstream literary stages because of their specificity — since queer is still considered a special literary interest group — or because of the graphically erotic nature of the material, or, some would argue, because of the revolutionary potential in the content, regardless of the writer's identity. Readers are invited to return a second time with more polished and sophisticated work and in this way, as you'll read from the writers themselves, the event is as much a literary workshop as it is a reading series. As organizer, I have offered to meet with beginning writers for editing and moral support, checked in with every first-time reader afterwards and incorporated others' suggestions for change into the series.

When I started Clit Lit I had no idea that I would still be curating it four and a half years later. All I knew then was that I wanted to be part of an intimate writing community. In Vancouver, where I'd just been living, I had attended Dyke Words, a regular lesbian reading night which ran successfully for a number of years, and upon returning home to Toronto I'd assumed there must be something similar. I soon realized that there was not, and that if I wanted to find a regular and ongoing community of queer women writers I'd have to create one myself. I began making calls. Art spaces and queer bars wanted to charge a large fee at the door, one that I couldn't afford and that would have made the event economically inaccessible. I couldn't find a venue that would take a chance on the series that wasn't also institutional-looking (the local community centre, for example). Managers and club owners didn't believe that enough people would show up to make it worth their while in sales at the bar. The only space I was offered for free at the time was called the Red Spot, and only on a Monday night, when traffic and sales needed bolstering. Fine. If the event was going to succeed at all, I reasoned, a Monday night wouldn't be the deterrent. The place had a stage and a functioning sound system. Local artists hung their paintings on the walls. The cook made amazing food. What else did we need? So I committed to one year and assured the owner that the audience would buy lots of drinks. (Coming from me, someone who doesn't drink ever, this was said with extra conviction to make it sound like a sure thing.)

Sitting on the parquet floor of my bachelor apartment in 1998 I then began to get nervous. Could I really get people out to listen to writing? I spent a lot of time thinking about what would make Clit Lit unique. I decided that by attaching a theme to each event I would double interest, and that I would see my role as one of host rather than strictly MC, offering support for new writers if they wanted it. I would maintain regular contact with those who read, by phone and later with monthly e-mail announcements. Just maybe with enough effort it could fly.

A couple of months later my partner and I sat on that same floor toying with potential names for the still-hypothetical series. I didn't want to promote the idea of esoteric lesbian poems full of fruit or water metaphors. (Enough of those already!) I didn't want to sound too highbrow either, and risk alienating folks who might just try the series because it was queer but who don't usually attend literary events. I wanted a short catchy title that stood out and suggested queer, women and literary but didn't take itself too seriously. I won't bore you with the many bizarre and downright dreary names we came up with that day, but finally Shannon blurted out, "What about Clit Lit?" I liked it. It's bold, I know. That's exactly why it works. Like it or not, nobody ever forgets.

Then came postering, which I did on roller blades for the first two years, speeding across Toronto, popping in and out of stores and agencies. At home I called everyone I knew each month. At work I used the fax machine to announce the series. I sent press releases to the media, and as a result Clit Lit readers have been filmed, televised and broadcast on radio numerous times. I carried flyers to every cultural and artistic event that I attended during 1998 and 1999. I handed them out. I had to push to actively create a community. It worked. At the first event forty audience members showed up — double what I'd expected. I was pleased, but not satisfied. More publicity. More calls. More flyers went up all over the city and further afield. Sixty people turned up at the second event, and today the house is routinely packed.

It has been important to me that Clit Lit partner up with grassroots arts and cultural organizations. For example, the May editions of Clit Lit have joined with the Mayworks Festival of Working People and the Arts in past years. The series launched a collection on lesbian parenting with the Association for Research on Mothering — a York University group — at a night entitled Dykes with Tykes. Clit Lit has hosted the launches for two anthologies from Arsenal Pulp Press and peddled books by local authors. All of this serves to keep the series fresh, dynamic and socially relevant, and to bring in new blood. Over the past two years I have sought to continue diversifying participation and so have asked for proposals from guest curators, who take on the responsibilities of hosting a particular month's event. There have been guest-curated Black History/African Liberation Month events, a night of writing by youth aged sixteen to twenty-five, a Trans Sex Fiction event focused on sexy work by transsexuals. Increasingly I am encouraging multimedia approaches to word-based art: video, visual arts, radio. By broadening the scope of what is considered "literary," I have been able to extend the series' reach beyond my own grasp and see new artists and audiences become involved.

So here it is: living history on the printed page, some "how-to" information and the book *Bent On Writing*. Welcome to Clit Lit. We hope to see you out one day.

Elizabeth Ruth, Toronto, 2002

ENDNOTES

1. Tulchinsky, Karen X., Ed., *Hot & Bothered: Short Short Fiction on Lesbian Desire,* Volumes 1, 2 and 3 (Vancouver: Arsenal Press, 1998, 1999, 2001) and *Queer View Mirror,* Volumes 1 and 2, eds. James C. Johnstone and Karen X. Tulchinsky (Vancouver: Arsenal Press, 1996, 1997).

2. Brant, Beth, Ed., *A Gathering of Spirit: A Collection by North American Indian Women* (Toronto: Women's Press, 1984).

3. The Lesbian Writing and Publishing Collective, Ed., *Dykewords: An Anthology of Lesbian Writing* (Toronto: Women's Press, 1990).

4. Silvera, Makeda, Ed., *A Piece of My Heart: A Lesbian of Colour Anthology* (Toronto: Sister Vision Press, 1991).

5. Taste This Collective, *Boys Like Her: Transfictions* (Vancouver: Press Gang Publishers, 1998).

6. At her 1998 Music Hall reading in Toronto, Canada, author Dorothy Allison spoke to the audience about the power of words, about the fear of exposing personal experience through fiction and of burning her writing for years before a friend finally interevened and saved the manuscript that later became the award-winning debut, *Bastard Out of Carolina* (New York: Penguin Books, 1992).

BENT

ON WRITING

❧ KATHRYN PAYNE

IN NOVEMBER 2001, I finally got to take my clothes off onstage. Are you hooked? Good. Now, flash back to a few weeks earlier when I received an e-mail from Chanelle. She's one of those fabulous loud, sexy, smart and able women — you know the sort. Her note said that she and Karleen were guest-curating the next Clit Lit, the theme was "Hussies for Humanity" and they'd love it if I'd read. I was flattered — a night about sex and politics curated by those two was sure to be interesting. I quickly threw a reply back at her: I'd love to. However, when I got home and went digging in my "recently-written" file, I wondered if I should have waited until the "Long Rants About Your Relationship" theme night. It's not like the file was bursting with racy porn or even caustic slut-talk. Unlike a few years ago, when my wee book of poems was published, I'm not hitting the double digits when my annual lay totals are added. I'm not writing an angst-ridden poem about each of the digits either. Instead I have been writing prosy rants about whatever has most recently made me indignant, character pieces and the odd quirky poem.

What the hell was I going to read? My girlfriend was definitely not ready to stand at the back of the bar while I read a poem about her tits and tummy, that was for sure (although the training is progressing nicely). I couldn't do my best piece of porn, because I'd already read it at the launch of Masturbation Week. The fuck-corporate-rule rants are good, but seriously neglect the whole hussy element. I did have a piece I'd written about the last bathhouse — but it was one of those rants that I mentioned above, and I didn't know if I could get up there at Clit Lit and chastise my own community for being chicken shit prudes when I wasn't exactly the Wonder Woman of sex these days.

The bathhouse — the Pussy Palace — had been a major coup for the Toronto dyke community. No longer the sole purview of fags, bathhouse nights had been held maybe four times a year over the past few. The organizing committee had done a great job advertising the events, getting

1

KATHRYN PAYNE

volunteers to do everything from work the door to lap dance, and they had even managed to make a bit of money from the bar proceeds. Two bathhouses ago, however, we'd been busted. The Toronto police force had sent in two undercover chicks and then, despite the fact that these are *women's* events, sent in five ogling, rude, power-tripping male police officers to investigate supposed and very minor liquor-licensing violations. The upshot of this had been that two of my friends (whose names were on the liquor permit) were charged, and nearly every woman at the busted bathhouse felt violated — like our one safe sexy spot had been pissed on. It was decided to skip the booze at the following bathhouse, so the cops had no excuse to drop by. Unfortunately, the spirit of the whole thing had taken a beating. Our initial confidence that the cops wouldn't bug us like they did the fags because it would just be too politically volatile had been proven naïve. The court case[1], still going at the time of the next bathhouse night, seemed to make the atmosphere, well, restrained. This was the subject of my rant.

I spent days mulling over the piece. See, I believe that part of the writer's task is to piss people off. It's an artist's job generally to stir stuff up, challenge assumptions, take risks and cause trouble. But there's a line to be walked. Because it's also our job to respect those we try to represent, as many an insulted ex-lover has told me. It is our job to tell truths, to say things others won't or can't or don't, but it's also our responsibility to take ourselves to task and hold ourselves to the standards we illuminate for others. I decided that I could use the "'Barring' of the Bathhouse" rant for Clit Lit, but in order to mitigate my own hypocrisy and emphasize the point of the piece, I would take off my clothes to read it. So that fateful Monday when I got home from work, I didn't change straight into my PJs, but set to work putting on garters, stockings and G-string under an otherwise not-exceptional outfit. The underthings were intended to minimize the legal risk to the bar, something I might not have worried about before the bathhouse was raided. My girlfriend, Patty, was charged with the task of writing that evening's bio while I packed a towel to wear in case I was freezing onstage, and off we went.

The time between arriving at an event and reading is always excruciating. I love reading my work out loud. I am a teacher and I stand up in front of rooms full of folks every day and perform/present with hardly a thought.

But waiting for your turn at the mic is my personal idea of hell. Wrestling with butterflies while you're trying to listen to the other readers, unable to drink a beer or blow a spliff because you mustn't slur, your lips mustn't stick together, you must be able to focus and enunciate and put expression into the (suddenly very dull-seeming) words you wrote. Wondering: Is it a good piece? Will I insult people? What if no one listens? What if I look stupid? What if I trip getting onstage? The bar was packed, and loads of the folks I like were there. I was up right after the intermission, so, well, the first half of the evening is a bit of a blur in my memory. What I do clearly recall (ah, the memory-enhancing qualities of narcissism) is being introduced. Chanelle got up to do so, and began to tell stories about things I'd written, meeting me when we were at the same university and things I'd said that had shaped her coming out, the direction of her queer-grrrl politics and sex radicalism. This flattering intro was followed by the equally complimentary bio Patty'd written. The combined effect of all of this was to wash away my nervousness in one big wave.

I took the stage and read my first two pieces — being careful to "eat" the microphone so the audience could hear me. When I was done with them, I set my papers on the stool and explained that I had to take off some clothes to read the next piece. Since I met with no objections, I took off my shirt, my shoes and my pants, apologizing for my lack of stripping skills, and climbed back onto the stool in G-string, garter, stockings and erect nipples to read my rant. The only other thing I want to tell you about was what the applause meant to me when it rose rather satisfyingly at the close of my piece. Well, above all, it meant I was done and could stop being worried. But it also meant that I wasn't the only one who saw what those asshole cops had done, and that it was all right for me to write and say what I saw, even when it was difficult and didn't cast us in the best light. And it meant that I can continue to take my clothes off in front of those people, can risk telling my truths, can keep on pushing and challenging and cherishing. Not all writers are that lucky enough to have an audience/community to give such personal, immediate feedback, to be able to look at the reasons they write, so clear in those faces as they walk off the stage.

3

KATHRYN PAYNE

ENDNOTES

1. On January 31, 2002, all charges against members of the Toronto Women's Bathhouse Committee were dismissed by Justice Peter Hryn. In his decision, Justice Hryn stated that the organizers and patrons of this event had a reasonable expectation of privacy vis-à-vis men. He was very critical of the police's failure to look for and use female officers. He said that police actions were analogous to a strip search — humiliating, degrading and devastating, particularly for women and minorities — and that the breach of the charter rights was very serious — flagrant and outrageous.

He further stated that the charter violations would shock the conscience of the public, that police actions contradicted fundamental notions of justice, fair play and decency, and were patently unreasonable. He said that the police's actions displayed a blatant disregard for the quality of humaneness which is valued by the Canadian public. And finally, that the actions of the police brought the administration of justice into disrepute.

"Barring" of the Bathhouse

What is it with dykes? Here we have our one opportunity to be big naked sleazes, to avoid the infamous pitfalls of lesbian intimacy (U-Hauls, drama, merging — for those of you not in the loop), to have anonymous sex but still call ourselves muff-divers, and what do we do? Hang around the pool in our usual cliques, with our dress-up clothes firmly on, dance like we do at every other women's event, contemplate (but never follow up on) approaching that cute unknown chick with a salacious invitation and clear out by 2:30 a.m. OK, so it's not like the rooms were empty, or no one came, or got spanked or sucked, but come on girls, where was the roaming libido? Besides the unfulfilled potential of the architecture (and the absence of booze), what made this evening radically different from our average night at the bar?

Let me tell you what I saw. I saw a bunch of sheep too timid to walk through an open gate into green green grass. I saw a kind of contagious fear, disguised as tough-assed poise, keeping its clothes on and conformities intact. I saw a communal inability to relax and get sexy without alcohol or nuptial vows. These bathhouses are our chance to break new (every-where but in Michigan) ground, to find out what a bunch of naked women hanging out in a comfy, caring, sexualized setting could get up to — but we're too cool to try.

I think the first step is getting naked, which loads of folks didn't. And, just to piss people off, I'm gonna blame the butches. Get some balls boys!!! It doesn't make you any less a man to ditch the jeans, take off the tank top and let a bit hang out. How is it fair that you won't even show us your navel when all those sexy femmes, etc., are wandering around in towels or less? Do you need that much body armour all the time? And, as it often goes with pack masculinity, y'all seem incapable of rising above the lowest common denominator. One butch I talked to told me she

5

KATHYRYN PAYNE

couldn't strip down cuz so-and-so wasn't and she couldn't be the only one with her belly showing.

The next step, I think, is getting over ourselves. Our community is just like any other grouping of folks. We have our own social structures, our stars, our status and our own sets of borders. We prefer the familiar, the similar, the already-known. We don't know how to take the risks of mixing it up. The leather girls play with each other, the artsies stand together in their well-put-together-ness, some of us cling to our girl-friends like the floaty-toys in the pool. Strangers only get small talk if they're standing in the same line-up, sitting in the hot tub next to us, or providing one of the excellent services available that evening. I mean, be honest, how many of us even met anyone new that night?

I want to know what is happening here. I mean, I think sociologists could have a hoot with this phenomenon, call it "the dyking of the sexu-al sea," the "barring of the bathhouse," or maybe "de-clawed pussies." Maybe they'd put it down to the way that we got busted last time. After all, most of us have had to work through enough of our own crap and shame and fear around having sexual agency, have practiced enough repression on ourselves, to need any help from a handful of power-trip-ping ogling pigs. Hell, I remember the flurry of get-yer-nerve-up pep-talk phone calls among my friends before that very first bathhouse, and we're not the shyest wallflowers in dykedom.

See, just like some of us shook our asses onto the streets to tell the police that it's SO not OK to disrespect our spaces, not OK to try to make us hide our fucking, we need to call our inner cops on their bullshit. We dykes are a collection of some of the gutsiest, funniest, most loving and creative people on the planet. I believe that we are a special people because nearly every one of us has had to take a good hard look at who and how we are. We could be holding each other hard in the abundant dark cor-ners of that bathhouse. We could be whispering our pride and pleasure to each other while hands move in heat and labia open in wild, willing risk. We could be breaking down the walls of fashion and association, taking strength from the common currents of our desire, flipping a sweet and naked bird at those who would have us marinate forever in shame.

But instead, most of us stood around like we're stuck in the norms of bar culture and terrified of touching too much.

Champagne Socialism

As if fisting
could cleanse all those
oh-so-classed
assumptions
out of us.
I would not be
the guilty liberal one
nor you the angry trash.

Maybe you could,
in your curled hand,
catch hold
of my expensive education
white-collar wardrobe
& property-owning aspirations.
Pull them all into the air
to rot with every other product of post-industrial capital.

Leaving me free of my
upper middle-class baggage,
no longer threat or symbol
unlikely to suggest you go back to school
or we eat out again.

If your scrunched fingers could fit
in this uptight princess cunt (lubricated with too much champagne)
you could clench,

KATHRYN PAYNE

in work-callused palm,
half of what keeps us apart.

But I can't hold your hand
inside me
any more than I can hold
my alcohol.
End up alone beside the toilet,
cocktail dress as undone as my composure,
unaltered and ashamed.

➥**KATHRYN PAYNE** is a writer, activist, teacher and slut. Her work has been printed in the *Church-Wellesley Literary Supplement* and the collection *Written in the Skin*. Her book of poems, *Longing at Least is Constant*, was published by Broken Jaw Press in 1998. In her spare time she facilitates erotic-writing workshops, is creative editor for *Torquere: Journal of the Canadian Lesbian and Gay Studies Association* and is a member of the writing group Stern Writing Mistresses. Kathryn has work forthcoming in the anthology *Brazen* (Arsenal Pulp Press, 2002).

●€ CHANELLE GALLANT

I CO-CURATED A CLIT LIT NIGHT about sex and activism entitled "Hussies for Humanity." I'd never before curated a reading event nor had I performed in public. Coordinating the event was much more fun and less stressful than I had imagined, possibly because I was coordinating it with a friend, and also because it seemed much, much, easier than the risks I was going to take with my own performance. A number of ideas had been brewing inside me for almost a year, and they seemed to burst suddenly into my head early one morning while I was showering before work. My piece was written while I was completely naked at the kitchen table, still damp from the shower, full of the zeal of inspiration. I wrote about how feminism and gender and sexuality had changed for me since my partner had begun to transition from female to male.

After years of studying and thinking about sex and gender I was damn pissed to discover that I had learned almost nothing to prepare me for trans-sexuality. Instead, when gender became a massive struggle for the one I loved, and not simply an academic parlour game, social-constructionist feminist and queer theory turned out to be totally out of touch and stunningly incapable of accounting for biology, personality and spirituality. This shocked me, and I became furious when I saw how this was affecting the women I knew in my own community.

In my community, transgendered (trannie) boys/bois who rightly unsettle the link between sex and gender have become fetishized as the ultimate symbol of gender revolution, even to the point that queer women will brag to me about their latest trannie conquest. At the same time, however, ostensibly trans-positive dykes are repelled when I talk about how my partner's transsexual experience has demonstrated to me the clear link between biology and personality. They are even more mortified when I talk about how this applies to my femininity and (gasp!) its positive relationship to masculinity. That's when some lesbian feminists leave the room. I wanted to talk to the other queer chicks in my community (straight people, not dogmatically attached to linguistic politics, are often less confused about his transition), and Clit Lit provided me with a perfect venue to put on my own show.

Underlying my desire to perform were the love, compassion and eroticism that my lover and I shared. I wanted the audience to see and feel it too, so rather than simply stand and read, I decided I would record my writing over music and have this play in the background while I performed a lap dance/striptease for him onstage. I'm not a pro dancer, but having been a bathhouse organizer, I know queer women can get into a sexy show. So we did it and the audience seemed to love it. I was selfishly thrilled to find that one transman in the audience had to run out in tears because, as he told me later, he'd been moved by the support and love evident between my partner and me. I was flooded with enthusiastic feedback, which convinced me that I must be hitting a true note. I've since considered filming the show…hmmm, still thinking about it and hunting around for good filmmakers.

Standing By My Man

I heard this woman talking about her girlfriend. She said her boy didn't even know if she wanted to be a girl, and either way isn't it just so *cute*? I wanted to cry and scream: oh yeah, dear girl do you realize what you're talking about here? Do you love her enough to stick around while your cute trannie boy sets off a bomb in your life? Do you know what it's like to tell your grandma that the girlfriend you just moved in with is now your boyfriend? Do you know how to shift, concede, re-examine everything you know about how to love a woman, a man? Have you got the balls to fuck it up over and over...and try again because she is worth that much to you? I look back and it was me I really wanted to scream at. I want to go back and shake myself and say: lord, you have NO idea what you're in for. So hunker down and take stock because a forest fire is about to race across your life, the dead wood will be set ablaze and bright hopeful eager new truths will emerge. But a fire is only pretty from a distance, so you will be scared and devastated and you will feel like a fucking champion at the end. My lover appeared, I think, to help me heal the split — the confusion about who I am and who I imagine myself to be.

My feminism has for so long been founded on the premise that gender is a social fiction, that there are no essential genders. This is the Gender-is-a-Sex-Toy school of thought. For me, a femme, this meant the freedom and ability to morph into and out of genders, turning them upside down. Gender was about ideas, theories, feminism, fun, activism. All good things. One experience of gender. One way: the queer feminist way. But not the only way, and now I see that it has very little to say to transsexual reality. Having a transsexual come into my life really was like having a bomb dropped. It set off seismic shifts underground, far from my queer theorizing brain: I knew that there were femininities that didn't work for me, but the question of what womanhood *did* mean remained unanswered.

Femininity for the feminist is difficult, dangerous terrain. What is it to be a woman? Why do I only seem to know how to play with it, articulate what it *isn't*, subvert it ironically? Feminists are tasked with redefining and reclaiming feminine gender while remaining detached from it at a deep level. I know what I'm supposed to be: independent, tough, a leader, never a follower. When I was topping in my sexual relationships I was catered to, cared for, respected and advertised. But when I got on my knees and sucked a dildo in public, for fun, cuz I like to, my feminism was called into question. Was I setting us femmes back? Should I have pretended that some of us don't like to suck cock? The feminist insistence that gender is nothing more than an elaborately maintained performance produces notions of "the bad old-fashioned and deluded transsexual" who holds a quaint belief in the fundamental truth of gender. Feminist transphobia.

Here's my truth: with my boyfriend, something started to shift. With my defences down, because I thought I was in the safe space of lesbianism, a different woman came out...tentatively at first. He brought out this woman. Long ago, the first night we met, I topped her and refused to let her buy me a drink or talk when I didn't want to listen. But at 3:00 a.m. I cried after I came and she held me saying, "I gotcha baby, I gotcha." No one calls me *baby*. How did she know? Days later, I was sitting listening to Nina Simone sing "You'd Be So Nice To Come Home To" and for reasons I can't explain, I sobbed and moaned thinking of her, imagining our lives together. I didn't understand why that felt like agony. Now I know it was because s/he reached into me and put her strong hand around all my squishy bits — my sex, my love, sadness, rage, my sadist, my desperate needy seven-year-old self, and just pumped until my creaky veins coursed with love. I had finally met my match.

A transsexual appeared in my life at the time he did and I welcomed him because my body and the universe finally concurred: the splits between my thoughts/ideas/theories and my feeling body and its place in the cosmos were eased. This is what loving a transsexual did for me; it revealed the dissonance, the lies I had placed over my body's truths. It was for me a sign of hope. Irrepressible. If I let it, if I was open, the truth about my own gender could emerge more clearly. My partner and I used to joke that he came into my life to teach me about femininity and I arrived to teach him about masculinity. We thought we were being funny and wasn't it all so ironic? We were right, but neither of us knew that this wouldn't turn out to be an academic exercise. Neither of us knew then how our changes would wrench us from the inside out, connect to all our fears and anger, sadness, love and sex. The struggle now, my purpose, is to allow my body to tell my mind, rather than the other way around, what it is and always has been for me to be a woman.

•• **CHANELLE GALLANT** is a worker-bee, writer/performer type and organizing member of the Toronto Women's Bathhouse Committee (a.k.a. the Pussy Posse). She studies sex, class and post-structuralism in her spare time at York University, where she is completing a master's degree in sociology.

13

◆ TRISH SALAH

OF COURSE I DON'T HAVE A CLIT. Not in any conventional sense. Perhaps in the future. The simple fact that I've read at Clit Lit on three separate occasions therefore might seem remarkable. It is less remarkable than the fact that it was never an issue. I've read on a lot of different stages, published in a variety of places, many of them marked as queer/feminist or women's in one way or another, and usually I've had to fight to do so, or at least I've had to bare teeth to write a not-too-polite letter. This is because I am transsexual and because non-transsexuals, particularly queers and feminists, have been, by and large, rather uncomfortable accepting us transsexuals among their ranks. Those of us who've wanted to be counted amongst them, that is. So it is very refreshing to perform in a space that is recognizably, markedly a queer women's space for making literature, and not have any grief about it. Whatsoever. Quite the reverse.

The other thing about Clit Lit that I really have loved has been the atmosphere of workshop, the fact that it is a space to bring something about which you are still thinking, working on and through, to test out. I'm not just saying that the audience members are generous and gentle in their reception of the work that is read, though they are. What I'm aiming to say is that the crowd is comprised of people who are actually attentively listening to and thinking about the work. That is, sadly, rarer than you might think at literary events, especially reading series that take place in bars. At Clit Lit I've received criticism as well as praise from audience members, really helpful, some of it. Why is the audience such a good one? In part, the curator has set the tone, very respectful, very careful — and because the people who come are, many of us, writers ourselves and we attend regularly. A certain collective competence has been fostered.

Teenage Trans Vamp

(Montreal, Fall 1987)

I masturbate in lunar cycles
with your bleeding, agile thighs
big tits in red mesh crushed
the gravity of your love
and our doom, in mind.
In the donut shop
we argue over which of us
should wear the dog collar
go down on the other.
In a room full of cops
speedy acid lets you dance for hours
round the corner at the Thunderdome
I make out with fourteen-year-olds from Longueille,
Dorval, the outer limits
At La SuperSexe you're the new favourite:
corkscrew blonde curls, ballerina body
except those tits you hate —
why you're not a ballerina —
and a face too young to be legal.
But best, with brains, they like that:
one of the regulars brings this magnetic chess set.
On slow nights the manager lets him play you
while other girls are onstage.
You gunk up my face and put me in your dress,
ripped fishnets. I look awful. I cut my face
in the bathroom mirror. You suck the glass out,
smoke me up and promise
someday I'll have tits like yours.

Love, the collusion of teethlike needles
cutting up in the backroom of the Café Commune,
velveteen seats, piles of pamphlets from the rally.
The sleaze gets me hot,
too much like work, you say.
I take my pills, the depression rolls
over the futon, I say my mantra:
idon'twannadieidon'twannadieidon'twannadieidon'twannadie
You kick me out of bed — obviously, the futon —
it's okay I masturbate in lunar cycles.
Who gets the bed,
who's on the floor tonight?
The working assumption.
After I give him head, and you, her
in some artguy's loft
I push you down stairs.
Not jealous just unable to fathom
why are you so nice to me?
Still drunk you don't remember.
My uncle, the cop, drives us home.
First you, then me.
He sticks his bony finger through a hole
in your fishnets, tears them from my thigh to
ankle, calls me Mauditte tappette.
He's not French, so it's unlikely,
him being in Montreal, in this poem
you can guess what he means.

Ghazals, from The Book of Suicides

I

Sometimes death begs permission to approach
Sometimes we are confused, death and I

As to your desire, I've lost the language
Fire whispers, tongues of black sun.

On this anniversary, of the flood, of mourning
Muddy earth rises, mute cushion to the fall.

A ray of light, your face, run amuck
It's just, the moon in shards, for shame.

Veiled, pressed to the ground, and proud,
I fell long hours to endure this peace.

II

A change of sex is not a suicide note
Or, it goes across death, to a particular word.

Veiled, you lie in the sun, your eyes wet
With what body are you leaving?

(Turning earth over, a sign, you hope, of dawn.
Sigh for the last words, the night she left behind.)

Suppose, when next we meet you do not know
This face or flesh, suppose my name is changed.

Reincarnated, skipping over death, the lovers.
I know you distrust the tale already.

III

Where who is dead is a different dead
Or word for who is a rose has arisen.

Where this death is not spoken
Or a name that we stumble over, apologize after

Your Rose kissed close, her friend and the room
How low and red, our young lips to that light.

My book of suicides began with the thought on your brow
With wine, and snow, a country house and poetry.

Neither Ghalib nor the world did imagine —
But they knew three sexes, tangled bodies' heat.

Words read in your mouth, on that night
First love, its death, forsaken, your promise.

IV

The third sex is always dead to the first,
Transcending, to the second, susceptible.

Where seducing is a virtue of finitude
A rose is kept for your garden.

And wilder growths allow you to imagine
Vast expanse beyond slant pale of headstone.

Neither the world nor Ghalib dead, imagine —
Your promise fulfilled, snow rising to heaven.

Roses bloom inward, a miniscule infinity
Bubbles of earth aflame, efflorescent with air.

V

Sometimes the dead are known to wonder
At this pass, or their past, with love

Veiled, in your room they cannot help
But want, what you've wanted, as if you

And they were in love, and your tragedy
Warded their own, gave language where

Before there was only slant pale of moon
Empty dark pierced with empty light.

Sometimes the dead are found wandering
Wordless, and dismembered, failing to recollect.

VI

A change of sex is not a suicide note,
What is a crypt? She heard him with his word.

Veiled, crossed out, divide of his mouth still open
He made her up — a language — we can only imagine

For the future, divide of the world still open
Not man or woman then — angelic, childish, feral, undead

Language keeps its own secrets, pink tongue roses, blooming
The intoxication of death or you, a body becoming its own

Name or sounding it out, slivers of cool wrists
Broken, inscribed as accident, an accent encrypting

A change of sex, the languish of your shadow,
Or the sounding bell of this word's breach:

What a sex is, is forever misled.

↝ **TRISH SALAH** Unlike most transsexual activist poets, Trish has a union job in the education sector and is damn proud to be Lebanese. Her writing has appeared in various publications, including *Border/ Lines*, *Descant*, *Tessera*, *Brazen* and *Ribsauce*, and her work is forthcoming in *Fireweed* and *Torquere*. In addition to performing at Clit Lit, Trish has performed on a number of stages including YAWP, Jerk Off Cabaret, the Free Verse Area of the Americas, and Scream in High Park. Trish is a member of the Stern Writing Mistresses and is a former editor of *index: Montreal's Literary Calendar* and the *Moosehead Anthology*. Trish's first book of poetry, *Wanting In Arabic*, will be published in fall 2002 by TSAR Books.

⬤⬥ NALO HOPKINSON

THE FRENCH POET Charles Baudelaire had a black mistress, a light-skinned woman named Jeanne Duval who worked as an entertainer and used powder to make her face even whiter. Her mother and grandmother, also black women, were prostitutes in the port city of Nantes. Before she took up with Baudelaire, Duval had a roommate, a woman who may or may not have been her lover. The following, based on that information, is an excerpt from *Griffonne*, my novel-in-progress.

Griffonne

Paris, 1842

A tiny pulse from Lisette's thigh beat under my ear: stroke, stroke, stroke. I contemplated the thick red bush of her jigger, so close to my face. I breathed her scent in deep.

"You smell?" I said.

"I smell of cunt," she laughed, making my head shake as her body shook. "And spit, and that honey powder you wear. And I have your face-chalk all over my skin." She raised up one elbow. I hung on to her uppermost thigh for purchase. Oh, so warm, so fair, her skin! She said nothing, just reached a hand. I felt a tug along my scalp. She was stroking the length of my hair, spread out so all along her legs. "Beautiful," she breathed. "My beautiful Jeanne."

"Mm." I burrowed my head in closer and tunnelled my tongue into her gully hole. Lisette giggled, then sighed, my girl, and spread her knees wider. The salty liquor of her spread in my mouth. I lapped and snuffled, held her thighs tight as she wriggled and moaned. Pretty soon she was bucking on my face, calling out and cursing me sweet. All sweaty, her thighs clamped to my ears so that my hearing was muffled. My hair was caught beneath her and it pulled, but I cared nothing for that. I reached behind her and squeezed her arse, fat as a pumpkin, and used it to pull her closer. She wailed and shoved herself at me, until to breathe at all I had to breathe in her juice. And she pitched and galloped like runaway horses, but I held her, held her down and sucked her button in, twirled my tongue around it. Then even her swears stopped, for she could manage words no longer, and only panted and moaned. The roar she gave at the end seemed to come from the pit of her, to bellow up through her sopping cunt. Back onto the bed she collapsed, and released my head. She was sobbing; gasping for breath. I wriggled up beside her and held her until she was still again. I licked my lips, sucking salt. I ran my hands through her ruddy cornsilk hair, blew on the wet place where it was plastered to her shoulder. She shivered.

"Ah, damn," she said, all soft. She kissed me. Our tongues played warm against each other. She broke from the kiss and grinned at me as if it was she, not me, who was the cat that ate the cream. "So good," was all she murmured. Then, louder: "Let me up. I need to piss."

"Go to, then," I told her. I lay and admired the smooth white moons of her bum as she climbed out of the bed. Bourgoyne was away on business, so the theatre was closed. All of us free for a time. In the corridors and from the rooms beyond this one, I could hear the voices of the other girls, high and happy with their temporary freedom. Feet scurried and there was men's laughter, too. Lise and me had scarce been out of bed for two days now. The plates of half-eaten food on the dresser and floor were getting a bit strong, and the smell of hashish filled my brain.

Lisette reached under the bed, pulled out the chamber pot, squatted over it. "What do you want to do now?" she asked.

"Bring you back to bed," I told her. She giggled. The tinkle of her piss against the pot made my bladder cramp to be emptied too. And the ache in my belly was starting back. I reached between my legs and brought my fingers away stained with red. "Fuck," I said. "Time to change the bung. You done there, Lisette?"

"Yes." She flicked the last few drops off with her fingers and wiped them on her thigh. She moved aside so that I could use the pot. I knelt over it, reached up inside myself and took hold of the plug of wadded-up bandages. It was so soaked with blood that it came out as smooth as you please. My womb heaved with it and a gush of blood dripped out into the chamber pot. I dropped the plug in too, to be washed later. "Cherie, fetch me another, would you?" I asked Lisette. "In my purse, on the dresser."

She brought it back for me and sat, watching me insert it. "I could never do that," she said. "I like the rags better."

"They smell and I can feel them wadded between my legs. I don't like none of it. Why must women have courses?"

She frowned. "Because we have babies, I guess. I don't know how it works."

"I don't have babies. I won't. So why I need this nuisance every month?"

NALO HOPKINSON

Lisette was combing her fingers through her hair and twisting it into a plait. She reached for the hookah by the bedside and pulled on it merrily. The pleasant bubbling noise grew and bounced between my ears. I inhaled the smoky air and suddenly came all over dizzy. I grabbed on to the side of the bed. My fingers left a red smear on the sheets. Lise took her mouth off the pipe and coughed a racking hashish cough. Face red, she said, "You don't want babies? Ever?"

"Never. Stillborn baby nearly killed my mother."

"I do. I want them. A girl and a boy." She edged herself to sit at the side of the bed, an eager look on her face. "I know how to tell who will get them on me, too. Shall we try it?" I pulled myself up to sit beside her. Dried my cunny off with an edge of the sheet. Time to have those sheets washed soon. I took the hookah from her and sucked its dreams into my lungs. I could hear my heart pounding in my ears. "You want to see who your true love will be?" I said, amused some and piqued some, too. "You're sure?"

She pouted, sighed. "Well, there's nothing else to do. It's hours before we meet the men at the cafe."

"Huh. I could keep you occupied, but maybe you tire of my sport?" Suddenly I was sad and dull, with that dark mood that hashish can bring on. Lise scuttled her bum close to me and hugged me tight. I turned my face away, but, devil that she was, she only took the opportunity to nibble on my ear. "We'll do it again and once more again before the night even falls, sweet," she said. I giggled at the tickle of her breath in my ear. "But I like to play at other games, too."

I kissed her. "So we shall, then. And how will you scry for your true love?"

She reached for the wine bottle on the night table; held it up to the light. There were a few sips left. "Not enough," she said, then tipped the bottle to her lips and drank down what little there was. She rested the bottle in the bed and looked around her, frowning. "We need water," she said to me. Then she smiled. Holding her plaits out of the way, she leaned over the bed and came up, triumphant and red-faced, with the chamber pot. "We can use this."

"What?" I looked with her into the chamber pot, at the orange liquid that swirled there, stirred by the unfolding plug; her piss and mine, my blood. "And what shall we do with it?"

"Oh, it's easy." She put the chamber pot down amongst the sheets. "Hold it, make sure it doesn't spill." She clambered carefully out of bed and blew out one of the candles. "Not too dark," she said. "Can you still see the liquid in the pot?"

I chuckled. "Yes, my pagan girl."

As she came back into bed, Lise told me, "Claudette showed me how to do this. Here, put the chamber pot between us."

I did as she said, and now we were both sitting cross-legged with the piss and blood between us. A faint acid smell wafted up from the pot. Yellow and red swirled in tendrils inside it.

Lise reached for the hookah, grinned at me and sucked on it until even in the shadowy room I could see the tips of her ears get red. She coughed and handed the hookah to me. "Suck the smoke in deep," she said. "It will help your sight into the otherworld to be more sharp." I giggled, and Lisette slapped my knee, sharply. "Jeanne! You must be serious."

So I bit on my lips until the urge to smile had passed, little bit. "Very well, I am sombre as a prelate." I sucked from the hookah. The warmth of the drug spread all through my body, bringing blissful ease to my aching belly. I felt I was floating. In the warm dark with my Lise, no one to bother us, anything felt possible. "What do we do now?" I asked her. My voice could have been coming from the ceiling, so far away I felt.

She took the hookah from me and put it back on the night table. She kissed my fingers, then said. "Hold my hands."

I did. So nice her hot, soft little palms felt in mine.

"Now we have the water in the chamber pot sealed in a magic circle," she said.

I was giggling again before I knew I would do it. "This is so silly, Lise!" She squeezed my hands in hers, not hard. "No, it is not. You simply must decide that it is not."

The seriousness in her voice made me sombre again. "All right. And then?"

"While we are scrying, do not break the circle of our hands. Whatever you do, we must keep hold of each other."

Suddenly I was apprehensive. "Else what?" I asked her.

"Else the vision will dissipate, and I won't see my true love!" she said. "Do you wish to scry for yours after me?"

I thought of Charles's high, pale forehead and petulant mouth, of his scribblings and his moods; his raptures and his miseries both. "I think I have done as best as I may," I told her.

"So you have," she replied. Her eyes were pink from the hashish, as though she'd been weeping.

"Oh, Lise, his family has land! He says he will take me travelling sometime! I have never been away from France."

She smiled, happy for me. "He treats you well. Me, I have no rich gentleman yet to buy me gowns."

"You will, beautiful one. Shall we do this thing now?"

"Yes. No, don't leave go of my hands! Remember to hold on." Her fingers held mine tight. "Look into the liquid in the pot, and let your mind wander, but keep one idea always before you: that you wish to see a vision of my true love."

"And he'll appear in the pot? He'll get his feet wet."

"Silly Jeanne. A vision of him will appear, as though we were looking in through a window."

"Very well." This scrying business had a flavour about it of my Grand-maman's juju, her African magic. Cleanse the floors with the morning's first urine, always keep a silver coin in a bag around your neck, with some sweet herbs in it. Harmless. I relaxed and did as Lise asked. I took a pull on the hookah, let the hashish fill my brain, open it wide. Hot, so hot in that room. I breathed out smoke. It flowed from my nostrils, seemed to swirl in the piss pot, floating on its bloody waters. I stared into the pot.

When there was money, Grand-maman would sometimes buy live chickens in the market for us to eat. She would cut their clucking throats on our back stoop, let the blood fall there. For the spirits to drink, she said. Blood was life, she said. It's life we had put in that pot, Lise and me. The smoke in there writhed and wound about the blood and piss. Something began to form. I should have been frightened? Not when sweet hashish filled me even to the tips of my fingers. I could feel a pulse ticking in Lise's warm thumbs. The smoke in the pot began to drift away, and something, an image, was moving in the orange liquid. Lise gasped, her hands clutching tight to mine. Me, I felt only a lazy, sly curiosity. Yes, show us this perfect man, I thought at the spirits swirling in the foetid pot, this man who will love my sweet Lise as though she were the frailest doll, the purest virgin.

Eh. There in the still liquid, as in a mirror. A black man. Dark as coal, as mud. "What is it?" asked Lise, then "Oh," she said; a little, sad cry.

Is this what she will come to? Making black babies? I whispered, "Hush, sweet. Don't jerk, or you may disturb the image. Maybe there's more to see."

I knew faces like his. My Grand-maman had had skin like that, and that nose. He stood in a simple, empty room. Not a chair, not a lamp. He was poor, then. He wore plain clothing, a working man's trousers and heavy shirt with a stained apron knotted around his spare middle. I felt a wash of shame for my Lise. Her hope, her true love, was an ugly black butcher. And poor.

The wash of the liquid in the chamber pot made the image shimmer. The man had a hat of some kind in his hands. I think it was a hat. Hard to tell, for he had twisted it into a mere screw of fabric between his loutish hands. He looked nervous, as well he might. Was that his house? Whose, then? Had he a right to be there? Perhaps he was a thief?

He turned at some sound we couldn't hear. He gazed off to my left. What he saw there made his face brighten as though angels had come to bid him enter heaven. Joy transformed him. They knew him in that house, then.

His lips moved; a greeting, perhaps. He reached out his hand to someone. A hand reached back towards him; a woman's hand? Was that a pink sleeve? Difficult to tell in the yellow-orange piss water. The hand placed itself firmly in the centre of his chest and pushed. He stumbled back some little bit. Oh. The woman wanted him to leave. A lovers' quarrel? His face got sorrowful, dignified. His shoulders dropped. He nodded, smoothed his poor hat out, jammed it onto his head and turned away.

The woman — Lise, I wager — was moving into the circle of the chamber pot. I could see more of her arm, the jut of a firm breast. I leaned forward. Soon I would see her face. Was my Lisette old? Was she still beautiful?

"Oh!" the real Lise exclaimed again. She picked up the pot, and before I could stop her, before I could see, she threw it across the room. It hit the wall with a tinny clang, spraying its mess everywhere. "It's not true!" she wailed. "It's not!" She clutched my hand in one of hers, and ground the heel of her other hand into her eyes. She sobbed.

I gathered her into my arms. "Hush, Lise," I said, gently this time. "Hush. Let me hold you." I rocked and rocked her as she wept storms.

"He was so foul!" she wept. "Black as the devil!"

I said nothing, only thought of the soft creases of my grandmother's face. Once Grand-maman gave me molasses in a plate, and when I ran my fingers through it, it left lines like those around her eyes and mouth. Sweet lines.

"And that apron!" lamented Lise.

I felt near to swooning from the hashish, and I was the more dizzy from the way I was rocking her, but I tried to think how to comfort her.

"Maybe it was a mistake," I said.

"No," she cried, sobbing harder. "I am to be wedded to a black, and toil all my days killing pigs, and have nigger babies."

Something, something was working in me, making me think thoughts I don't think. "Well then, my beauty," I told her, "they will look like me."

At once she grew still in my arms. She was silent some little while. Then: "Yes," she said. "Yes, they will." She turned her tear-tracked face to me and smiled, too wide. "My beautiful Lemer. I am sorry." She pulled out of my arms, scrubbed her face dry with a corner of the sheet. "This is not a day to be gloomy," she said. "We are meeting the gentlemen at the cafe, after all!"

Gently, I pulled a lock of her long, fair hair through two of my fingers. Like silk. "You won't sulk any more?"

She giggled, too loud. "How foolish of me! No, no more. It's just that I'm tired. Let me doze a while?" Even as I was nodding, she was lying back against the bed, pulling the covers over herself. She was asleep very quickly. I covered her bare shoulder. She didn't like drafts. I put my head out the door and shouted for someone to bring us some water. I went and sat on the bed, just regarding Lise's face as she slept.

A few minutes later, there was a quiet tap at the door. I opened it to see Maryvonne, holding a jug of water. To look at her always reminded me of home, of all the brown and black and teak-coloured faces of we who lived near the docks in Nantes. She smiled at me and held out the jug in her lovely plump arms. "You and Lise liking your furlough?" she asked in the French of the Nantais coloureds.

I know my smile back was rueful. "Perhaps too plenty," I said. "We are become dull and womanish." I took the jug and closed the door again. I found a discarded chemise and used it to clean the stained wall.

This week I shall send some things for Maman. The emeralds, perhaps, that Charles gave me. He's so distracted, he won't notice if I'm no longer wearing them. Maman could get good money for them. Buy herself some new shoes, and some of the good brandy for Grand-maman. Grand-maman thinks it eases her coughing. It makes her sleep, at least.

Charles has been talking of setting me up in an apartment here in Paris. I scarce dared to hope that he would. Oh, how I would love him if he took me off the stage and away from Bourgoyne!

The wall was clean again. I opened the window and tossed out what remained in the chamber pot. It was full dark. We would have to leave soon.

The sound of the window opening must have woken her. When I went to return the chamber pot to under the bed, she was awake; yawning and stretching. I sat beside her. She just looked up at me, her waking eyes blank. Not enough of her in her eyes. Almost like she didn't know me. I said, "You mustn't make the vision frighten you, love."

She frowned. "Vision?"

Little picky points rose on my arms. "Yes, the vision in the chamber pot. The man."

She giggled and patted my thigh. "Oh, my Lemer. Such sharp eyes, to see a man. Was he a gentleman?"

"You saw him, too," I whispered.

She only shrugged. She sat up and kissed my cheek. "I saw hashish smoke, dancing in front of my eyes. Shall we dress for dinner now?"

She heaved herself out of the bed and went and sat at the mirror. So soon she'd forgotten. Grand-maman used to tell me that people only see what they see. Used to vex me, for it made no sense. Children like for their adults to speak plain, to help us make the world come clear. But I understood now.

NALO HOPKINSON

→ **NALO HOPKINSON** is an internationally known, multiple award-winning novelist and short-story writer. Her first novel, *Brown Girl in the Ring*, now in its fifth printing, won the 1997 Warner Aspect First Novel Competition, the 1998 John W. Campbell Memorial Award for Best New Writer and the 1999 Locus Award for best first novel. Hopkinson's second novel, *Midnight Robber* (also published by Warner Aspect), was nominated for the Hugo Award, The Sunburst Award, and in 2000 was named a *New York Times* Notable Book of the Year. Hopkinson edited the anthology *Whispers From the Cotton Tree Root: Canadian Fabulist Fiction* (Invisible Cities Press) and in 2001 published *Skin Folk*, a short-story collection. She has held several writers-in-residence positions in both Canada and the United States and is currently teaching a science fiction and fantasy writing course through the continuing education department at the University of Toronto. Nalo Hopkinson holds an MA in Writing Popular Fiction from Seton Hill College. For a complete biography, please visit: www.sff.net/people/nalo.

⚫ ANURIMA BANERJI

"MONOLOGUE OF THE MANDIBLE" premiered at Clit Lit as part of the "Science Fiction and Horror" show. It was a night of debuts — it was my first performance there, and the poem received its first (and only) reading at this venue. The monologue itself has a strange history of "firsts." Originally commissioned by a modern dancer as the textual accompaniment to a performance piece he was directing on themes of war and violence, the poem was my first real paid piece of writing, so I was thrilled! But through a series of twists and turns, the dance production never got off the ground and the whole project was ultimately shelved. Still, writing the text was a rewarding experience.

As the inspiration for the writing, the dance piece was incredibly experimental and complex in its early stages. This was the sole time I had tried to write with poetry imagined not as the principal text, but as the context, placed in the background as enhancement for another artistic medium — dance. This presented certain challenges and I responded by writing at the scene of the dance rehearsals. In the winter I travelled to Montreal, met the dancers who would eventually interpret the writing and music and collected raw ideas for the proposed commentary. Then, on the train back, I played with structures and words. The images had to be simple and strong enough to make an impact separate from the dance, to complement the stark, abrupt body movements of the dancers without interrupting their flow. The poem had to be easy enough to memorize, and long enough for the speakers to fill the time in each scene. Finally, the text had to be sufficiently literary and meaningful to support the overall theme of the performance. So it ended up being my first piece of "long-distance writing," where I tried to connect what I had seen as physical practice in one city with words and images conjured in another — an ironic and literal moment of "fleshing it out."

At Clit Lit, I was amazed by the diversity of queer imaginings. In my piece, I used the image of Kalki — a millennial figure representing the tenth and last incarnation of the South Asian god Vishnu — as the central icon and soliloquist. Kalki is a phenomenal figure, richly represented in ancient texts and familiar to thousands of Hindus. Invoking his form, I made him into a cyborg and made him speak English to translate him for a millennial Canadian audience. Until now, only patrons of Clit Lit have heard the "steel autobiography" I wrote for him!

Monologue of the Mandible

I

sleepless, I am out for blood, the night avenger,
beginning with om. outside the revelation
I come.

I have bared my skin for metal. *what have you done?* gliding through miles
of smoke and dust, bones distilled from poison and mercy. And I know
you will be mourned, you cannot be saved. fear grows through the city of your skin.
Too much noise for the eyes, too many insomniac lights.

fate nailed me here, or faith?

II

my skin is braided with metal and sex, altered by alchemy. I've lost
my senses to synasthesia. there are times when I taste memory.
and there are times when I capture the killing scent, destroyer
of the earth, faithful to a beauty not my own. then dazed by the life
of this world. *the knife is for this*

cut: I don't have a real part, don't have a scene,
cancel my characters. all ten of them. a decade of my selves. *cut:*
these baboon hearts, artificial limbs, all organs
vestigial,
the futile fugitive from my own senses.

and while I stab: I am the blood bandit. I rob soft skulls,
in another light's country, the continent of foreign stars.
the curse: you will come back.

III

all my parts come loose. take my photo now: machine
makes memory flesh, memory, the untamed monster of me,
the exit. face amputated by the metal eye. need the machine
to remember, dismember. I've been edited, soundtrack
of the future on my blade, small orchestra of replicant twists,
spontaneous combustion of saliva and flame —

made my disfigured self from warehouse parts: a lock of hair,
crushed foot, broken arm. *mortal embroidery for the divine.*
how copper fits into a hand — the painted eye — the stump of a leg —
minefield of ambushed cadaver. my resplendent armour of human
remains. android in the abattoir with so many pieces to choose from:
unhappy cyborg, slaughterhouse-born.

IV

I am a dancer and I burn the world around me,
tearing at skin and shards, never poised,
always on the verge of vertigo,
surprised to hear my own skin speak,
the unnatural tongue.

I confess. *I've bared my flesh for metal.* (steel autobiography.)
made all the elements and made of all the elements.
this hybrid atlas of the body: claw, beak, liquid, follicle, cimeter
(smells I like? the sharpest resins. lemon and asphalt and acid)
all organs intact, synthetic spine, plastic mouth, muscled robot heart.
spliced animal drinking chaos. mutant god.

sometimes sensation comes back, surreal river of shock and nerves.
untouchable. that's the secret. immaculate calcium scales and shells.
immaculate wife. tusk and axe. bow, arrow, blade, weapons shining
in panic, diagnosis: disorder. emergency. *Kalyug.*

you think I haven't loved? my passion for incarnation:
I have an alias, an address in each time, Kalki, hostage of tomorrow,
flash into the centuries roped around me, see my hand, proof of nostalgia
fingerprinted, spiral tattoos of time. estranged from myself and multiplied.
search my lifelines: Kalki, also-known-as (a.k.a millennium healer: not yet,
Kalyug: now), yellowing evidence of past life, *no, I haven't been here before,*
committed no crime, these are my sepia alibis:

fish to fly over: half-lion to eat: boar to hide: dwarf to dance: turtle to swim:
no. I've lost my senses. try again:
fish to eat; lion to hide; boar to swim; turtle to dance; dwarf to fly over
no. I've lost my senses. try again:
fish to crawl through sea turtle to hide boar to dwarf to dance against half-lion
eating to rip no one to fly over (break) the half-god to mother to life to father
to brother to lotus to blood bandit and no one to swim through or fly over.
yes. that's it.

time is my choreographed solo. strange monologue of the mandible.
"*pralaya payodhi jale, dhreet vanasi vedam.*" you came back,
full replay, exact imitation through temperature and sign.
once it was Matsya, then Baaman, and Balram. backward now.
Buddha, Parasuram, Narsimha. forward. "*tat tvam asi.*" pause.

v

it's not the truth i saved
but the thread of my tongue,
sewing scraps of the world into story.
I am each witness, each form,

though I don't remember (always).

VI

remember me: equine boy, black albino. body raining blue from fear
and pheromone. *premonition: in three minutes you will marry steel.*
you will fuck music. grief has its own semen song. hear me.
give me the birth of ethereal horses, mongrel-dark bodies twisting in light,
the slow eyes, astonished by night. give me the epic of bones.

VII

the sun, galloping on water
and the earth, falling towards fire

there are times when I taste memory,
capture the killing scent: we are all enchanted
by histories that speak for us.
(even the gods) (even the mutant gods)

but all that has been committed to memory
wants to be abandoned.

all the pure
are kidnapped amnesiacs.

After all these lies and nocturnes
I saw you glowing, ashwin, cornered by the dark

Illuminate the world with my word:

Shanti

pray to me for another beginning
of the universe, pray for the murdered beauty
of me, skin and metal myth.

for I am the revelation, the night avenger,
I am the sleeper, I am om, I am the knife, I am divine,
I am the sun, falling on water, I am the world
galloping on fire.

for I am the revelation. I am the world
galloping on fire.

⤳ **ANURIMA BANERJI** is the author of
Night Artillery, a collection of poems
recently published by TSAR Books. Her
work has also appeared in several literary
journals. Currently based in Toronto, she
has performed her work widely in Canada,
the U.S. and India.

37

ENDNOTES

1. The line "*pralaya payodhi jale, dhreet
vanasi vedam*" is from the *Dashavatar*, a
Hindu text relating an account of the ten
incarnations of Vishnu. Matsya, Baaman,
Balram, Buddha, Parasuram, Narsimha and
Kalki are all various forms of Vishnu mentioned in the text. *Tat tvam asi* is a famous
pronunciation from an ancient Sanskrit
text, literally meaning *You are that*, roughly
meaning that every living being is a part of
the divine. *Ashwin* means horse; Kalki is
said to be arriving on a splendid steed during
the age of Kalyug, or darkness.

ANURIMA BANERJI

☙ MICHÈLE PEARSON CLARKE

FOR SOMEONE WHO DOESN'T consider herself to be a writer, the idea of not only writing words down on paper but also reading them in front of assorted friends and acquaintances was intriguing. I mean, of course I write. You don't get through grad school without wearing out a keyboard or two. But sharing my ideas — sharing me — was something new. I can't imagine that I would have agreed to do it at any other venue but Clit Lit. I had been there as an audience member many times. I had seen and felt the love and overwhelming support these dykes show for one another's work. We gather and listen and then debate what we've just heard. Pride marches have been described to me as the show we put on for others, whereas other cultural events, like our film festivals, are more like campfires we build for ourselves. That's what Clit Lit is too, a place where we come together and talk.

Black Men and Me

It's a Friday evening and I have been driven across town by a craving for a chicken roti. Regular of course, with the bones in. That's the sweetest part. I leave the East End and head west to Ali's at Queen and Lansdowne. I have had the same arguments here in Toronto as I had in Trinidad, about where the best place is to get a roti. We all have our favourite spots, and as I walk into mine, there's that busy Thank-God-it's-Friday no-way-I'm-cooking-tonight thing going on. I make my order and I take a seat to wait. I'm just taking in the cricket on the television when I feel eyes on me. I turn and look at him, cap turned backwards and collar turned up. He smiles that slow, lazy smile. "Sweetness, yuh real pretty yuh know, whus yuh name?" He's a good-looking boy and I'm in a good mood, so I smile back and I tell him my name. "Yuh from Trini, eh? Which part?" I tell him I'm from Diego Martin, and he says, "Yeah, yeah, I know you from home, man." They always do. He's just about to turn up the charm when my order's called and as I stand up, my legs tremble a bit. On my way out, I flash him the coy, flirty smile that I reserve for black men, in particular black West Indian men. The smile that offers up so much promise with no possible chance of follow-through.

Whenever I have an exchange like that, I'm not sure what's more interesting to me — the attention that a man pays to me, or my response to that attention. I mean, the whole thing fascinates me really. Straight white men never hit on me — they're not interested and they seem to get that I wouldn't be interested either. Gay white men sometimes hit on me, but most of the time it's because they think I'm a man. Straight black men, on the other hand, they never make that mistake. They always know that I'm a woman.

Last month, I was riding my bike along Commissioner's on one of those mild January days, bundled up in hat, coat and scarf, with barely

MICHÈLE PEARSON CLARKE

any of my body visible to anyone who was interested. The only person I saw was a black man who winked and yelled, "Stop and talk to mih, nuh gyul!" as I passed him by. I couldn't help but stare back in disbelief. I was truly amazed at his cunning skill.

And when black men do recognize me as a woman and they choose to look my way, shall we say, either they don't read my queerness or they just think that they're irresistible to *all* women, lesbians included. I'm never quite sure which. But they smile, they flirt, they tease, they make offers. I've tried to explain this to friends and I only have real success when I can point it out to them in action. Once at a boxing match in Cabbagetown, I was sitting amongst a large group of dykes who had come out to watch some women fight. Shaved heads, tattoos, hand-holding, it was all there around me. But a friend had herself a good laugh at the way in which some of the male spectators managed to pick me out from the sea of lesbianness. She watched them watching me and she watched the ways in which we engaged with each other.

Usually, I try not to be rude and to at least acknowledge with a nod or a smile. They're my people, black men are. Growing up in Trinidad, they were my first vocal admirers. Even though I couldn't understand then why their desire was so unimportant to me, they offered me my first lesson in being wanted. That has its own place in my personal history. Mind you, it was nothing like the first time that a woman gave me that look. You know the one; it says: You. Come. Now. *That's* when I truly understood desire, but I digress.

With me and black men, there's a particular commonality between us. I recognize myself in them. That self-assuredness, that cockiness, that sense that they're God's gift to women. Yes, I admit it, there's some of that in me. It makes sense, because when I was younger, I thought that I was going to be a black man when I grew up. And in some ways, that has come to pass. So when I hear a line, what we call lyrics, or I watch a man acting all cool and trying to get my attention, I see myself and I get a glimpse of how other women might see me. This is not always a good thing, by the way. Sometimes I look and I wonder, am I *that* cheesy? And I guess sometimes I am. Although they probably have no idea, I'm responding to them as a contemporary, as someone who is in some way like me. My brother, indeed.

And then, every so often, depending on my mood, depending on the way in which I am approached by a black man, I find myself — *me* — acting all shy and girlish and flipping about imaginary hair that I don't have. What the hell is that? It used to really freak me out, but I've grown to accept that it seems I have been socialized just like every other woman. It's incredible the power that that holds over me — that I would revert to some automatic script and behave in a way that I don't normally associate with myself. I've never slept with a man and I have no desire to sleep with a man. Well, not a straight one anyway. And yet, it's like, I'm not a heterosexual but I could play one on TV if I had to.

So what to make of this coy, flirty response? A couple of things — I think that it gives me a chance to try out the role that I rejected a long time ago, to step outside of myself and play a bit — to be a woman and to exercise some power over a man. And by behaving in a way that I've seen my mother and my sister and my straight girlfriends behave, for a brief moment I am able to connect to what their sexual lives might be like, and that brings me closer to them. I like that. Recently I've begun to think that in some way this response is also a defence mechanism: I present myself to the world in a certain way and I assume a certain level of visibility as queer, as gender-variant, and there's comfort and security in that. There's something about a black man coming on to me that makes me feel exposed, unmasked and ultimately ordinary. I haven't quite figured it all out yet, but I do love thinking about it.

The other piece that I find really intriguing is that I have had many black men tell me that I look just like Tiger Woods. Actually, all sorts of people have told me this in the past few years, including my father, who calls from Trinidad on a regular basis to ask me if I have the television on, because my "twin brother" is about to win another championship. Uh, yeah Dad, sure. But when a black man tells me, "Dahlin, yuh does real look like Tiger, yuh know?" and then proceeds to hit me with some lyrics, I have to wonder, exactly what kind of homoerotic thing is going on here? Am I serving as an outlet for repressed homosexual desires and fantasies? I have to tell you, I really, really hope so. I find the absolute kinky queerness of this scenario to be simply delightful. I get to be a gay Tiger Woods and I get to indulge in some truly layered gender play. Of course, that's all going on in my head and who really knows what's going on for the fellas, but a girl can hope, can't she?

41

MICHÈLE PEARSON CLARKE

When it comes down to it, this is where the interest and the appeal and the fun of it lie — it's about opportunities for play, whether all the participants realize it or not. Black men give me all these ways in which I get to stretch and explore my gendered and sexual selves. Not that I don't get that from women as well, but it's a different kind of risk. Men don't make up my immediate community, I don't have to worry if someone's keeping score or not. I can be a girl or a boy or butch or femme, purely on my own terms. I'm probably never going to see them again; I'm not going to have to account for my behaviour. We just run into each other every now and then, dance a few steps together, and then move on into the night. I like that.

↝ MICHÈLE PEARSON CLARKE was born in Trinidad and Tobago and came to Canada when she was nineteen. Usually she just tells stories, but she wrote this one down because she couldn't get it out of her head.

☙ SINA QUEYRAS

BEFORE CLIT LIT, I had given several readings — at UBC, Concordia, Banff — but my shyness and stage fright were so painful that for days prior to the event life was unmanageable. I had all but given up on the exercise. But the truth was I loved reading. I wrote and continue to write poetry to be read, to connect with other people, and it was painful not to have this final communion. To watch the poems stack up on my desk and, granted, sometimes end up published in journals that people might or might not read was such a waste — the poems, it seemed, were living half-lives.

When I was working at the Jewish Vocational Service of Toronto, I started reading *The Vagina Monologues* to some of my co-workers — several of whom had grown up in Brooklyn and were women of that generation who deeply understood what it meant to say simply "down there," "my down there, you know…" The lunch hour that I read "Flood" to them I saw the recognition on their faces and though they laughed — we all laughed — I knew that none of us, not even me, a thirtysomething lesbian, could say the word "clit."

Then I heard about Clit Lit. I was writing a series of love poems that would make up the first half of my first collection of poetry, *SLIP*, and was dying to read them out loud. I called the organizer and left a message. I thought this would be the perfect place to try them out. I went to check it out and loved the vibe. There were confident young women who had no problem saying "clit," or "dildo," or "come on baby fuck me now!" There were writers who fantasized about Wonder Woman. There were serious, earnest writers, and there were those who were trembling and green, brave and utterly overwhelmed. One night a former student who I recalled was a zine freak, a heartbreaking cap-girl who hardly spoke, was there with her girlfriend. "Sina," she said, "I have a poem burning a hole in my back pocket."

On my night I went alone. I listened to the women who went before me (all much less repressed than I, of course) and when it was my turn I walked the length of the club feeling like a doting old woman and apologized for changing the tone to something more romantic. What can I say? Ultimately I'm a romantic. I love being in love, and I love to write about it. The audience seemed okay with my work once I started to read, and I felt like I'd stepped into another skin. The light was in my eyes and I couldn't see. I sunk deep into the world of the poems as if I was hearing them for the first time myself. There were lines that went bump and words that struck odd chords, and yet reading and hearing those poems that night I knew that there was a place for them, and that they *had* to be read, to be spoken in order to fully live. Now I'm a public-reading slut. I can't get enough. I'm still a little nervous beforehand, but I have discovered the public world of my poems and that it's a safe one I can inhabit.

In the night, suddenly

1.

It is 6 a.m. when I open my eyes in your bed. When you turn,
open your eyes, every muscle and vein in me expands.

If I open my mouth you will see my heart beating, how
lost I am; you pull my head to your chest. I tell myself

this is only one night, I have an island to return to. Later
in my basement room, my nose full of you, cat scent,

where your tongue has touched I glow. I'll lie here contained
in the sonatas while you lick your fur and purr

your possession of me. Already you have touched me
more than anyone, ever, everywhere. Prodigy. Beethoven

tongue.

2.

All day I feel your breath in the rub of my collar, on
my cheek and jaw where I expect your downy fingers still.

I long to kiss everyone on St-Laurent, to buy every flower,
every fruit, every book, every chocolate, and lay them

at your feet. Impossible behaviour: the cashier at
Warshaw's clucks her tongue, but I feel only Lust

with a capital L, and what is lust but the transformation
of obstacles to winged things, adoration of ascent,

muscled haunches overhead. O, the first time I've
gazed outside myself in months! There'll be no

talk of sin now, and to celebrate, new lipstick, a glass
of St-Emilion, a tomato flown from Provence to

the palm of my hand.

3.

In the reading room I feed you slices of papaya, painful
to lick the juice from your chin and not follow the line

drawing me down. How can I survive this untransformed?
Why describe desire when I can reach out to you? And

who cares about other people? My hands seek your hips,
lips, ribs, the half-shell of your underarm. What I need is:

a phone call from L., a crack in the ice, two mating
elephants, my hands in earth, seven popped balloons,

my Visa bill, reservations on the space shuttle, a trip
to Roswell, night shift at a shelter, to hear Sylvia Plath

laugh.

4.

What Cixous has to say about jouissance makes sense
in the flash of skin, your legs when your toes scrape

the full moon, a whole ocean pulling at my tongue. But
outside of thighs I have nothing to say. Impossible

to concentrate on the reading. When you caress your pen
I feel your fingers on my thigh and when I moan finally,

it's not because the presentation has moved me.
What do I know of Margaret Cavendish? That she did not

have the pleasure of your mouth on the inside of her elbow.
And I won't disagree that women invented the novel since

poems may not be large enough to contain them. When
you raise your hand to move a curl from your mouth I cannot

contain myself.

5.

The phone's pierce and crackle. My spine, my sunflower head
droop, shoulderless. This is the last time we will sleep together.

Just one more time is all. Each time you slip into my bed
it is the last time I will see your elbows lift; you slowly remove

your blouse. Let the arms linger, let me take in every hair
and mole, burn—the texture of you will become my tongue.

What I say when you sleep: this is another island,
in the St. Lawrence, between St-Laurent and St-Denis,

an oasis, each kiss a granule of sand underfoot or
this can't go on, can't be spoken of, and I would stay

on my knees
all night.

↝ SINA QUEYRAS was born in Manitoba and
spent her childhood in the back seat of her mother's
Chrysler. She has worked in restaurants, in gardens,
and with at-risk youth, and lived mainly on the
West Coast before completing a BFA at the
University of British Columbia and an MA at
Concordia in Montreal. Sina's poetry has appeared
in numerous journals, including *Prairie Fire* and
the *Malahat Review*. Her first collection of poetry,
SLIP, was published in October 2001 by ECW
Press. Sina is currently an instructor at Rutgers,
The State University of New Jersey.

ᵉᶜ JULIE GLASER

CLIT LIT. ON STAGE. The dress is my Oma's, circa 1965, shortened to reveal more leg than she would have during the onset of the sexual revolution. It amuses her in the same way disbelief can sometimes be amusing that I should want from her closets selections of four decades of well-preserved fashion history. I never take from the '80s — baaaaaad karma. The garments hold our history: of gatherings (funerals, weddings, various familial celebrations); of work (thirty years on the upholstery line at the Chrysler plant, smuggling scraps of vinyl and leather and carpet interior to make purses and skirts); of home dirties (cooking, cleaning and pregnancy frocks, homespun with sturdy, brightly printed cottons, large pockets and big industrial zippers up the front).

She would have worn the hausfrau smocks whilst shaking out the asbestos dust from my Opa's clothes, after making him undress in the garden like a small boy. Her instincts told her even then, despite that plant's assurances, that he was covered in toxicity. She would have worn these same dresses years later, to bathe him when he could no longer bathe himself, and administer the morphine that distanced him from the cancer pain. The "for good" dresses, party dresses made of classic woven wools and '70s polyfibres, purchased in stores for special occasions, cloaked her in the dignified armour necessary to stand up to my Opa's alcohol-induced behaviour, unwieldy, aggressive, mean. She put on pretty dresses and a brave face for these festivities, Christmases and family celebrations that could result in calamity. Row upon row of black dresses, varying lengths and styles of the decades, mark the passing of family members, my Oma attending to everyone's grief through food, ordering the pallbearers around, comforting. Each of these dresses signifies another buried secret, another link safely locked away.

I fit these dresses like they were made for me, our shapes so similar. And they appeal to my femme sensibilities of historical subversion, play and desire. I wear them with occasion, fully aware of the power they have to transform an event into an experience. I chose my outfit for the Clit Lit reading with all of these things in mind: the night's theme, "Mothers & Daughters;" my reading of "Eat & Disorder," an examination of my relationship to the matriarch in my family, and of my own desire; and the audience, a room packed with (mostly) dykes, hungry for words. Stepping up to the mic to share with a generous room of queer literary appreciators the secrets stashed away in my family's closet, the dress I wore embodied its own critique. Costumed in history to read about the relationship of food, racism, sexuality and the matriarchal keeper of family secrets, the dress motivated me into performance mode, and the audience egged me on. They laughed, and understood, and wanted more. The energy generated by words and want and understanding that night moved my reading onto a level not previously experienced. The dress was on fire, alive and kicking with lesbian desire, secrets unleashed, story told. And, as its author, my relationship to the piece transformed. My own sense of what I had written deepened. I understood the relevance of its historical context, not just because I lived it, but because as queers, many of us have lived it, as we make decisions to live otherwise than what we have been taught.

My Oma, however, most likely will never appreciate such transformation, the reclaiming of history. She would not be amused at such a subverted critique of what has been worn and re-worn. Her dress hugging my flesh under the gaze of a hundred or so dykes would no doubt cause her some distress, and probably some confusion. But not me, n'huh. There was no confusion for me that night. The images I released from the stage were carried by the energy of such a queer-positive crowd, clearly and tenderly and passionately to the back of the room, and passed back to me. Empowered, mesmerized by the room's reception, I stepped away from the mic, femmepowered, and transformed.

Eat & Disorder

PART I: EAT.

They link her to my rejection of meat. Days of plates of cabbage rolls, fried moose steak, the Thanksgiving bird, rabbit I was told was chicken, deer meat, steak tartar, goose, the Christmas bird, breaded veal, glazed ham, stewed beef, the Easter bird, head cheese which is not really cheese at all and once, bear. Not ones to waste, make haste and make room for the organs and innards: kidney and liver and tongue and tripe, stuffing up arteries like bursting, bar-b-queued bratwurst, dripping slow deaths of ambiguous hunger. My brain cells waded through the pools of fat in a last-ditch effort to digest reality.

Years ago, while still in school, I felt the need to cleanse my system of pigs and deer and bear and cow and moose and rabbit and turkey and goose and chicken. Flush my soul of creatures consumed against their will. That year I learned how to cook and eat without grimace, tofu and chickpeas. It was the same year I first read Foucault and stopped shaving my legs. At Christmastime, I received four angora sweaters from various family members and an Epilady. They saw me off at the train station with a case of sardines weighing down my suitcase. I couldn't explain to their satisfaction that I was feeding myself with a steady diet of fresh herbs, ginger root and Virginia Woolf. I bartered the sardines for marijuana and tickets to see experimental theatre.

On weekends, I paraded an array of boyfriends by them. Mostly skinny, much to their disappointment. The melodrama and sensitivity and situational poverty of the young, budding actor or artist were underappreciated in my family. Once or twice I brought home bigger ones, athletic types, good feeders and polite, always accepting seconds and occasionally thirds. Watching them eat was the highlight of our relationships: they filled me to no other capacity beyond entertaining my family with their voracious appetites. My Oma would ask: what is their last name again? and what nationality is that? are they Jewish?

God forbid I bring home to their table a Jew, or a black, or an Indian or a dirty gypsy. Eye-talians were pretty much suspect too for that matter. And later, as I pushed the meat around on my plate and eventually passed it by altogether, they added to the list socialists, environmentalists and academics. Artists continued to invoke laughter much like the gag reflex. It just never occurred to them at all that I might bring home a girl.

Flesh not of my own brought to my lips makes me a carnivore. Hands and lips and breasts and tongue and thighs and sighs from flesh of my flesh make me a lesbian. Dirty, sick, shameless. Condemned to death by my own blood, thrown onto the heap of bodies akin to me in our difference: gypsies, Jews, homosexuals, crazies. Warming me in our criss-crossing faggot of fire, roasted to perfection. They'd rather have me eat another than love my own. Pile my plate with Nazi propaganda. Learn by rote the family recipe for normalcy, the ingredients to a good girl who'll grow up to work at A Job, buy a house in suburbia close enough to all relations to make them neighbours and consume goods from the mall. Lick the plate clean after each serving.

I starve there: skin breaks out and hair falls out and teeth rot.

We made pudding our first greedy night together. Not enough eggs to double the recipe, we multiplied the fractions and added the remainders to form a thick, chocolate brew. Laugh and argue over the calculations, counting on fingers. Numbers making us dizzy, banter making us breathless. Turning up the heat to a slow boil. Her hand brushed against my back and the world
    stopped.
Tastebuds explode on the exotic fruit.
I have fallen far from the family tree, plump and tart, juice dripping

between my sapling limbs at just the thought of another like me. Some fucked-up genetic imprint on my rain said: Girl, you will not be a Nazi, nor will your cleanliness be next to any god's godliness. Grinningly wickedly at my own lusty indulgence, I rolled early and eagerly to the wayside and began the descent to disgrace. Not once did I stop to pick the lint from my sweater. And she, any she, banished she, all. I dream while she sleeps. I am nine.

Sensing the badness of something I know nothing about, innocent lips curl around a hiss as I ask the Grand Mother: Was Opa a Nazi?

Twenty years later the Grand Mother hisses back at me: Are you a lesbian? Evil wearings on my back, I bade the beasts before you. I know what lies behind those eyes. Locking me up, charged with your indignities. Member ship lost at sea, salty like my earthly endeavours, dissolved in tears that followed. Outside to your inside, peeping Pam I am. When I arrived home it was to her. Two women, she & I, makin a go of it, eh? Hopeless-chest china and newspaper all over the floor. Dog hair and little pebbles of kitty litter woven into the carpet. Save it for later. Vacuuming's the last thing on my mind.

In his backyard, accordion and lederhosen hung out to dry. Guilt, crusty mud cracking in the seams.

It seems that I was out of order, out of line to suggest such a thing.

A Nazi?

A Nazi?

A trisket a tasket, a green and yellow basket.

I went to bed with a lump on my head,

And didn't wake up in the morning.

Don't mention it.

Don't   ever   mention it   again.

I didn't.

Until I could sleep no longer.

And so...

Once upon a time, years later in a place not too far, far away, I rose from my bed of thorns and imported duvets (German ducks produced the best feathers, they said) and tasted the fruit before me. She was sweet, and she offered me cups and bowls and spoonfuls of her. A geyser of seductive

53

JULIE GLASER

truth poured forth from her and I wept with acceptance. Lustily, I led her to the kitchen, where I could eat my fill of her. We set our bed up where the table should be, and began the feast.

PART 2: DISORDER.
Prepared for the questions they do not ask, I carry on as usual. Usually I just carry on.

And what I expect is what is to be expected. The phone doesn't ring. Just the proverbial pregnant pause while they await my change of mind. As if I would change my mind. And then a voice croaks through the dusty receiver, full of warning and shaming and saving my soul. As she did her own, I suppose, half a century ago. Her eyes grey steel. Were they blue once? She tells me they are blue, but she maintains that she is taller than me too, which she has not been since I have been a fraction of her age. There are pictures I have seen: first years in Canada mostly, a few of herself as a girl in Germany. Taller, rounder hair falling loosely from her head in curls. Bosom soft, eyes laughing at something away from the camera. She was a girl once; I have seen the evidence. There was a boy too, whom I have not seen, but heard about. Once. And I have seen the evidence of this too: a silver band, melted down and shaped to fit her finger, gently hammered by his own hands. He joined up with the German army, she said, and died shortly thereafter. She told me this only once. And at that moment she transformed before my eyes into a woman I had not known but had been waiting to meet my whole life. Her beauty and passion cleared the kitchen of its antiseptic and sauerkraut smells. The room awhirl with her hopes. I hoped for her too.

And then the ring is snatched from my hand as she dashes up the stairs, to hide it away in her piles of things hiding other things. I try when we are alone together to get more scoop out of her. I try other family members for details, but no one seems to know what I'm talking about, including her now too; she looks at me like I'm crazy when I bring it up. Apparently I don't know what I am talking about. Apparently I am crazy. I am always the crazy one. Of course I am; how quickly I forget. There are the things we remember and the things we forget. And then there are the other things that exist to prompt the remembering or secure the forgetting.

My shape mirrors hers: hearty Russian peasant bones, big hands for the size of us, nose and chin that will meet in time. My bosom, however, pales in comparison. My skin is darker too. Popped out like some brown and hairy little foreigner. The gypsy, they called me. Defects attributed to my mother's gene pool. Imperfections abound in the British; years of scandalous trading with the colonies. Sugar and spice, all things nice.

I add garlic to everything.

I am nine. Summer of 1976. We — my parents, a cousin and his wife — are packed into some sort of hot-rod car, travelling west to Vancouver. We eat Niagara Bing cherries out of a paper bag and spit the seeds out of the widow. It's so damn hot we strip down to what is legally permissible. I am conscious of growing out my bangs, which is probably more conscious than my parents believe me capable of. I marvel at the way my father rockets determinedly across the country, never consulting a map, never losing us. I marvel too at his silky armpit hair, catching some breeze through his crooked arm out the window, his hand beating a rhythm on the door to a seventies soundtrack. Freddie Mercury, a blazing streak of groin lust turning up the heat in our hot rod. The women fall asleep, sticking their thighs to mine. In their purses I dig out tampons, fluff them out and marker wee mice faces on them. Line them up on the back dash. I keep my eyes peeled for prairie dogs, imagining them trainable rodents. We stay over at the farm of our cousin's cousin, somewhere in dry and dusty Saskatchewan. The cousin's cousin has produced a herd of children, none of whom appear to ever brush hair or teeth. They are strangely quiet and screamingly hysterical at the same time. They sleep everywhere. I sleep on a couch next to the kitchen table. It smells like beer and wet dog. I wake up early and the girl nearest my age takes me out behind the barns, through a field, into scrub brush sprouting rusted appliances. The doors should be off, I think, all panicky. Hasn't anyone told them that the doors should be off? Else children crawl into dryers and freezers and ovens and get locked inside. They suffocate there on their own exhale, in darkness and the echo of quiet.

The girl beckons me behind a line-up of refrigerators, only a couple with doors hanging open on their hinges. I lurch past them, eyes spinning to the back of my head on the lookout for small, withered hands emerging from a Westinghouse. The girl is behind the wheel of a burnt-out vehicle.

55

I crawl in next to her, perch on a crate where a seat should be. There is a sleeping bag in the back. She pulls out a pack of cigarettes from underneath what remains of the driver's seat. This is where we do it, she tells me. Sometimes they give me nickels. I stay on the porch awhile gathering air in my lungs. The girl has gone inside to get a plate of bacon and toast. I think I should tell my parents before we leave about the children who might be trapped in the appliances. But then I think that our cousin's cousin might not let us go if they know that we know. And no one would know where we were, in the middle of nowhere, Saskatchewan, severed and roasting in prairie-sun-powered ovens. I feel a fever coming on and lie out on the porch, one eye peeled on a sorrowful black dog eyeballing me, and one ear tuned and alert to the footsteps of a mangy teenage boy. When we say our thank-yous and goodbyes to our cousin's cousin's family, I can barely wait to get in the car. I am so unsteady on my feet that my father insists that I use the outhouse one last time before we go, otherwise he's leaving me here.

The girl catches me on the way out of the hut that up until now I had been peeing behind. She pulls me close and my lungs catch on bacon grease and cigarette smoke and wet dog. I could come visit you. We could be pen-pals, and I could visit you in Ontario. I give her my hair barrette that is holding back my bangs and tell her, OK. Our cousin's cousin gives my father directions back to the main roads. He tells us to roll up our windows going through the Indian reservation, just like the man at the ticket booth at the African Lion Safari told us to. We emerged from the African Lion Safari with our soft-top roof torn to shreds by the monkeys. I sat horrified mute throughout the entire experience, holding back tears for captured beasts on display. I anticipate the worst going through the reservation, and for the remainder of the trip keep a close eye on our cousin. I discover a feathered roach clip in his wife's purse and add an Indian tampon mouse to my brood. Twenty years pass and my cousin and his wife are travelling the Yukon in an RV equipped with an oxygen tank. They have routed their journey according to oxygen-refill stations, and my cousin waits for a lung transplant. Twenty years pass and the GrandMother's cellar is lined with an armour of cans: cherries and ham and tomatoes and corn and beans steeling themselves against some unprovoked, anticipated attack, multiplying in the dark. How long before their insides poison with ancient aluminum? How long before decaying ham and corroding metal bubble a life of their own?

Twenty years pass and I know no more about family secrets than I ever did, other than that I have become one. My sexual orientation is about as well tolerated as my preference for not eating meat. It is never acknowledged, nor taken seriously. Apparently if they ignore these things long enough, I might revert. I might just conveniently forget that I don't eat hormone-injected beef or by-products, that I sleep with girls, that I need to know where I come from. Discontent with silence I create my own noise. I make my own dinner and my own bed. I piece together my family history like a raggedy old quilt, a thing of purpose, not of beauty. It doesn't keep me particularly warm at night, but I feel better knowing that it's there. Twenty years pass and my CV is filled with acts of disobedience, challenges to social structures, mind-sets and political whimsy. Twenty years pass and my neighbourhood demographics brag of Indians, bikers, queers, and around my Thanksgiving table assemble my friends: socialists, academics, poets, deviants. We thank the good farmers of Ontario, and eat.

JULIE GLASER

⇢ JULIE GLASER has had work exploring themes of sexuality, gender and food recently published in 2001 editions of *Fireweed* and *Tessera*. Her short fiction has received literary awards, and the creative non-fiction piece "Eat & Disorder," read at Clit Lit, was short-listed in 2000 for a CBC Canadian Literary Award. Julie currently curates queer cultural studies workshops for youth in London, Ontario, and is producing a film to document the lived experiences of these youth. She also hears the ocean calling ...undulating, beckoning...and wonders how long it would take to ride her horse across this country.

●◗ BRIAN DAY

I READ AT CLIT LIT less than a week after my first book came out. It was a remarkably inviting place to read, and it felt much more a community event than other readings I'd taken part in. It was exciting to sign and sell my first books — and to be in an atmosphere that was literary and stimulating without being pretentious.

Bake me

Sweeten my skin with dark vanilla
Grate me, a fragrant acorn of nutmeg
Hold me, a naked yolk in my shell
Whisk my breath to a fine peaked froth
Spin me in a dizzy tornado of blades
Squeeze the cries from my mouth with lemon
Scent me with cinnamon
Mould my corners with your fingers' strength
Flatten my back with the tines of a fork
Bake me

Plant a fortune of oranges around me
Brush my skin with a film of honey
Dust me with sugar
Indulge me with cream
Garnish my throat with a raspberry's beads

59

In Others' Skin

Having known the cool pink pill of athletics
to bolster the sexual wattage of my cells
and sweeten by teaspoons the raw sugar in my blood,

I crave other creatures shaped by exertion,
whose bodies are crafted by disciplined practice,
engorged in each of their packets of pleasure.

Strolling the rows in carnality's orchards
I've reached for men carved hard with work,
polished their strenuous, constructed shapes,

tasted them as fruit might taste its own flesh,
pressed my limbs beneath each of their weights,
known my pores beaded with the sweat of their effort.

I've boasted their bodies, delicious as marble,
been lit by their nerves and wires of gold,
felt their power like quicksilver licking my veins.

I've glowed with rewards of their hard repetitions —
and the labour of training that peaked in their cries
is laid as bright ore in the records of my flesh.

⇝ **BRIAN DAY**'s first book of poetry, *Love is not Native to my Blood*, was published in 2000 by Guernica Editions. He is working on a second book that draws extensively on stories from South Asia.

KARLEEN PENDLETON JIMÉNEZ

I WENT THE FIRST TIME because she told me to go, and she was cute and had kissed me before. I went because my actual girlfriend was still married to a man and she was spending that night with him. I needed to get my mind off of her and fill my time well. Bumping into this other cute one could do the trick, I thought. I went because I was a dyke and a writer in a new city and this was where I could meet more of my kind — in a bar, on a weeknight, over a dinner of chile verde, huddled together from a cold outside that I had never experienced growing up in California. I was searching for context.

When I first came to Toronto, I knew no one (besides the married girl-friend). So I came to a bar for poetry. A bar. I've read in bars before. I had my worst reading ever in a bar. Nobody listened for the first half. Shushing filled the second half. I kept right on reading like I didn't notice. I have a thing about people not listening. It makes me crazy. I stepped down from that gig happy, because I knew it was the hardest reading I would ever have to do and I hadn't blown it. I decided I would give Clit Lit a chance despite my other experience, and because of the earlier-mentioned lack of a life. Besides, in San Diego, where I had just been living for four years, people hardly ever go to readings. You have to keep coming up with innovative food and alcohol bribes. And even then we searched for tiny venues so it would seem like we had half of a crowd.

I was astonished at the large, packed bar. Dykes slipped into every crevice. Quiet, attentive, cheering dykes. One big butch was presented to me as the new girlfriend of the cute dyke who had kissed me. Damn. I eyed her during someone's poem about the lesbian appropriation of Bo and Luke Duke. I was so jealous; she could kick my ass. It was ridiculous. Being jealous at a poetry reading where no one knew who I was, let alone would notice that I was jealous over a pretty girl I dated only a couple of times. Focus. I needed to focus, not on the back of her large shaved neck, not on this butch, but rather on the Duke boys, or at least on the man that was still married to my girlfriend...

When I left that night, I was extremely happy that all these dykes were hungry for writing, and that I was a writer. When I left I walked and kicked at the snow, and wanted my girlfriend. I drank a shot of whiskey at a Portuguese sports bar on College Street. The old man who served it to me called me "son" when he told me how much I owed him. It made me smile. I came back to Clit Lit a month later with my printed out pages and read about the Portuguese man who called me "son." I also read about my beautiful girlfriend and how she picked me up over an afternoon of writing together on a patio, and about sex, about flying over her body (through a lesbian appropriation of superheroes) and digging in deep.

The audience cheered. I smiled and glowed and stepped off of the stage and bumped briefly into a dyke or two sitting on the ground. "Um, sorry guys," and tried to look humble when they didn't care and instead just told me that my words were good, were important. I tried to look humble, when for weeks after, lesbians would catch my eye at any given Starbucks and say they recognized me from Clit Lit and they'd liked my stories. And on the first day of class when I was a teaching assistant, a student came up to me and confessed she had also heard me read at Clit Lit. I was nervous because one of my students already knew about my sex life. I think she was too.

Two and a half years later I have context. I have a job, a home, the girl-friend without the husband and my first book published in stores. But if a stranger catches my eye and starts to speak, I know she'll begin with, "Have you read at Clit Lit before?" So I keep going back to read into the microphone in the red bar that hides my nervous blushes, where we flirt and listen over a beer. I take in the bitter, dark taste with trans science fiction from Newfoundland, gutsy tales of psychiatric-institution seduc-tions and a handsome dyke's Manchester childhood. This is where I've been able to share some pieces of my growing up, or my family, or my passion, in a city that otherwise holds such a brief part of my history. It is one queer place where so many dykes have come from everywhere to share a memory of their lands. One queer Mexican bar, in fact; one of the few places in this city where I can get food that tastes like home.

My Dad in Pink

My Dad is standing in a French maid's dress on top of my piano. It's not the first time this type of thing has happened. One year it was Elvira, another time it was Raggedy Ann. Over the years there were also a few average middle-aged housewives and one shiny green-tighted Peter Pan, who is always played by a woman anyway, so really it's the same thing. Halloween was the major holiday when I was growing up. My Dad, my brother and I searched for make-up at the pumpkin-patch outlet and on already-torn-apart thrift-shop racks. We'd open the cases to smell and sample before my Dad reached into his normally hidden, limp wallet. We'd fill our bags with blacks and burgundies. We'd spend the afternoon in front of the bathroom mirror, applying and reapplying dark lines and soft powders across our cheeks until we felt fit to earn candies from the neighbours. I never questioned that my Dad dressed up too or that Halloween would somehow extend for several weeks in October. We needed to practice to get it right for the big day. It all seemed to make sense at the time.

I remember the first time it actually occurred to me that something was off. I was only about twelve or so, and my best friend from across the street and I watched our fathers talking together. They were standing in a small driveway and the sun was going down. "Look," Donald told me, "your Dad's not really a man like mine." He spoke what I was thinking. I didn't really know how to describe it with words, and I don't think his were adequate either, but it was obvious we had both recognized the same thing: something queer was happening in my father's gentle pose, in his awkward positioning of hands and feet. He didn't know where to put them, or maybe he did and was trying not to. Donald's father was six inches shorter than mine, had a solid muscular body and talked about his gun collection a lot. My Dad looked like a fancy, long-legged flamingo tilting over him.

63

KARLEEN PENDLETON JIMÉNEZ

I got a letter from my Dad last night. It documents a lifetime of secrecy as a cross-dresser. "From grammar school through college 'til I got married," he wrote, "there were many times I wanted to dress as a woman, but this was kept in my mind and I did not discuss such things with my parents." His mother in turn honoured the silence, overlooking mysterious losses of rouge and extra wrinkles in her favourite gowns. A sixth-grade play provided colourful candied oils spread across his cheeks and a whole day of drag. The car ride home full of laughter from a neighbour girl only turned him on more. It was meant to be punishment on the first day of high-school, smearing lipstick across the pink faces of freshmen boys. My Dad had only wished it could have lasted longer. Then there was boy-scout camp — one young, blond queen sashaying through the mountain tops, my Dad left only to stare and envy. Badminton practice became a game of kisses from a female classmate, her honeyed lipstick spread across his face, his crotch wet for the first time. At one fraternity bash, a fellow brother arrived dressed to kill and my Dad remembers each layer of sequins and his special nipple-blinking bra. While serving in the army, he watched a film that showed a man cross-dressing and he counted himself lucky to be appreciating the moment in the dark. Then, a second later, his buddies turned to him and joked that he was the one flickering in flowered silk across the screen.

These are only a few of the six pages of memories I received stuffed into a plain white envelope. They chronicle every time my Dad watched silently, hoping to be the one in the dress, and every time he wore the dress and pretended not to care. Because these other men who wore dresses, including his father and uncle, presumably did so as a joke. It was supposed to be funny to pad bras with toilet paper and lay make-up so thick you could be a clown. He now explains his shyness around cross-dressing as a lack of assertiveness. I would add that he had something to fear. There was nothing funny about the warmth that shot through his body when succulent-smelling make-up oils were applied to his lips and cheeks. It always goes back to the smell, the ecstasy, the fear. I knew his eyes lit up when he talked about lipstick colours, but he did not openly admit the sheer joy and terror to me until a few weeks ago, when I sent him writing about my own gender identity. You see, while my Dad knows more about make-up than I do, I am more of a man than my father will ever be.

Recently I confessed to him about my life as a boy and how horrible it felt every time people laughed at me when I was a kid, and how exhilarating it feels today every time my girlfriend sweet-talks my little-boy stature. I did not write these stories with him in mind, I merely wanted to share a bit of my life with someone I had almost entirely cut out. You see, my father molested me when I was young. I've gone through years of therapy and rage over the memories of betrayal. When people find out, they often ask me never to introduce them to him. They do not understand how I could keep this man in my life. Even now I question how I can write lovingly about a man who hurt me so profoundly. When someone you love molests you, you have this intense love/hate thing eating inside you your whole life. I hate the man who pulled a ten-year-old girl to him on weekend nights in his bedroom. I love the man who always made sure he had my favourite food in the pantry and who took me to movies and concerts.

Today very little has changed. I hate the man whom I yell at for making sexually inappropriate comments at family events. I love the man who gives history to my passion for cross-dressing, the person in my family who understands my absolute pleasure in ironing my slacks, twisting a silk tie around my neck and buffing out my shiny black shoes. For a long time I used to think that I could not speak to him any more, because the abuse had destroyed everything. Lately I think we've finally found a place to begin knowing each other again.

I know that child molesters are often weak men, men who do not feel any other source of power. It makes me wonder...all those years of not being able to embody what he felt in his heart. What did this do to his soul? I think of Audre Lorde's essay "Uses of the Erotic."[1] She argues that if we could openly express who we are as sensual, sexual human beings, we would expect nothing less from every other aspect of our lives. We would be strong and dangerous to the rest of the world because we would be unable to tolerate dishonesty in any other form. How different might my life have been if my Dad could have donned his lacy gowns in grace? At twenty-six, I can finally offer him the world of cross-dressing I have loved freely for the past seven years. At sixty-five, he can finally offer me a father who is honest.

I keep the eight-by-ten glossy French maid portrait of him because it brings a smile to my face, and because he's got nice legs. I look at his rosy

65

KARLEEN PENDLETON JIMÉNEZ

cheeks and blue eye shadow and think of the final words of his letter: "I was too shy to do any of this — so I'm making up for it nowadays. My manicurist used to buff my nails, now she finishes by putting four-second drying clear polish on them and you can probably see the shine in San Diego."

➳ **KARLEEN PENDLETON JIMÉNEZ** is a writer and teacher originally from Los Angeles. She is a member of Lengua Latina, a creative writing group for Latinas in Toronto, and a doctoral student in education at York University. Her book, *Are You a Boy or a Girl?* was named as a finalist for a 2001 Lambda Literary Award.

ENDNOTE
1. Audre Lorde, "Uses of the Erotic: The Erotic As Power," in *Sister Outsider: Essays and Speeches* (Santa Cruz: The Crossing Press, 1984).

⊶ JEFFREY ROUND

Queen for a Day

There was always petty jealousy among the drag queens. You felt it the moment you entered the dressing room. The room itself was the problem. The amateur contest was held one night a month and there was just one change room. How could you make a surprise entrance when everyone already knew what you were wearing? By curtain time there was so much pent-up hostility in the air it felt more like a wrestling match than a beauty contest.

The competition was always fierce. If you were young, gay and effeminate there weren't many options. You'd never be accepted in a profession where masculine behaviour was required. Nor were you likely to find yourself on the receiving end of a happily-ever-after romance. The ads reading "straight-looking/straight-acting" meant one thing: queens need not apply. And most queens quickly became too independent to keep a sugar daddy happy for long. So if you were a queen with no interest in cutting hair or waiting on tables for a living, you learned to fade quietly into the woodwork of some interior design firm or else go into fashion merchandising. Otherwise you got loud and tough and went out and bought yourself a dress. There was no midstream. The drag circuit could support only a handful of the best queens in any city.

George Timson, owner of the Box Club, watched the monthly displays of ego and ambition with amusement. To him they were only kids. What had he known at their age? He'd fought in a war by the age of twenty and that had toughened him up, but all the really important things he'd learned later, through love. George had his favourites at the bar. Some claimed he could fix the contest for favours. But George was into the "straight-looking" kids who eventually became his table dancers, the young punks who came in saying they hated fags but eventually got themselves straightened around by an older, patient man like George who gave them a job and a little self-esteem in return for their affection.

To George the queens were a different sort. Just as tough, maybe, but less likely to be tamed. They had more pride than the punks, who, once they'd been to bed with a man, could no longer proclaim so loudly their anti-gayness. But a queen could hate you whether you were gay or straight, man or woman, friend or foe. And it made no difference if you'd ever worn a dress or not. While a street kid could be worn down with patience and a few bucks, the queens burned fast through life with a cheap sense of drama all their own.

That night's show featured the usual unknowns — kids who'd hung out in dark corners of the bar for months. They watched the contest night after night until envy got the better of them. Bursting with an I-can-do-better-than-that pride and going through their mothers' closets, they would return, rouged and haughty, to show the world what a real woman looked like. In the line-up, George recognized Miranda, a young tart with a mean mouth. She'd been on the scene four or five months and had talked about entering the contest, flirting with George in the usual quee-ny sort of way. But this was one queen who thought she had the edge over her competition. It wasn't a question of asking for favours from anyone.

Miranda sat at a make-up table lit by a row of bright bulbs, applying the feature-enhancing paint. The other queens chattered loudly to each other, glancing nervously around the room. There was an occasional high-pitched, "Oh, honey, it's fabulous!" as a dress was displayed for the first time, followed by the inevitable, bitchy "Fabulous for a Barbie doll, I mean." In the mirror they could see the door through which each would make her debut. Once a queen appeared in public there was no turning back. They all shared a look of grim determination contemplating this door and the instant success or dismal failure facing them. All but one, whose gaze was focused intently on the face in the mirror. For Miranda there was no one there but herself.

Miranda finished her make-up and fussed with the folds of the antique gold satin gown. It was a magnificent piece, trimmed with white silk and real camellias that had cost her last three miserable paycheques from the drugstore where she worked days. She wore a blonde chin-length bob with a sprig of baby's breath held in place by an amethyst aigrette. It had been tough choosing between the satin dress and the red velvet number with black pompons. She looked ravishing in red and the lace on the collar had come from her grandmother's wedding dress. But at the last minute she chose the gold. She knew some other queen might show up in red and spoil it all. She absolutely had to stand out that evening. Everything depended on winning.

And she was right. The last of the contestants arrived, a very large girl dressed in red. She looked a sight. The others made faces to one another in the mirror. Why would anyone who looked like that enter a contest? Miranda looked in the mirror. Her make-up was perfect. Her hands were cool and calm. She hadn't been the least bit nervous. The hair was just right. A relief since that bitch of a wig had been so much trouble lately. She'd over-sprayed it at New Year's, but it was finally getting its shape back. Miranda stood and surveyed herself, taking a tentative step forward and back. Better to test the heels before going out and falling flat on your face onstage. That would spell doom to any bid for grace and beauty. Beauty queens did not fall. Beauty queens did not fail at anything they did. Character tells, Miranda thought. And that is the dividing line between me and the rest of them.

Onstage an announcer introduced the contest. Cigarettes were stabbed out with great finality as each girl took one last look in the mirror. They primped nervously, lining up in the order on the sheet pinned to the back of the door. Each one had chosen her own song, the winner to be declared on the basis of applause. Miranda listened as the first few numbers went by, spelling the halfway point in the contest. The applause was tepid, nothing to compete with at any rate. She already knew these queens – she'd watched them strutting on dance floors in the after-hours clubs. They had neither faces nor moves. There was no mystique, no secret allure. And dresses! Nothing compared to hers. A princess couldn't have been married in anything more fitting.

The fourth contestant was greeted by laughter. Miranda feared for a moment she might be outdone by some ugly queen who won the audience over with cheap jokes. That was always a danger. She'd seen it happen before. A queen could be the most beautiful thing in the world, but it did no good if the audience wanted to laugh instead of adore. Miranda peeked through the doorway and saw the fat queen in red. Poor thing, she thought. She has no idea how terrible she looks. Of course they were laughing — she was ridiculous. But they were laughing *at* her, not *with* her.

Two more numbers and then it was Miranda's turn. She entered slowly to give the dress its full effect to a soft flutter of applause. Her timing was perfect. The song rose in volume. She felt as though it really was her own voice singing. She didn't miss a beat, striking her final pose as the music faded in the speakers, just as she'd practiced every evening for the past month. A moment of silence, followed by applause. She deserved more, but it could wait till the judging, where it really counted. Miranda swept offstage to the dressing room. The other queens looked exhausted from nerves or fear. A quick check for make-up. She gave a pull on the hose to keep them up. They would start to itch soon, but there was no time to worry about that right now. The announcer was calling them back as the audience readied for the vote.

The applause was polite for the first two girls, who looked alternately shy and defiant at being received so coolly. The third queen got a fairly solid hand — she had a pretty dress and her hair was gorgeous, you had to admit. She returned the applause with a large smile, enjoying the response. She'd been a hit, Miranda thought, but still no danger to her. The trouble started when the fat queen was called on to bow. Four loud punks in the front row began hooting and yelling. The queen took it as encouragement rather than ridicule, bowing again and again. The response went on for a full minute. Surely the judges would discount it, Miranda thought.

Numbers five and six were again no contest. When Miranda bowed, the crowd was more than generous, making up for the lukewarm applause after her performance. She'd triumphed! Soon she would be competing with the real queens. She smiled and contemplated her win and how she would be the envy of every other queen in the city. She would be talked about. And of course she would be hated for her daring. There was no doubt about that. And that thrilled her.

George came up to the microphone and stood looking over the crowd. "Ladies," he said with a wink towards the contestants, just as he did every show. "And a few gentlemen," he continued. "I think you'll all agree there was a fine display of talent up here this evening and I want you to put your hands together for all our lovely contestants." The crowd cheered and clapped as they waited for George to read the verdict. He held the paper that he'd been handed by the judges aloft. There were gasps onstage when he declared a two-way tie between Miranda and the fat queen. Miranda's eyes blazed. Surely the idiot knew those punks were causing trouble and hadn't really intended her to win. George asked the audience to applaud again to help choose between the two semi-finalists.

The fat queen came on first. The same young punks hooted and hollered again, pounding on the tables with their beer bottles as she bowed, extending the applause to well over a minute. Miranda was incensed. Her nostrils flared. Then Miranda stepped forward. Again the crowd stamped and applauded till the place seemed it would burst with noise. Out of the corner of her eye she saw George check his watch as the applause faded and died. Miranda stepped back, her mouth closed in a sickened smile. Nothing happened. George stood there grinning, making them wait. He approached the microphone and burst into a silly giggle. "That's the most noise I've heard in here since I bent over and my girdle burst in three," he said. "Should we try that one more time?" Scattered cheering. "Just kidding — I think we have our winner."

And then Miranda was incredulous to hear him call the number of the fat queen. She tried to smile warmly as the ugly thing took her place at the front of the stage and embraced the bouquet, kissing George on the cheek. There was laughter and cheering as the one-hundred-dollar prize was handed over. Miranda felt nothing but contempt and disgust. Back in the dressing room one of the other queens came over as Miranda removed her make-up. She looked around at the others and gave her a big wet kiss on the cheek. "You were robbed, honey! You deserved that award." Miranda took a long time getting undressed. The disco beat upstairs told her the dancing had begun. She still hadn't finished by the time the others left. George passed the dressing room and looked in. "Better luck next time, Miranda. You looked wonderful," he said with a smile, and walked down the hall. Miranda picked up a shoe and threw it at the wall. "Next fucking time? You people should be so lucky to have a next time!" She peeled off the hose and shook her penis free from where it was tucked between her legs. She pulled on jeans and a T-shirt.

Without make-up, out of a dress and wig, Miranda was Murray, a very plain-looking boy with thin shoulders and pale skin. Someone nobody would even notice. Murray stared hard in the mirror, thinking about his lost triumph. About the fat queen in red crushing the bouquet to her chest. Life isn't always fair and it's seldom kind, he told himself. And no one had said it would be. But I will be back, he promised his image in the mirror. And I will win this contest. Just to show all of you. And next time, he vowed, his eyes narrowing...next time *I'll* wear red.

JEFFREY ROUND's first novel, *A Cage of Bones* (Heretic Books), was an international gay best-seller in 1998. He has written and produced for television and theatre, and recently completed his first film, the comic short *My Heart Belongs to Daddy*, which was based on *Queen for a Day*. He hosts a radio show on psychic matters for CIUT in Toronto, where he lives.

☙ SUZANNE ROBERTSON

to drift,
to soar

I

Usually it begins with a quiver in the voice,
a little coo clearing
the throat as I find a current of breath
up
face to face with that bright round sun
to scoop and lift me
is all mine as I shuffle
and for a moment its shining
the pages and begin to read,
the quiver holding steady
my voice now a rudder drifting through the years these poems have travelled.

73

II
I think I've read at Clit Lit three times. Each one memorable. Each one slightly altering my inner gravity. One of these readings took place on the eve of a huge snowstorm. It was beautiful, how the pink-black sky silenced the incessant motor of the city, the huff and puff of cars abandoned for invisible sidewalks. Rush hour reduced to the hearty clouds of breath from people trudging home through knee-deep snow.

I remember wondering if I should call the venue to find out if it was open. Or call the curator to see if the reading had been cancelled. But I didn't. Like the one hundred other women and men who attended, I just locked my door and walked through the omniscience of all that snow, bundled in the faith that my poems would find an audience...and they did. All of us squeezed into this nook and cranny of a bar, where we gathered close, hip to hip, shoulder to shoulder, words cajoling us to listen. Words reminding us to leave no one behind. And perhaps this is what lies at the heart of Clit Lit: it attempts to provide any who dare to dream a tiny stage to stand on. These readings give us the opportunity to experiment, to be outrageous or timid, burlesque or heartbreaking, they create an essential space of articulation, where women's words, the unique, oral curve of them in the air, are finally let loose:

to drift,
    to soar

What can happen in 78 hours

Inside the first 24

I

My mother leaves the doctor's office, hoping
to lose her fears at the casino.
Not knowing what else to give,
her partner buys more time,
places a cup of red chips at her feet.
Slowly her breast unthaws
as she plays the one-armed
slot machines, kisses
each coin for luck.

II

I smoke cigarettes on my backstep,
read poems to the naked
apple tree and an anonymous brown
bird who talks to no one
but the darkening sky.

Meanwhile the red puff
of her heart beats
its frantic rhythm
as a tantrum of wind shakes the branches.

75

SUZANNE ROBERTSON

Hour 33

I lie awake.
Wait.

Make a list of things to believe in:

the clear empty jar on the windowsill
the wisdom of three-legged chairs,
moonlight in its snail's pace
journey across the walls,
the dark,
roving hours before dawn.

Above my dresser is a black-and-white
photograph of my mother and me.
We are standing in the shower,
giddy with exposure as
my sister adjusts the aperture.

Light from an unseen window
pours across our chests.

What I remember is her smile
opening between my palms,
the look in her
hand-held face,

what I stare at now
are the blue veins
navigating
the astronomy of our breasts.

Hour 65: Winnipeg

As the plane descends I stare
out this porthole to the sky,
feel the engine's ungodly hum
surround me, and I wonder:
What am I doing
1000 miles away from her?

In the airport the Invisible Man
waits for me to find him.
I hide in his arms,
press my forehead hard
against his chest.

We step outside and the air
burns a clear path into my lungs.
I've forgotten how it can hurt
to breathe here.

Hour 78

Before my mother picked up the phone I knew
she wouldn't want me to fly home.

So I remain hiding in the bathroom
of a beautifully decorated house
on a neighbourhood street lined with
oak trees that grow old and symmetrical
in the frozen earth,
in a prairie city that waits
and waits for winter's stubborn release.

I take off my shirt
and my breasts stare back at me —

77

cold and shy in the fluorescent light,
wanting soft cotton or the heat inside
my lover's mouth to cover them.

I trace the contour of my right breast
that has ached for weeks.

Cancer, I say.
Not mine.
Hers.

A Mastectomy

I

Last night I dreamt the surgeon
found my mother's cancer,

small as a nut

he said, and opened his fist
revealing the hard brown
hat of an acorn in his palm.

II

We arrive at the hospital, check in,
and my mother changes into blue
fatigues.

I hold her hand,
watch the dark wet struggle
in my sister's eyes.

All I can do is concentrate on her beautiful
smooth nails, how they remind me
of grandpa's —
grooved like almonds,
and without thinking
I take her breast in my hands,
kiss it goodbye.

↝ **SUZANNE ROBERTSON**'s previous poems have appeared in the anthologies *A Room at the Heart of Things* (Vehicule Press) and *Vintage* 1999 and 2000 (Ronsdale Press).

CHRISTINA STARR

I AM A MOTHER whose monday nights are always occupied by my daughter, which means i rarely go out to mingle and flirt, have a drink, listen to music, be a dyke, hear what other writers are reading. i stay at home, i make dinner, i help with homework, i march self-righteously into the living room and snap off the tv, i absorb the latest playground gossip, i read stories aloud snuggled under a quilt and an amber nightlight fixed above the bed.

i don't think i had been to clit lit before the one i read at: "Dykes with Tykes" — a launch for the "lesbian mothering" issue of the *journal for the association for research on mothering*. the association is a feminist organization devoted to the topic of mothering, and was founded at york university by a woman who shared a class with me when i did my MA there. at that time, i wasn't queer. i wasn't a mother, either, until just before the end of my last course.

my pregnancy grew throughout the weekly seminar meetings of eighteenth-century women's writing until one day in march i didn't show up. i made it to the last class, an informal potluck on a sunday afternoon held in the residence of the professor. i brought my baby daughter, one month old, and watched her curled and trusting sleeping body get passed around the room for everyone to cradle. as a tentative writer, then, who had published small bits of work, as a new mother, deliriously happy with my precious progeny and as a waning heterosexual, increasingly uninterested in saving the relationship — i had no idea that in a few years' time i would be reading my work aloud at a notoriously lesbian salon.

it being monday, my daughter attended the clit lit night with me. she sat close up front and paid enormous attention to the words i read, afterwards telling me that some of them made her uncomfortable. it was about her, after all. she is cursed with being the daughter of a writer. i respect her immensely and i will fiercely protect her, but i am not likely to promise not to write about her. which means that a lot of people in the community know about my daughter, how i feel about parenting, and how i combine that with being queer. i've been approached a number of times by lesbians thinking of having children who want to hear the real dirt from someone with experience. will they lose all their friends? will they ever have a social life again? is it really as hard as people say? i tell them it's like apples and oranges. you can't compare not having a kid to having a kid. you can't know what it is to be a parent until you are one.

a year or so after i read at clit lit i met a couple who were thick into alternatively inseminating, hoping each month for the magic pink indication that a sperm had hit its target. they remembered me from clit lit. remembered my reading, but more so remembered the attendance of my daughter, her rapt attention, and the way we received each other once i stepped down again off the stage. they told me something i've not forgotten. they wanted, they said, to have a relationship with their child like that.

night duty

limp in the looseness of childhood
you breathe warm against my chest
your head heavy
on my demanded arm

this your assumption of comfort & safety
this body of mine
your minimum condition for surrendering
into the dark

this body of mine & the lock on the door
battlements you devise between
you & the monsters
who keep you from sleep

monsters as real as the one you have seen
& others
of war & murder   little children gone missing

easy the air falls in & out
the night blind bucks in the breeze
my sentinel sleep takes up its quiet place
only as your eyes cease
to drift open

& there are those who say I'm
fucking you   up
feeding too much dependence & needing

83

CHRISTINA STARR

those who believe I'm creating the monster
in the nightlong embrace of my child

in the small shape of your legs
tangled with mine
the back of your hand in my palm
in the stories & games & trespassing laughter
that giddy their way past the clock

they don't know

we conquer the monster
each time under blankets
& the courage of quilts
we curl into our sleep

we draw down the dragon
with the rudeness of love
and two bodies bold
in one bed

→ **CHRISTINA STARR** is an eclectic writer and performer who currently pursues a paycheque (with
benefits!) by donning a brown UPS uniform and
driving a matching truck a few hours each morning. Her original works for theatre have been produced across Canada and in the U.S. and she is a
regular columnist with Toronto's *Xtra!* magazine.
She is also a freelance writer and editor and a passionate mother to her eleven-year-old daughter.

✒ MARGARET CHRISTAKOS

THE ROOM, MORE LIKE a never-ending corridor of luminescent women's faces, was packed. The audience gave me a sense of pleasure and divergent convergence, if that makes any sense. There was an attitude of flexibility to the material presented, and I was able to comfortably collage theory, poetry and fiction. I go to many reading series and have read at numerous other series, and have done so for many years. Clit Lit has a potent double-edge of exclusion and inclusion, wrapped up in pleasure and repercussive erotics.

85

UNCOMFORTED

Little Miss

Mother's not listening to vast thinking allowed so
flew over known hall sounds or faces most
chancing is our heart of failing who better
just right! Unflattened those voices had air filled
sides even which it flatters sadness to lucky!

Givingness

Since we are lucky! Moth's air the headlights!
Girls are luck to a mother not failing!
It is much sadness not with us though!
Seriously, if or how listening makes uncomfortable where
or who you flatter to be true just
mistaken and why it must be so! Given
what she gestured! Which thinking about it did
confirm the probabilities even allowed good margin for
erring on both sides of those issues! (It
is great how we can talk about that
so openly!) It is so great! But your
hand-flicker up butterflied! Fled, flew, it hurt, not
mysterious, by yawning air or constellatory proof of
grief's silliness! We had our chances at her
bodies! Some young voices know better behave herselves!
Heel-click tonic-flutter on a hall or runway outside...
(How'd you make those sounds travel like that,
sitting here!) Regards unflattened faces or thinking or
not remembering it right! Not honest since girls
faking makes you just more gestured! That beyond,
far now, or better chances sear us proof,
how sitting or who is truer about reasoning
uncomfort! But let's fail us, each her burdens!
That you're not of her herselves! Outside that!

87

Deferred lament of the inadequately mothered women friends

The headlights not failing, us though uncomforted where true just so.

Given it did margin for issues.

(It about that but your hurt, not proof of, at her, behave herselves, runway outside...

Like that, thinking or since girls that beyond, us proof, about reasoning her burdens outside.

That.

➩ **MARGARET CHRISTAKOS** is a Toronto-based poet, fiction writer and mother of three young children. She has published four collections of poetry: *Not Egypt* (Coach House Press, 1989), *Other Words for Grace* (Mercury Press, 1994), *The Moment Coming* (ECW Press, 1998) and *Wipe Under A Love* (Mansfield Press, 2000). In the spring of 2002, Coach House Books will publish her *Excessive Love Prostheses*, from which this sequence of poems is borrowed. Christakos's first novel, *Charisma* (Pedlar Press, 2000), was short-listed for the Trillium Book Award. She received the Bliss Carman Poetry Award in 2001, and took second place in the Queen Street Quarterly Lit contest that same year. As Toronto representative for the League of Canadian Poets, she organizes Poetry College, a one-day festival along Toronto's College Street. Christakos taught creative writing from 1992 to 1997 at the Ontario College of Art and Design, and worked for many years as an editor and production coordinator in the feminist and art communities. She regards Ondaatje, Marlatt, Nichol, Brossard, Scott and Mouré as in-formative influences. Her present writing circulates among subjectivity, bisexuality, work, mothering, technology and love.

♣ ELIZABETH RUTH

IT USED TO BE THAT BEFORE EACH EVENT I was filled with dread and worried that no one was going to show. I was nervous to MC. What if someone cried? (Happened a couple of times.) What if someone read for double the allotted time? (Happens far too often.) What if the microphone finally fell apart? It used to be that I couldn't eat dinner beforehand, could hardly enjoy the readings because of my sympathy pains for readers who were knocking knees on stage. But that's all changed. Now if a potent moment occurs I know I'm not alone — the audience will be gracious. If the audio system quits we'll just have to raise our voices. I know how to interrupt a reader if necessary. I have grown in confidence with public speaking and am no longer at all nervous in front of large crowds. I still get that zip when the first Monday of the month rolls around, but now it's pure enjoyment. I'm proud that Clit Lit has grown and developed along with me — or me with it. It's gone from being a lesbian affair to a queer one — one that encompasses greater diversity but still gives space to marginalized content. One whose audience continues to expand and diversify.

From time to time I booked myself to read, usually if there was a last-minute cancellation, sometimes if the theme was of particular interest to me. The excerpt below is taken from my published novel *Ten Good Seconds of Silence* (2001), but drafts of it were read at Clit Lit on two different occasions. You need to know that the prologue that precedes this chapter shows the protagonist as an active (albeit idiosyncratic) contributing member of society — a single mother working as a psychic finding missing children for the police. She "works" in gardens and greenhouses. However, the Lilith Boot presented in this section is twenty years younger, recently released into her parents' care from a psychiatric hospital where they'd placed her. She became pregnant during her hospital admission. No one knows who the father is, and she will not tell. In this scene Lilith realizes that she must forget the past in order to step fully into the future where she belongs.

Ten Good Seconds
of Silence

In 1968, just weeks after my eighteenth birthday, I was standing at the entrance to Mother's kitchen in Vancouver. My muscular legs were spread as wide apart as I could keep them, hands over the material of my dress covering my privates. A wooden bowl full of bananas and crab apples sat in the middle of a pine shaker table with three Windsor-back chairs on either side. Our brand new electric stove was on my right, and a four-tiered spice rack was hanging next to it. Mother was scraping carrots at the counter opposite, scraping their brown outer layer clean with a paring knife, flicking the shavings onto a newspaper in the sink basin. She'd lost herself in the repetition and the satisfying sound — like a new razor on a woman's legs.

"It's time," I said. Mother looked out the window, the sunlight reddening highlights in her hair, which was pinned into a massive six-inch beehive. "It's time," I repeated.

"About time, you mean." She wiped gritty orange hands on her apron. Turned to face me. Mother had been against this from the moment she realized, when she saw me drag that old bassinet up from the basement, and repaint the chipped white wicker. It was just like me to muddle this too, she said. Bad enough getting myself knocked up, refusing to name the father. But dragging the whole ordeal out into the tenth month just seemed like rubbing salt in a wound. And keeping it? Mother had little patience for girls who wore their mistakes so proudly, unapologetically, she said. Like churchwomen donning new Sunday hats. I ignored her remark.

"Must be my water's broke." I was still holding myself between the legs and standing on the outsides of my feet.

"Well, you think clutching onto it like that will make it any easier?" Mother turned away, ran some water at the enamel sink, and put the kettle on to boil. "You having pain?" she asked.

"Some. Right here." I pulled my hands away from between my legs to show that the pangs came from higher up. Mother turned only to gasp and step back, digging the edge of the Formica counter top into her kidneys. My hands were coated in a thick, dark red paste. The front of my skirt stuck to the insides of my thighs and now that I'd removed my hands, blood splashed onto the yellow tiles underfoot. Looking at Mother's horrified face, next at the floor, and then at my own hands, I started to scream.

Blood hit the floor in slow motion:

Drip.

Drip.

Drip.

Then my brain sped wildly to reconcile what I expected with what was really happening. I hadn't seen this coming, hadn't imagined tearing the lining of my body, wounds that would take time to heal. It never for a second occurred to me that I might lose the baby. I scanned the large open room to catch my eye on something for reassurance. I saw the old ice box Mother used as storage for pots and pans, the glass shelf filled with her collection of salt and pepper shakers and the yellow eyelet curtains billowing in as the breeze blew through the open window. Nothing helped. My contractions came closer together and lasted longer, and blood trickled in a steady brown rust stream, smattering into small puddles, like clay deposits marking warm earth. I wanted to cover my ears as my own tissue fell away. I wanted to stop time.

I didn't know then that time never really stops; just disguises itself as progress, another chapter closed, old memories. It slips through fingers like dandelion heads in the wind, spiralling up and zigzagging back down, sometimes you can't catch it but it's always there. I was about to learn though; memory *is* stoppable. Memories can stunt like a malnourished newborn and take on fresh powdery interpretations.

Each contraction spiralled me further into the past. Flashes of my recent life with Randy and Mrs. Moffat mixed with blinding glimpses of the coming child, see-sawing me into the final stages of labour. I reached my arms out on either side of myself for balance. I wasn't certain I'd readied myself well enough for labour. Motherhood yes. But the in-between stage, the passage from single to double, that seemed to be splicing me in two. *A genetic time warp,* I thought. I swear, I sensed Lemon enter into the world the moment the *idea* impregnated my mind, but there was unnatural suffering with her physical arrival. It isn't too often that a body opens to the universe. Legs spread wide to mark change; past from future. A red sea parted at my feet as I walked across the yellow squares, birthing a miracle.

I lost more blood and Mother's voice faded to a muffled irritation, an underwater noise to remind me I'd moved on to a deeper place. I stopped focusing on breathing, my lower back pain and the ringing in my ears: like one hundred wind chimes or the sound of a vacuum cleaner at close range. Instead, I swooned, sucked oxygen inside my lungs until I thought they'd burst and held it there as long as I could.

When I fell forward my bare knees buckled and I landed on them. Hollow thud! On all fours, I stared at a reflection of the ceiling fan in the pool of blood. The fan sliced through the kitchen air, dividing my life in measured strokes. Round and round. It was reassuring, spiralling Bridgewater and my psychiatrist well back into the past, and my whole miserable childhood further behind where Randy always said it belonged. I was making space for a new life. New priorities. So I stared at the fan which was like a metronome and kept a sane pace propelling me into the future.

It wasn't an easy task, letting go. I felt like I snagged on thorny corners of experience and was being flung against the mossy walls of time. I gagged, becoming dizzy. But I was no longer afraid. Babygirl, I thought. Here you come...I screamed again.

"Bloody Hell." Mother muttered under her breath.

Bloody universe.

Then Mother gathered the soggy newspaper from the sink, careful not to leave carrot shreddings to clog in the drain. She lifted the refuse with both hands, opened the cupboard door in front of her and dropped the rubbish down into a bag. You didn't hear her carrying on like a wounded animal at the time of my birth — not even a peep. And, she'd lost my twin. Daddy told me the story so many times. You think anybody came around with flowers or get well cards for her? Not a chance. Just said be happy for what she'd been left with: me, Lilith. A gift from God. Mother closed the cupboard door with her foot, and wiped her hands over the sink. See? Pain runs in the family.

As my uterus contracted I pushed myself up, balanced on my knees and held my swollen belly with love. Mother watched from behind and I tried harder to focus on the final moment of the task. A sudden torrent of water and blood mixed and evacuated my body at once. Baby pink. I held tightly to consciousness through my vision of a healthy newborn. Sweet and tender. Honeysuckle red. Checkerbloom pink. Fireweed, burning in my belly. *Not long ago I was nothing but a child myself*, I thought. *Now mine is raging to be free.* Baptizing Mother's house. Forcing herself out through every pore. I was covered in sweat, burning up. Temperature well above a safe degree. I felt like I was being torn inside out, my contents turning to liquid and running away from me. Even my nose was dripping, taste buds were over-stimulated and I couldn't help the saliva filling my mouth from drooling down my chin. *Stay*, I told myself. *Stay until she gets here.*

I tried my best not to panic. Tried to distract myself even though my uterus *was* bleeding into my cervix, which was ruptured and leaking down onto the linoleum. I thought about snow-capped mountains and the magnificent view of English Bay from Lion's Gate Bridge. I thought about friendship and Randy, and the last time we'd seen each other. How Randy refused to look me in the eye, how she hid under her baseball cap and pretended she was glad for what I'd done, fine to be staying behind at the hospital with Mrs. Moffat. "We all do what we have to," she told me. I figured that next to me the baby belonged to Randy. Maybe by recalling her at that precise moment, Randy's best qualities soaked into my placenta and birth canal, passing Lemon her loyalty and courage. I felt Randy there like she was my mental midwife, so I closed my eyes and visualized her smile, remembered strong hands and a tidal wave laugh. A laugh to drown in. I slid onto my back and raised my arm to block the white light from my eyes. I spread my fingers apart and observed a sticky paste connecting the inside of each digit to the next, giving the appearance my hand was webbed. I'm turning into an animal, I thought. *A turtle, who takes home along when it leaves. Or, an ostrich able to bury its head.* Ancient creatures. Back to the beginning.

A woman giving birth is as round and resourceful as time.

I remembered the details of Randy's expressions and gestures. Thin brown hair, clinging flat against a pronounced, angry jaw. The way she rolled her own cigarettes like she was making a great scientific discovery with the tobacco machine. How her wrinkled forehead gave away her concentration. And most of all, the special way she'd sacrificed herself for me. *The child must never know what sacrifice smells like*, I thought. *Urine-soaked sheets, stale semen and salty tears.* This child deserves her own life. But, can you ever really be free of your mother's history? I clutched my stomach again. *Why won't the baby come to me?*

I knew this wasn't just any pregnancy — Lemon had chosen me. I reached out behind for Mother, who was standing a few feet away, but she stepped back, leaving my hand flailing in the air. Then, almost as soon as the thought crossed my mind about the child needing something more before she would arrive, I had my answer. Lemon wouldn't come until I really had forgotten. Not bits and pieces, but all of it. *Forget everything*, I told myself. *You promised you would. It's better for everyone if you move forward. Only forward, and accept what you were never allowed to. Open to finding. Clairvoyance.*

And so I replaced my memory with the future.

Randy faded feet first, knees, collar bone and finally, her laugh. Mother put the receiver down after calling for an ambulance. No need to become frantic. Someone should remain calm. She could see I was bleeding to death; anyone could have seen that. But what Mother did not envision was that my life would be saved not once, not twice, but three times. And this was only the second time that my Babygirl would rescue me. Blood stopped flowing the instant I made my decision to forget. That was when I started to lose consciousness, and that's when Lemon's head crowned.

When the ambulance arrived the paramedics covered their mouths and noses to filter the odour as they rushed into the kitchen. They found me dripping in my own liquids, so much stale blood that the beige house dress I was wearing seemed black. One of my hands was between my legs, protecting the baby; the other was waving good-bye to Randy before it fell limp at my side. Mother was on her knees next to the table, with an unopened package of sponges in her lap and a pan of clean water and vinegar. Lemon and I had marked the bottom legs of the table and chairs, the counter cupboards and Mother's clothes, and she intended to remove all evidence with both arms fully extended. "You made your bed" she spat. "Now, you'll lie in it."

After I delivered and was taken to the hospital, when Mother was also satisfied that the past was well behind us, she scrubbed herself in the bathtub until her skin was furious pink, and raw. When Daddy got home from work he found her there. Later that evening, Mother got out the mop and pail again and then put a load of laundry in the washer.

↝ ELIZABETH RUTH's debut novel, *Ten Good Seconds of Silence*, was short-listed for both the 2001 Roger's Writers' Trust of Canada Fiction Prize and the Amazon.com/Books in Canada First Novel Award. Her work has been widely published in literary journals, anthologies, and print media. She is also the founder and curator of Clit Lit. Elizabeth is an editor with *Fireweed Feminist Quarterly* and teaches short-story writing at George Brown College. She holds a BA in English Literature and an MA in Counselling Psychology from the University of Toronto, and is a graduate of the Humber School for Writers. For more information please visit www.elizabethruth.com.

95

ELIZABETH RUTH

✒ KIM TRUSTY

IF MEMORY SERVES ME (which it often doesn't), I read at one of the very first Clit Lits. It was a few years back and came soon after my first appearance in "Strange Sisters" — a lesbian cabaret at Buddies in Bad Times Theatre. What both of these experiences had in common was that they took place in queer-positive spaces, with tons of energy and good vibes. At the time I remember being a little hesitant to participate at either venue because, as a straight woman, I thought it was unfair for me to fill up queer space with my privileged, straight-assed self. I decided that it was necessary for me to "out" myself to the organizer, and at least give her the opportunity to fill my spot with someone who, in my mind, had "earned" it. Elizabeth kindly assured me that I would be welcome at Clit Lit, and I am incredibly grateful to her for urging me on. The experience was intimate, enthusiastic and accepting — not to mention *fun*. My heart-felt thanks to all those involved for creating a safe creative space for us — gay and straight — to grow in.

RHYME SCHEMES AND SIMILAC

She lets her weight rest against my legs, hooks her arms over my thighs and breathes deep. I clench the comb between my teeth and continue braiding — real hair over weave over real hair over weave...a rhythm that nearly put us both to sleep. This silence is round and warm like breadfruit roasting on an open flame and Jaleel is in his playpen, asleep after 20 minutes of straight up hollering and I wish she'd just respect this quiet, but no, Nicolle gotta get all up on her favourite topic — makin' babies and how makin' babies made her complete. She tells me I gotta get me one, like a baby is a set of Ginsu knives I could buy off of Home Shopping Network, sale price $69.99. I concentrate hard on finishing this braid, concentrate on the sound of the pink, wide tooth comb pulling through her hair. When she asks me if I at least love my godson, I'll only go so far as to say, "I like the smell of him."

All Johnson's Baby Powder and dried milk

And I'll concede

"I don't mind the weight of him"

7 lbs in the cradle of my arms

Nicolle says

"you should be breast feeding one of your own by now, not givin' birth to words that don't even rhyme!"

I don't blame her for judging.

That's what she knows from

a mother and older sister

both pregnant and manless at 17

but we've been girls since knee high

she's supposed to know

my creation ain't stewin' in my loins

I can't help thinking that if she'd just listen to one of my poems

but she can't hear my flow over hungry cries and *Jenny Jones*

blaring from the TV

And I think that if she could just see me onstage on the mic

but she is a

single mother

in the ghetto

with no baby-sitter

no baby father

and I am a

ghetto superstar

who will leave Nicolle

fatherless sons and

dirty diapers far behind

to flow the trail

of alphabet love.

I Wanna Flow Elemental

This brother's flow is momentous   like the Yangtze during monsoon
winding   swelling   taking life   He's talking conceptuals like   time
space   memory   are places he visits often   So befitting for a man
whose father   pulled the sun across the sky behind him   giving us all
light   and there is enough for my 2 eyes to see   that I will never
flow elemental like my brethren   cus I don't parlez with the gods on
Mt. Olympus

I talk to   the Maytag man
    who still hasn't   dragged his ass   over here to   fix my
        washing machine
I talk to my boss
trying to tell him   that   OT   is out of the question   b/c   the sitter
won't stay   past 5
I talk to   the professor of   my night school course

impressing upon her   the importance of   an extension   for

this   worth 35%   of my essay mark

And I talk and talk   but these words don't flow   from my lips

to the God's ears b/c

I don't flow elemental

So I ask this of you   man who treads firmly   above

the stratosphere   while you are creating   the universes

from synaptic responses   gaseous constituents   and the particles of

light   could you   please   find the time to give birth to a rhyme

that will   explain to a 5-year-old   the possibility of his existence   in the

total absence of   someone else's son   in his mother's life?

↝ KIM TRUSTY is a big-haired "attitudinous" poet who has performed in venues across Toronto since the late 1990s. A member of the Rovolution Girl Style guest collective for *Fireweed*, Kim (and her writing) is consumed by the grey areas of racial and sexual identity. Currently, Kim is at work on her first collection of poetry, and is simultaneously filling out applications for graduate school. In 2001 Kim won first place in *Fireweed*'s national poetry contest.

☙ ANDREA NÉMETH

THE PLACE IS ALWAYS jammed to the rafters, women sitting on the floor, on each other's laps, standing at the bar and cluttering around the doorway. There is barely enough room for the readers to make their way to the stage when their turn arrives. And it's always silent. The sound of so many people listening is one of my favourite things about Clit Lit. I had read in public before but not to such a large audience nor to an audience that was so thoroughly attentive. Clit Lit is peopled by lovers of fiction, poetry and performance who get hooked and return month after month. I've never gone to Clit Lit and not heard something that somehow changed me.

My reason for first going was because it was a queer women's event; the fact that it was also a literary event seemed like a bonus. I kept going back to Clit Lit because it was such a joy to be a queer woman writer in a place where that was the norm, where the different identities — queer, woman and writer — didn't have to compete but could appear as complementary parts of the whole. I had never experienced a place where many parts of myself could come together seamlessly: it was both comforting and thrilling to have found a community.

I wrote the story "A Lifetime" for a night centred on the theme of "Mothers and Daughters." Having studied and written about adoption as a graduate student and having been a reunited adoptee gave me a particular perspective on a theme with which we are all, in our own way, familiar. "A Lifetime" surprised me by being the story that I had wanted to write for several years, the story of a birth mother's initial meeting with her now-adult daughter.

A Lifetime

When I see her all my carefully planned lines fly out of my head and the only thing I can do is stand still and open my arms. She hesitates only for a second, an awkward second that allows her a quick, shy shrug and me to wonder if this is too much too soon, and then she steps into my embrace and tightens her arms around me too. She's wearing some faint sweet perfume, perhaps it's only the scent of her shampoo as her hair brushes against my cheek, so faint that I sense it only for a moment before the hug ends and she steps away from me. It's over so quickly, I haven't even had time to consider the key element of this meeting, haven't had time to savour the feeling of holding my child in my arms. I want to call the moment back already, play it over again and again like a favourite videotape, press "pause" for as long as I need to think about how it feels to hug this woman, this veritable stranger, and know that she is mine, my child, never held before in my arms.

My child. My daughter. How to reconcile the permanent infant of my memories with the adult standing quietly before me? Intellectually, of course I understood that she wouldn't stay a baby forever, of course twenty-five years is a lifetime, the entire journey from infant to adult. But intellect means nothing here, this is all about emotion, this is all about the memory of a high-pitched wail rising from a white hospital blanket, carried quickly out of the delivery room before I could crane my neck enough to see what it contained. All the mirrors covered to hide my shame, protect me from the reality of what I might have seen reflected in them.

"It's better this way," I was told. And who was I, at fifteen, to question? I'd already been proven to be unable to take care of myself, shown that I wasn't ready for the adult responsibilities of love and sex. Who was I now, strapped arm and leg to the table, to say, "No, I want to see. I need to see." I was no one.

"A girl," they told me. "Give her a name." And I cried, not knowing how to name something that I had never seen, something that only the pain in my breasts and between my legs told me existed at all. Tears blind-ed me to the typed document that I was to sign; the date leapt out at me, April 1, 1969, and I mumbled, "April is the cruellest month," thinking sud-denly, bizarrely, of my unfinished English essay. "April" was all they heard and "April is just fine" they said, the form whisked away for other hands to inscribe the name upon it.

This is all about emotion and how it feels for a woman who has long considered herself barren, even though her fertility was demonstrated at too early an age, to have her own flesh and blood beside her, there to be touched and kissed and caressed. I want to grab her and clutch her to me. I want to seize her, feel the solidity of her form, know that she's not a vapour that will vanish when I awake. At the same time, I want to keep her at arm's length, look and look and look upon her, examine her face for traces of mine, for traces of his. Does she look like me? How can I know? I have suddenly forgotten what my own face looks like.

There are a million words that I need to say to her. I'm inclined to beg her forgiveness, though I don't exactly know for what. How can I be for-given for doing what I needed to do, for doing the only thing I could do? Can your choice be wrong if it's the only one? I need her to know that it was right for me and right for me meant right for her, though I have no way of knowing if indeed it was. Is her presence here a sign that it was not? I know so little, as little now as I did then. "When they cry, it means they're healthy," said the only friend to whom my teenage self entrusted the knowledge. "It means they're breathing and they have strong lungs." Strong lungs, the sum of the knowledge I had for twenty-five years about the daughter I had inadvertently named April. I've imagined her a swimmer, a scuba diver, an opera singer...might she be any of these? What if she is? Is there any way for me to make her understand how it was, any way for me to create empathy for her father and I, living in a different world twenty-five years ago, still children in our suddenly adult bodies? Will she have pity or only scorn for our naïveté? "It can't happen the first time," people said in those days, and we believed them until it did. Can she hate me? Can her late twentieth-century-culture have immured her from the conventions of the world that she was born into?

Has she lured me here under the guise of goodwill only to despise what she considers my weakness? If only she could know the strength it took to live each day not knowing what had become of her. My grief so fierce at first that I sometimes wished her dead instead of gone. There is mourning for a dead child, even an illegitimate one, there is mourning and there is comfort. No mourning or comfort for the teenage girl that I was. I had "done the right thing." I was expected to "get on with things" and "forget about it." Which I did, as instructed, though not the forgetting part, her absence resonating so that even if I'd wanted to forget, the echo of my ever-after empty womb wouldn't allow it. Punishment, I thought, for giving away my child and then later, protection, the body wiser than the brain, refusing to allow me to undergo that ordeal again.

"I have a grown-up daughter," I've been saying to myself in the week since we first spoke. I have practiced saying, as if to strangers, "I have a grown-up daughter" instead of "No, I have no children." I have a grown-up daughter and she is standing before me, looking at me with what I suddenly recognize as her father's eyes and smiling at me with what I suddenly recognize as my own smile and without remembering what my own face looks like, for I'm still unable to, I suddenly know that she looks every bit as much like me as I do my own mother. And I wonder if she's doing the same thing, looking at my face and trying to remember her own. How inconceivable it must be for her, to have never looked like anyone, to suddenly find there are strangers who bear her face and speak in her voice.

My grown-up daughter extends her hand, an oddly formal gesture between people who have just embraced. She clasps my hand tightly between both of hers and speaks so earnestly, so anxiously. "I'm so very pleased to meet you," she says, and my breath, which I seem to have been holding, releases. Shared blood doesn't make us anything but strangers and it's this place of politeness that will be the starting line on our journey towards family. "I'm very pleased to meet you as well," I reply. "Shall we walk for a bit?" She nods and takes a step, her arm reaches forward as if to link mine, then drops beside her again. Touching is suddenly too intimate and we settle into step side by side, brushing against one another from time to time as we proceed along the path.

"Tell me..." I begin, then pause.

"What?" she asks.

"Tell me what you'd like me to know," I answer, replacing the "everything" that had been on the tip of my tongue.

"I want you to know I've been happy," she answers, without hesitation, and as if she knows that these are the words I've been hoping her whole life to hear.

ANDREA NÉMETH has a BA in English and Creative Writing and an MA in Interdisciplinary Studies, in which writing fiction supplemented an analysis of the representations of adoption in contemporary popular and literary fiction. Her work has been published in *Focus, Quagmire, Womyn's Words, Existere* and *A Room of One's Own*. She has taught queer creative writing workshops and is involved in adoption advocacy, through both her fiction and her work as a board member of the Adoption Council of Ontario. Since 1996 Andrea has been employed in the non-profit co-operative housing sector.

ANDREA NÉMETH

◦◦ SUSAN GOLDBERG

CLIT LIT WAS MY FIRST public reading. I'd been onstage as a performer before, but never as a writer. As an actor, I'd spoken other peoples' words — sometimes convincingly, sometimes mechanically — but never my own. If the performance was less than stellar, however, there could be excuses: leaden dialogue, an unpolished script, an off night, misguided direction, fellow actors not up to snuff. I could remain one step removed from the successes or failures of performance. Reading my own work, however, provided no such buffer. Nothing between me and the audience except a few sheets of paper and the microphone. These were my words, my innermost thoughts, my prose, clunky sentences, embarrassing revelations. My joys. My pleasures. And pleasure, when I think about it, for me defines the essence of Clit Lit.

As an actor, I'd recognized too late for my liking the power of taking pleasure in being on a stage, that people enjoy watching just about anything if the actors take pleasure and pride in what they're doing. You can play the most miserable, suicidal character convincingly, I think, only if you genuinely love playing her. When I stopped acting, I had only begun to learn how not to take myself too seriously onstage, to lose myself in the moment, in communication with other actors. I had just begun to ride the pleasure and power of being onstage and bringing characters to life.

In my creative writing group my peers would repeatedly tell me to speak up, to read with more confidence, not to apologize for my work. What they were telling me, I realize now, was to take pleasure in the reading, in the writing. To slow down and speak up loudly enough for everyone in the room to hear and enjoy. To let them take pleasure in the sensuality and strength of my writing. To pause for laughs — and expect them in the right places. To breathe. To perform. And that's what I tried to do on that stage that night at Clit Lit. I know I had a good time. The pleasures of connecting with the audience stayed with me for days after.

At the West End YMCA

The Portuguese woman
sits in the sauna
heavy folds of flesh
obscuring each other
dark, pendulous breasts
glisten
as she throws one arm back,
covers her eyes,
in supplication to the heat.

And I wonder what pressures
her body has borne
what children
what burdens
what sacrifices hide
in the sweat that trickles like tears down her face

What hangs round her neck like that cross on her chain

And I want to think "Madonna"
But I refrain.

SUSAN GOLDBERG

SUSAN GOLDBERG is a Toronto-based writer and editor whose work has appeared in the *Globe and Mail*, the *National Post* and *Xtra!* She is the co-author of the non-fiction book *The Facts of Life* (Stoddart, 2002). Susan wrote and directed "Shall We Dance?" — a performance piece for the Strange Sisters cabaret. She writes with a group called the Stern Writing Mistresses.

Harbord St.

It was Mother's Day:

Harbord St. 1979

Or maybe it was '83 (I don't know)

But I know for sure that I was there
and that I was small.
So I think that it all
must have taken place
in and around that time:

Harbord St. 1979.

Now,
if I checked it out in the history books
or in the newspaper archives
I might know for sure.
But alas, I am a lazy poet
and Goddammit this is a story,
so I have liberties to take
with times and dates.
But I amend not the place

For I know for sure that I was on Harbord St.
and I think that it was 1979.

I wore a yellow dress
with puckered pink roses
embroidered across my chest.
I wore yellow barrettes in my hair
and like always,
one side flipped in
and the other side flipped out.
I was about six,
and I was big enough to carry a sign.

Harbord St. 1979 —
me, a small girl
marching in the picket line.

We were marching
Hallelujahs and Glory Be's
to God the Father Almighty
the Holy, Heavenly Trinity

On that Mother's Day,
we sang for the intercession
of Mary the Immaculate
Virgin Mother of myth
to beg on behalf of us sinners
now and at the hour of death
that her Father, Son and Lover
would rescue the world from
the wrath of Eve's Vicious Daughters —
those barbarous women
who would decide when, and if,
they would be mothers.

But I digress.
It was Harbord St. 1979.
I was six years old
wearing a yellow dress.

It was an assembly of Jesus on the Crosses
and Hail Mary Full of Graces
as we marched and chanted
The Lord is With Yous
there would be donuts and Kool-Aid
in the church basement, I knew
and I was thinking about what
kind of filling I would choose.

But there on Harbord St. 1979,
something across the street caught my
six-year-old eyes:

Opposite my picket line of spring dresses
and pastel-coloured ties,
were some curiously, contrary,
confusing signs

On the other corner stood three or thirty women
arms defiantly around each other's shoulders.
They were on every corner that we passed,
I think that they stared at me
and I know that I stared at them:

Trip —
trip —
tripping on the sidewalk crack,

Don't wanna break my mother's back

Almost drop —
drop —
dropping my mangled fetus sign,

My mother yank
— yank
— yanking me back into line.

It was their T-shirts that I remember
most from that day
and that the sun shone
brightly on their long hair
but what they sang I cannot say.
I saw the clothes hangers on their T-shirts
(a line through a clothes hanger)

no more clothes hangers?
It made no sense to my six-year-old mind
what these women and their clothes hangers
had to do with me and my picket line —

So I asked

Harbord St. 1979

From her tongue and lips
my mother's voice was a hiss.
Words pelted like
hail on that sunny May day;
her hard words against my cheek
like a smack not a kiss.
But still, I snuck a peek at
those "lesbian feminists"
or was it fesbian leminists?
I couldn't be sure,

T.L. COWAN

and although I knew they were
Godless Hussies
and not Immaculate Virgins
the sun on their heads shone with such a glow
that it seemed to me that those women were crowned
with fesbian leminist halos.

That is what I saw...
on Harbord St. 1979,
when I was six years old
walking in a picket line.

A few years later on when I called my sister a fesbian leminist after she
successfully stapled my hand...well, I was hit and chased and made
to promise never to use
those
words
again

I was spanked into submission;
I confessed and I was shriven.
Because I loved my sister
and so how could I call her That?

So, I promised to put those words away
onto a forgotten top shelf
and I left them there
until I was tall enough to reach for them again,
which is when it occurred to me to use them
in reference to myself.

So that was Harbord St.
In and around 1979.

When I go there now I still march.
Only now I march my saucy ass

straight into this little store I know —
it's one of those crazy fesbian leminist joints
that sells cocks for girls
and greeting cards shaped like vulvas
and T-shirts with slogans that read
"I like to fuck"
and
"When I grow up I wanna drive a truck."

And when you step through the door they always offer you a cup of tea
to drink as you wander around and take a little look-see
at their notorious wares
and I absolutely swear (on a bible)
that I once saw a dildo so big
that it made me

trip —
trip —
trip on the industrial-grade rug

almost drop
— drop
— dropping my hand-made ceramic mug;

but I collected myself,
acted cool, and sipped my tea.
Cuz I beheld another
browser and whatdoyouknow,
she was cruising me.

Thanks to this store I always smirk
as I turn from Bathurst onto Harbord St.
And although it is no longer 1979,
I still remember that yellow dress,
and the roses on my chest

T.L. COWAN

and the sign that I carried
and the Kool-Aid that I drank.
So, when I walk into that
Godless Hussy store,
I always thank
the woman who owns it
for choosing Harbord St.
because I believe that every time I walk through those doors
those fesbian leminists help me to redeem my soul.

So I buy a book about drag kings
and some interestingly shaped toy things
and I ask her if she knows of any immaculate virgins,
and in lieu of that, if perhaps she might have a
costume that would make me look like one.

Now that I paint the words on my own signs
and march in my own picket lines
I wish I had been on the other side
of Harbord St. that Mother's Day, in 1979.

↝ T. L. COWAN is a poet, storyteller, short-story
writer, spoken-word performer, radio programmer
and student who lives in Vancouver, B.C. T.L.'s
work can be found in publications in Canada and
the U.S., including Seattle's *PUSH* magazine and
Hot & Bothered 3 (Arsenal Pulp Press). T.L. is a
guest of Sister Spit's *Ramblin' Road Show*, and the
curator/producer of many spoken-word extrava-
ganzas including *Choice Words, The Malcolm Lowry
Poetry Stage, Just a Little Bit Harder Than Nice* and
Sex, Lies and Duct Tape. T. L. teaches spoken-word
and "art and activism" workshops. She has a BA in
English Literature.

☙ KRISTA TAVES

AROUND THE TIME I HEARD ABOUT CLIT LIT, my primary identity was bisexual and I was a dedicated bisexual political activist and community builder. I really didn't have much to do with the lesbian and gay community, except to write letters to the editor when I saw biphobia in queer publications. I'd been writing fiction for about three years by that time, but had never shown it to anyone beyond friends and a few family members. I didn't know if I was good. I didn't know if anyone would want to hear what I wrote. However, a friend of mine saw my writing and strongly encouraged me to read it at Clit Lit. The thought scared me because I didn't know how welcome I'd be in what I considered a lesbian space, so I contacted the curator and she emphasized that this was *queer* space and that I was indeed welcome to read. I then attended one reading just to check it out and really loved it. I liked the atmosphere because these women took literature seriously. The people who came were there to listen.

One month later I read and I was also one of the last readers! I was so nervous and so afraid that no one would be left to hear me. I underestimated the loyalty of the crowd. The house was still packed after almost three hours. When I finally stood behind the microphone, holding these fragile words in my hand, I felt something come over me, a power, a oneness with my story, and every word released from my lips exactly as I'd rehearsed it at home. I got a strong round of applause and some really positive feedback afterwards. All those long hours alone in front of my computer, seeing poetry dance around the screen, and finally it could be released into something over which I had no control, because you never know how people are going to hear you. That reading was the first time I felt that I had been a part of a larger queerness.

The Cold Pressed Baptism

The train is coming! Can you hear it? Thousands of pounds of raw tool and die brazed over with coal dust now diesel glaze. The kind that sears its way into the crevices of your palms, accentuates the sharp points of born-again hang-nails and turns your soft and vulnerable and feminine into pure masculine gripping and pumping potential. The sieve of unfiltered motor oil lubricating what used to need shovelling and burning into time compressed into black gold singeing the hairs growing out of pierced nostrils with a Christ-like post-Pauline full-submersion baptism. That's the sound of a train coming. No hydrogenized Crisco pastiness here. Real trains are cold pressed and virgin, verbs conjugated only in ripe presentness. Diesel fumes blackening the back of your throat with the filo pastry of ancient death reborn so that we may race through sunrises and into sunsets fermenting with unfinished business, our lists of wannabees and wishwe-bees and gonnabees whistling through the hair in my nostrils parted by a seam of stainless steel. That's a pre-Pauline baptism of the dunking kind.

The train track parted our farm in several ways. It parted my poet daddy's back fifteen acres from the front eighty-five. It parted my grand-father's first fifty acres from my muscle-bound daddy's hundred and there was no Crisco to make that parting smooth and fluid. That parting ripped sinew into flapping pieces of father/son wishwewere nevergonnabe but I love you and wish you hadn't criss-crossed my back with moulding me into God's child. That kind of unfinished business. Overprocessed iron rails cracking in the summer heat after a bitter winter laced with the unin-tentions of Menno humbleness bred through four almost five centuries of a new dualism Menno mammas and papas and never let Crisco hang off our underarms and never acknowledge the invisible hand that pulls us forward in time because we are the quiet in the land and somehow we forgot the virgin. Somehow we forgot the cold pressed and we got to care more for whether it was submersion or sprinkling rather than the raw baptism that simply means…"Ah…I have been reborn."

That's unfinished business, and the heavy quaking of a diesel-fuelled train slicing through fresh country air and fifteen/eighty-five and fifty/a hundred, panted, "Lots to do. Lots to do. Lots to do," as it cut my father's farm into heretical triangles in a land where squares meant business and success. That's why my father was a poet muscle-bound daddy and that's why the train said, "Lots to do" in pairs of three not four and why he felt in particular that the trinity spoke to him. He was a huge man, my daddy, and I'll bet he could have stopped the train if he'd ever realized he could have lifted his massive arms to the virgin heavens and said, "The invisible hand is not coming through this farm! Not ever! So please back up and go away!" Then the criss-crossed moulding gift from God might just have dried into dust and blown away and I would not have had to flee from the criss-crosses etched on his back by his daddy. I wouldn't have worried about diesel grime working its way into my soft palms, or developed ragged born-again hang-nails. I have attained salvation in the paved place I soak and suck into my body to escape the curse of the hundred and the fifty and hydrogenated Crisco.

But as it was, my daddy did nothing of the sort. No letting the Holy Spirit rush through his fingertips and into the front of the train and rust-ing the axles so it couldn't take any more of his rural presentness away into the urban future. He drew the diesel rumble deep into his soul and descended into the basement so we wouldn't have criss-crosses on our backs, so there would be no fifty/hundred or fifteen/eighty-five, just one big two hundred and fifty acres tilled by poet farmers, muscle-bound and being their own daddies. Daddies to the soil, siblings to each other, age as in only separated by 5/4 time in our mamma's contractions. Pop pop pop pop there we were, all four of us, ready to be the children of coal and diesel and four almost five centuries of Menno humbleness, dreading the pull of the invisible hand and the drip of Crisco.

Our very fertile and psychologically virgin mother had not intended to breed prolifically human beings made for Crisco glazing. Her progeny were to embody the wanderer spirit deep inside her cold pressed ovaries. So she breathed her poet hubby's triangular thick and sticky in through

117

KRISTA TAVES

her globe-like aesthetic and produced four beings with incredible chameleon potential. She problematized them with a programming of subversivity. No post-Pauline full-submersion baptism for her babes. No virgin halo for her daughter. No sowing seed through home-base pumping cloaked in reproduction for her three sons. She called down the Father Son Holy Ghost Virgin Mother Crone for all of us, and that is probably why our asses bodies are tinged with a light shading of purple.

She found herself in conception mode far too easily. One finger gliding over the muscled arm of a poet farmer rumbling with the power of an eastern-bound train and forget the eighty-five/fifteen and who cares about the fifty/one hundred and there's no reason for the quiet in the land. His criss-crosses would melt into her and she would pull their shadow deep inside her, screaming for the sheer love of taking diesel glaze and burning it into nothing, pulling oxygen into eggs made for laughing at arbitrariness. The non-allowable became matter and buried itself into molten rose and grew into its own hallowed beings unaware yet of quietness, humbleness, pain, fear and criss-crosses. Each of her four progeny made her turn into something else and she grasped that elseness like a freshwater fish swims into brine, because why the hell not.

For her first child, she soaked herself in orange, the colour of sky on nights predicting clear blue ahead. Vitamin C. Acid. Citric stuff. She stoked her belly and thought about people of the female sex who smoked like chimneys, didn't let anyone fill them if they felt like being a desert and wore lace and stilettos all the same. She felt in her the masculinity bred in women who spurned baptism of any sort and preferred instead the gauntlets provided by her fellow beings. For her second, she wore the lace and stilettos and breathed in cedar and sage and etched strange symbols in virgin oil dyes on the baseboards behind the kitchen table as her knees ground into old linoleum. She knew it was a boy and felt in her the femininity bred in man who spurned the gauntlets provided by his fellow beings and preferred baptism of any sort. For her third, she opened her legs more than she ever had and crooned to him and shook Vitamin E bottles filled with skin from her own body coated with poet thick and sticky. She felt in her the masculinity bred in man who spurned baptism of any sort and preferred the gauntlets provided by his fellow beings.

Her fourth son felt like a daughter and so it was back to citric and liminal green and woman power stuff. But this time, she felt like putting the family Bible between her legs. She placed the Holy Scriptures where it counted and he that she thought was a she would caress her in places only a pre-Pauline Christ would know about, and minus the stigmata to boot. He became a man who spurned gauntlets of any sort and preferred baptisms of his own making. Pre-Pauline, pre-pietism, pre- just about anything a train would snake away from. She was oval woman supreme, with a triangle branded on each ass cheek, clear and virginal. Not like no nineteen-year-old walking down an aisle leaving yellow sweat stains of nervousness on satin that her anxious mother paid way too much for so her daughter could have a wedding like real Canadians. My mother's purity perspired translucent. Clear as a stream screaming with the rebirth of a virgin baptism. Her translucence accomplished exactly what those who fought for opaqueness feared would be accomplished if human beings (especially the innocent) were allowed to see. Which was…Sight of course. We saw the Crisco, we saw the diesel glaze and the stupidity of eighty-five/fifteen and fifty/one hundred and thought we would much rather wear stilettos. We felt the salvation of smooth un-crisscrossed backs because our daddy listened to his poet self and tried to understand when his wife would take her inside him and then run outside and raise her arms to the north under the umbrella of all the parts of the sky that weren't north.

She knew where it was at, all right. She knew that a smooth back free of railroad lines and Crisco would not groan under the beauty of a full two hundred and fifty acres and its own tool and die iron power because wherever we went, we would paint strange symbols with dyes of virgin oil on the baseboards of our kitchens in urban places that became urban because trains criss-crossed each other. We would feel her knees through our own as they crunched against old linoleum and the tingling of the inside of her nose against filo pastry fumes as she conjugated us into a house that shook with the power of the gentle poet daddy in the basement.

And that's how it went.
And that's how it's going.
And now the train is coming.
Can you hear it?

↪ **KRISTA TAVES** grew up on a farm near Wheatley, Ontario, and landed in 1994 in Toronto, where she became one of the founding members of Bisexual Women of Toronto. She has written for *Siren* magazine and has published several academic articles. Krista's passion is fiction, and more recently, poetry. She understands her writing not as a labour of love, but rather a labour of life, a way of grabbing at the raw edges and massaging them into something bittersweet and tingly. Her writing has always intended to be spoken. She says it means something different when it slides off her tongue.

☙ EVALYN PARRY

The Revolution Song

(a response to the FTAA protests in Quebec City, April 2001)

Sunday morning, after the revolution
we drove home, made the beds we would lie in.
Pockets full of papers and the papers full of headlines;
took some pictures just to prove we had a good time.
Now I'm lying here, while the fires still burn outside.

Wake up in the morning, heads full of sleep and we
listen to the news as we drink our coffee.
Didn't need to be there, you can watch it all on TV,
but now we know that they're only telling half the story,
'cause we were there, we saw the dancing and the drums.

And what they are showing us looks like a battlefield,
but what they fail to mention is why they had to build a wall
all around the leaders, as if they were in jail
or as if they were an empire about to fall.

Friday night, before the revolution,
thought I should call you, thought maybe the solution

was to take my courage and to walk into that landmine,
but three in the morning came and then it was closing time,

and I know you well enough to know that it's too late to call.

And sure love, love can be a battlefield,
and sure I made my protest, tried to break down the wall:
Inside some countries people disappear, and maybe I am one of them,
or maybe we're the empire that's about to fall.

Five in the morning, sun's still rising when we
hit the road, gotta get there to make history.
The old Dodge rumbles toward the trouble in the city
we're dressed for protest like it's Halloween, we're giddy:
the sun is shining and it feels like it's a holiday.

Saturday, what a day for the revolution!
Walked into a wall of tears before I could stop them.
Everyone's shouting "Who's watching the watchmen?"
Everyone's crying 'cause the air's full of poison
but it's here we've travelled to and here we are going to stand.

And this revolution turns into a battlefield,
they have a tea party while we try to break down the wall.
Inside some people the revolution disappears,
and maybe that's just apathy, or maybe it's just easier,
or maybe it's the reason that we're gonna fall.

Monday morning, after the revolution
I never called you, my silence absolution.
But now the miles are flying and my eye's on the road at hand,
I keep on driving like the sea searching for land,
my tires spinning revolutions that never end.

And maybe you'd be hurt if you knew why I didn't call
or maybe you were marching too, holding your own sign

and if I had seen you there,
maybe we'd have put down our masks,
faced the fear and breathed the air
stood with the rebels by the broken wall

and watched the empire fall.

123

Profit in the Margins

Wait a second — just a second — did I blink? How did I miss this?
When did gay become a gold mine? When did homo sex go prime time?
When did my previously marginal identity become a marketable entity?
When did being gay or lesbian go from catching to cachet?

It must have grown inside the boardrooms of the mega-corporations:
"All right, gentlemen, now listen to what I have to say:
imagine two men, as a couple — sure it's disgusting and immoral,
but two white collar professionals together
means we're talking double earning power!

Then minus the dependants (since they've got no wives or children) —
what we've got here, fellows, is a cash crop!
All we've gotta do is convince this target market
that our company's on their side, and then they'll dispose
of all that income on our cars and clothes and gadgets,
they'll buy our liquor at the dance clubs,
and gentlemen, our net sales could increase by...ten percent!"

Sure, I can see the times are changing
but not like the Christian Right was hoping.
Seems family values don't hold a candle to our newfound market value,
since it's no longer economically viable to discriminate
against the previously disenfranchised but presently highly politicized
and extremely well-organized group of people that we are
because as it turns out,
we've got money.

And not only that:

we've got sex appeal. And in the open market...
well, as they say, all's fair in love and war.
And everyone knows a good war does wonders for an economy,
the way the battle against AIDS and HIV must have made the condom industry
go delirious with profit joy!

And sure, we all know sex and ratings go hand in hand, like lovers:
it's like bisexuals and fences, it's like Birkenstocks and dykes,
it's like gay men and their loafers
but if you walked a mile in my shoes,
you'd find me talking on the telephone
to my friend who's in a crisis, having split up with her boyfriend.
She says, "I wish I was a lesbian, it would be so much easier with women!"
And I say, "Thanks, but I think your analysis is lacking."

Seems TV's been airing progress:
shows like *Queer as Folk* and *Ellen* make it all look quite appealing.

But let me tell you that my "lifestyle" doesn't feel much like a sitcom,
since being queer still skates this fine line
where love and fear are deeply entwined.
The law's still no guarantee against violent discrimination,
people's fear still knows no regulation
and when you see me walking down the street
hand in hand with my girlfriend

we're not just a market,
we're a target
so don't tell me what you'd rather be,
that it's easier to be me
just 'cause your heart's broken and you've temporarily had it with heterosexuality.

125

EVALYN PARRY

My life's not just an alternative
and though there may be profits
lurking somewhere in my margins,

I'm not coming up with any spare change,
I am looking for some real change.

EVALYN PARRY is a musician, writer and theatre artist. She has been "Poet in Residence" on CBC Radio's *Definitely Not The Opera*, and her spoken-word pieces have been commissioned and broadcast on several other CBC Radio programs. She released her debut music and spoken-word CD, *things that should be warnings*, in 2001 (Ponygirl Records). Theatrical writing credits include *The Freelance Lover*, a "gay comic musical" (Independent Auntie Productions), *GRRRL Power* (Company of Sirens) and *Clean irene and Dirty maxine*, co-written with Anna Chatterton. Evalyn's performances are beginning to take her on tour across Canada and the United States.

MAUREEN HYNES

UNTIL I WAS ASKED TO READ at "She Works Hard for the Money" (an event co-sponsored by the Mayworks Festival of Working People and the Arts), I had never even been to Clit Lit, so it was quite a thrill when I walked up the stairs to find the pub packed with a huge and growing crowd — I was so used to the poetry-reading scene with just a handful of listeners. We had been asked to read work dealing with work issues, and all the other readers — poets, non-fiction writers, novelists — all of them stuck closely to the topic and spoke about how hard it had been to confine themselves to that theme. But to tell the honest-to-goddess truth, I really didn't — and still don't — have all that many poems that deal with work. I wish I did.

A really excellent work poem is something that can speak to so many people because many of us, especially women, spend such a large part of our adult lives undervalued and underpaid and out of place in a job that steeps us, like a strong tea, in a brew of banality, frustration, oppression or fear, and occasionally — I really don't want to omit these — in the joys of accomplishment, connection and making a positive difference in the world. A good work poem can distil and release the frustration or joy of a particular moment, send it out into the world where the recognition doesn't just make the reader feel a warm and fuzzy sense of recognition, but allows us all to see, or hear, or taste that work reality and its meaning so much more deeply and clearly. I envy poets like Wayde Compton and Philip Levine and Larry Leavis, who can do this so adroitly, and as the poetry editor of *Our Times*, I am always looking for poets who can do this.

However, in order to have suitable poems for that evening, I had to expand the idea of work to include the emotional work we do in our families (like "Nine New Undershirts") as well as a more traditional meaning ("Storks of Kampala.")

Storks of Kampala

(Uganda, 1985)

In the early morning, a massive bird attacks
our window: close-up of claws, huge wings flapping,
its pointed beak and pendulous throat sac
on a long bare neck — an image of terror, framed
and hanging in our hotel room.

I remember a baby's room back home:
above her crib, a blurred photo of storks nesting
in a European chimney. Here
they look like vultures, perched
on window ledges above the piles of garbage
simmering on every street corner. Grimy
sentinels, they keep watch

over the rotting stew of fruit peels and cellophane
for the quick dart, a rat, a mouse.
How can you run your shop,
I asked a hairdresser, no water or electricity
until dusk? We pay, she said, we pay.

Yesterday the hotel owner told us to come back
in exactly three hours, before the curfew.
We spent the afternoon with the taxi drivers
under the acacias in the railway station's park.
Could we imagine its perimeter lined with corpses —
starting with the edge of the parking lot,
could we get further than the torn clothing,
dried blood, arrested flail of arms and legs

in the larger heap, pile the mounds
all the way to the red brick station? —

                            no.

In the evening we looked down from the hotel room
onto the park, a yellowing clockface
spread below us, eight dusty paths radiating
from its centre. We settled in the damp, half-
painted room, the iron bed swallowed
into the corner, our packs open on the floor.
A thin trickle of cold water to wash
my hair as I knelt in the tub. In the suburbs,
machine-gunfire burst out at the stars. That night,
the phone in the railway station rang
steadily for four hours. How could we sleep?
But we did, until the stork woke us, we slept
through the sweet smell of garbage
burning and extinguished and burning —
a wasted, desultory conversation with the rain.

Nine New Undershirts

It was a kind of evasion, the way
I carried that chore past late August,
but his new undershirts for the winter
hardly seemed urgent, the days

still hot and glorious, the nights
not yet ripening to a chill.

Finally, early September,
I bought them, three packages of three
undershirts, low white scoops
at the chest, the armpits, the back,
entirely serviceable, male.
Nine tubes of cotton ribbing, bought
in a hurry, carried around all day,
even left in a washroom for an hour.

As soon as they were laundered and
labelled, he began to die. Two
weeks they sat folded on the windowsill
beside him, and I wondered,
was I bargaining, was I deluded? — *Oh, can't you
just wake up and put one on?*

Now they spill like tissues
out of a bag on my bedroom floor. I pull
them out, wear them one by one, a layer of readiness.

MAUREEN HYNES is a Toronto poet whose second book of poetry, *Harm's Way*, was released in 2001 by Brick Books. *Rough Skin*, published in 1995 by Wolsak and Wynn, received the League of Canadian Poets' Gerald Lampert Award for best first collection of poetry. With Ingrid MacDonald, Maureen co-edited *we make the air: the poetry of Lina Chartrand*. Her poetry has also appeared in several anthologies, most recently *The Edge of Time* (Seraphim Press). Maureen's memoir, *Letters from China*, was published by Women's Press in 1981. Maureen is the poetry editor for *Our Times* magazine.

MAUREEN HYNES

◂◉ MARGUERITE

I HAVE READ IN PUBLIC BEFORE at a variety of venues but for some reason that I cannot quite explain, I was really nervous reading my pieces that night at Clit Lit. I was very rushed. I raced home from work and had supper and then my partner and I dashed over. I had never read as part of an ongoing reading series before and that felt like a really big thing. Or maybe it was because the venue was so full that there wasn't even room to walk around inside. There were people everywhere, even at the top of the steps opening into the entranceway. Also, I had not read in public for a while, so that could account for the dry throat and the queasy, anxious feeling in my stomach. I didn't want to disappoint my faithful supporters (you know. The friends and the lover who drag themselves from one "poetry reading" to another so they can ensure that someone in the audience applauds). I had written new pieces and tightened them up for Clit Lit but I wasn't sure how they would transmit. Two of them were in my own dialect "from home" and I didn't want the essence of what I was saying to be lost because people couldn't understand.

The evening turned out to be excellent. I felt that we all gave our very best. The theme — Racism and White Supremacy in Queer Communities — was one that caused a lot of introspection for me, and after performing I stepped back to figure out what I was really writing about and in what genre my work fell. I came to the conclusion that I will write about whatever gives me pause in whatever way the "inspiration" brings it to me; be it poetry or short-story forms. I like to think of myself as a storyteller. That I *perform* my pieces instead of reading them, but I have only written two tiny (short) stories. I have come to understand that my poems tell stories also, and I am comforted by that realization.

I am not in the "scene" per se and I keep feeling like a part-time artist who is not a defined poet or a storyteller or an activist or…I just write because I like to and I have to…then I perform sometimes. There are thoughts and ideas that haunt me until I put them to rest on paper and that process gives me great joy. At times I feel that writing is the reason "for my being here." I've had to reconcile my own ideas about who an artist is or should be, and how I live my own "artist" life. I feel as if I have betrayed the mantle of "artist" because I am not dedicated like my colleagues. I don't write for hours on end, every day, and I am not consumed by writing. I don't live, breathe, eat, sleep writing and performing. I'd like to but I don't.

The experience of reading at Clit Lit was a very pivotal one for me. It made me stop and think about what I was doing as an artist and why. More importantly it provided a safe space for me to share my work and feel whole in all of my many selves as a woman, as a black/Caribbean/lesbian. The pieces I have offered here are in response to racism and homophobia within the "queer" community and the black community. Finally, I realized that night that had I been single, I could have had a lot more fun after my reading. Women seem to love artists and the attention would not have been wasted on me!

133

MARGUERITE

SUGAR MONEY

The people in Zimbabwe up in arms.
Dey beatin up de white man an
tekkin back dey farms.
North America say dat it's a disgrace.
Now anarchy will come an take ova de place.

Granny say "beat dem an gimme
back me granfader sugar money."

Back when they had de bible in dem han
an gun ina we face to tek way we lan,
It wasn't no disgrace.
Ah fine it hard to understan
de unfairness of dese europeans.
It's all good an well when dem did tief
Now we must give dem full reprieve?

Granny say "beat dem an gimme
back me granfader sugar money."

I know dat two wrongs don't make a right.
But if we don't act now change
will neva come to light.

Me Granny say "beat dem an gimme
back me granfader sugar money."

Nyabingi

Ban up yuh wais'
an tie up yuh head
Screaming batty man
an sodomite fe dead.
Wearing righteousness
as your conviction
burning the sinner
with a litany of diction.

Remember while you
hating with pristine clarity
De macabees say dat de
greates is charity.
Is it not red blood
dat I goin bleed
when you fork up me folly groun'
and plant your seed?

Do you really think
dat dis is de ansah
to the silent commands
from your supreme master?
Next time you iditatin on the weed
callin on Silaisse I to intercede,
Look in de mirror an you will see
de real difference between
you an me.

↪ **MARGUERITE** is a black Caribbean lesbian and a Peterborough survivor. She's been writing for the last six years to deal with the madness of daily living, preserve her sanity, cleanse her soul and keep herself at one with the universe. As a hedonistic Pisces she is happiest enjoying life and her partner. She is eternally grateful for the support of her tireless friends, who always encourage her to keep writing. Marguerite's work has appeared in *Our Words, Our Revolutions*.

☛ PERCY LEZARD

CLIT LIT HAS AFFECTED not only my life but the lives of other queer women and queer-positive folks who support the creative expression of this vital and awesome community. In moments of silence, sitting on the edge of my barstool awaiting the next stanza, paragraph or witty comeback, I have participated in the festivities. I have talked about race and class and about how as queers we can be just as cruel in our love and passions and in our self-hatred as non-queers.

137

Wannabe

Sooo...you want to be an Indian?
Visit our Pow Wows,
watch us dance our style
in fancy jingles and traditional dresses with long colourful ribbons,
be mesmerized by our footwork
and our eagle feather bustles?
But you turn a blind eye and scowl against the drunken Indians
soldiers of war
who line the fronts of your skid row.
Hmmm...honey...don't you know your class and privilege has got to go.
You wanna have some place to call home,
smell the sweetgrass and sage burning
and satiate your need to be replenished with the taste of Grandma's fried bread?
Witness and acknowledge our persistent commitment to each other,
our "nomatterwhatyoudoyou'refamilyandwewillloveyoutilltheldaywedie"
cuz we ain't got nothing but that to hold on to.
You've appropriated everything else.
We're left these small plots of grazing land; the OK Corral.
We're left overwhelmed by your charity and self-indulgence,
your attempts to extradite generations
with disease-infested blankets
and rotten maggot meat
first by your knights in tarnished armour, the cavalry
and now as you guiltily donate 71 cents/day to UNICEF
while we live on food stamps and pennies in your own back yard
and epitomize a developing nation.
Our traditional hunting grounds are stripped now
buffalo gone ghost on the prairies,

fish swollen with uranium and mercury.
It's tough competing for permits with the commercial fishery boats.
So?

Sooo...you wanna be a woman?
Hahahahahaha....you wanna experience what it's like to give birth
be a creator of life,
a power you've deemed so threatening?
You wanna give birth to that BOY-CHILD to carry on your namesake
cuz girls are here only to be left on a mountain side
or along that old country road
set to drift down the river
or become little old maids
waiting on you hand and foot,
and to top it all off be treated like shit and get paid 66.9 cents
compared to your boy-child's wage?
Mmm mmm mmm...you want to marry me cuz I'm your little princess.
Cuz you want your half-breed children to have high cheek bones
nice chubby cheeks
creamy, dreamy, chocolate skin
and big brown eyes...
trophies for all to see.
But you fail to see
the countless numbers of anonymous sisters
daughters
mothers
casualties on your stat sheets.
It's been seven generations since first contact
and still you turn a deaf ear to our cries each time we're raped
beaten and bludgeoned,
and that's every 2 minutes and 17 seconds.
You fail to read the 7th page small print news story
about how our sister Anna Mae's hands were severed from her body
and preserved in jars on your government shelves
in the name of national security.
And how gratuitous you were to send her body back to her people.

Sooo...you wanna be a dyke?
A woman of 2 spirits
lezzie
fairy
homosexual
gay
woman-loving-woman
clit licker?
The latest media craze,
fad propaganda splattered on the cover of magazines.
You wanna be shaved by a long-legged cover girl
beauty in a bathing suit and high heels
with a nice view up her ass?
Haahaahaa...when the shit hits the fan
and you lay all your cards down on the table
you don't really speak the languages of tongues
but the languages of pricks.
You're too scared to embrace the reality
of you
being an individual
defining the parameters of your own relationships
and not let some patriarchy define it for you.
You don't taste the fear we gag on
deep in the closet
passing for straight to keep job security
because some males feel masculinity is threatened
and some females think lesbians are out to convert every woman we meet
and hate men
don't eat meat
have hairy pits and legs
and are aggressive old hoes.
So, you wanna be a dyke when the reality bite of it is will our families
ostracize us
or institutionalize us
for what they call our little "phase"?
We won't be marrying the Jones boy, you know?

Or maintaining the national survey's quota of 2.5 kids
a dog
a nice house in the burbs
with a picket fence.
We know the Jones boy is a flaming queen
and in our small communities full of rednecks and homophobes
he might be the only support we've found for being different.
There are real wars waged against women, gays and lesbians,
First Nations, people of colour.

Sooo...you wanna be me?

➳ **PERCY LEZARD** is a 2-spirited Okanagan poet who lives in Toronto with an Anishnabwekwe. She rides her mountain bike, plays soccer, greets each day with thanks and is a woman in love with words and more words. Percy has had the good fortune to share her work onstage with others who have had great one-liners, metaphors and raves, all of which have inspired and changed her. She strives to be creative and wants to morph one day from only standing onstage in front of a microphone to seeing her work fill the pages of a book.

✒ VLAD ELIZABETH WOLANYK

WRITING IS ONE OF THE MOST IMPORTANT aspects of who I am. Words, woven together, reflect experience and location from many different angles. Clit Lit marked the first time I had ever read in public. I had just returned to Toronto from Vancouver and was beginning to see my life from a very different point of view. I used to go to a similar literary event in Vancouver called Dyke Words. I had meant to sign up to read there, but always came up with some kind of excuse not to. In the past, I had found ways to present my art without having to get up in front of an audience. I wrote and directed theatre for several years, happily getting high off the audience from the safety and comfort of the tech booth. When my films screened, there was nothing like sitting incognito amidst the audience under the cloak of a dark theatre. It was when I moved back to Toronto that I knew it was time for a change.

I had collected years of my writing in notebooks — from high-school crushes to tranny-boy angst to nervous breakdowns. I finally gave Elizabeth Ruth a call and was amazed by how accessible she was. But alas, my heart sank with relief when she told me that the line-up was full for that night, but to bring my work anyway, just in case someone backed out at the last minute. The night went like this: I smoked, drank thick ginger ale, smoked, listened as best I could and smoked some more. At the end of the evening there was just enough room for one more reader. What was it like? Quite honestly, I'd love to write about the exhilaration and gratification I got from reading, but it just wasn't like that the first time. However, it was one of the most important stepping stones for the person I was then.

Another Day Pounding My Own Head On The Pavement

There are so many reasons why I'm stone. That thick scaly flesh I use to protect myself from them. Because sometimes it's just easier to slip under my skin than use my stone to fight back. Today is just another day pounding my own head against the pavement. Standing in line at the UPS office, wondering out loud to the woman in front of me whether or not there's a poster of the perfect UPS worker on the wall of the interview room. "Yeah really," she says. The look in her eyes paints the same portrait I'm imagining, of Mr. and Mrs. Hetero Aryan-Nation proudly wearing their brown uniforms with the coveted gold insignia. Like me, the woman in line is clutching her completed application with visions of paying rent and buying groceries this month. We're both hoping that this time we'll get a job that doesn't pay slave wages under the table with some testosterone-pumped power-hungry foreman at the helm. She looks over at me again as a young Asian man stomps out of the room, shaking his head and mumbling, "What a waste of time!"

Earlier that morning, I had debated with my partner whether or not I should bind my breasts and apply as Vlad. Hey, a nice, young, clean-cut Eastern European boy could easily get a job like this. "No," she shook her head. "Too risky." Are we really living in 2002 or is our reality more akin to 1960 than our anti-discrimination rhetoric would have us believe? In a time when our community is taking the federal government to the highest courts with same-sex marriage issues, I can't even get a job that pays more than a buck or two over minimum wage and hides people like me away in dark airless warehouses.

As I was standing in the bread line, hoping for a chance at the brown and gold, a union job that pays all right with benefits after three months, I found myself asking, "Why?" Why should I foster white-male-hetero privilege? I thought about the woman in front of me? *She* could never

143

VLAD ELIZABETH WOLANYK

hide her skin behind a tensor bandage, a condom filled with hair gel and an eight-dollar crew cut. Her presence gave me renewed hope and it helped me get through the three-hour wait for the ten-minute interview. After finally meeting with the young, blonde and blue-eyed human-resource lady, the woman in line ahead of me came out of the interview room, and I knew from her face what I was in for. But she held her head high and smiled at me as she made a most fabulously dignified diva exit.

My turn next. Miss Tight-angora-sweater looked over my application, citing an error. I'd seen it happen to a few other "unposter-boy" applicants. She said I had to wait and fill it out again. "But here's the information you're looking for," I said, pointing to my freshly printed resume. "Well," she repeated in her best anti-discriminatory voice, mandated by the large, politically correct corporation, "you're going to have to fill it out again." "But I've been..." She cut me off and pointed to the stack of applications on her desk. "I understand, but you'll have to wait a little longer. I'll just be a moment." A quick smile and she turned on her heels with her thoughts trailing loudly behind. She came back before I could possibly be finished and happily interviewed a charming young woman who had been in line behind me and who was, ironically, wearing a similar tight, baby-blue sweater. Hmmm? I guess the college-boy look is out this year for girls. Have I committed the ultimate interview fashion faux pas?

Wondering again about my decision not to try and pass, I began to imagine myself in a poofy blonde wig, a busty, baby-blue angora sweater and a long, sophisticated black skirt. Now don't get me wrong, there are many women who would look stunning in an outfit such as the one I have just described. Unfortunately, even though my mother coerced me into dressing up for very special occasions well into my teens, my entire family would always say I looked like a "football player in a dress." The analogy continued while I endured sharp scoldings of "close your legs!" and "stop swaggering!"

The thought of precious adolescent memories helped me pass the time while I waited, yet again, for a chance at rent and groceries. Well, wasn't Miss Fake-smile-disorder just taken aback when she finally came out of the room again, expecting me to have moved and be waiting at the back of the growing line for another turn. "OK," she said mockingly. "Nice to meet you, I'm..." She extended her hand without making eye contact.

144

BENT ON WRITING

Oh no, what do I do now? I thought. Should I drop to my knees and kiss her diamond engagement ring to show my newfound submission, so she can drag me by the ear into the interrogation room and degrade me for being a he-she? Nah, I'd like that too much. Besides, she had spent long enough in her office after the last interview. Perhaps anticipating, preparing. I'd heard her talking on the phone about the applicants. Maybe after re-reading *The Politically Correct Bigots Guide to Dominating the Universe*, she was still a little shaky because I had the audacity to show some assertiveness.

She took a deep breath and allowed me to follow her into the interrogation/torture chamber. She was trying her best to look flustered and disorganized — aha — another deterrent. Why would I want to work for someone whose office is completely spotless except for a few papers she's frantically pushing around? I'm on to you lady. She tried to keep it short and simple. In fact, I'm not really sure she said much at all, with her mouth anyway. She even avoided telling me about the available positions. I smiled politely, but all I could hear were her thoughts escaping, or rather the Korporate Koercion Kaucus guidelines, repeating in her head like a mantra. Remember rule #1: They are still the enemy, you just need to pretend they're not and they won't hurt you. Fine, I told myself. But she can't deny my qualifications and experience.

"Okay," she finally said. "I just need you to sign here to say that you have attended the first interview." (Translation: "Look, we've filled our he-she quota, you're never gonna get this job but this can go in our equal-opportunity proof file for when those nasty equity-seeking groups come calling.") She pushed the paper over, rotated it and handed me a pen. I picked it up and began reading. After a five-second pause she spoke up again. "So, if you don't have any more questions." Basically showing me the door.

"Well actually," I said, "I'd like to hear a little more about the other two positions you have available."

"Oh — uh — yes, but you've got your heart set on driving, right?" I almost fell into the trap and said "yes." Sure, driving would be great, but I knew there were a lot more people applying for the driver positions, so I wanted to cover my bases — rent and groceries being *my* mantra. "Yes, I would love to drive," I agreed. "But I'd also like to apply for the customer service position."

She sat up straight in her chair, flipped her hair. "But it's not like people just come in and drop off packages and stuff." Whoa. Rule #2: They can be coerced into believing they're worthless, even if they think otherwise. I raised an eyebrow and still poised, I spoke.

"So it's similar to a Canada Post kiosk?" Her eyes quickly shifted back and forth from me to the speed-dial button she'd labelled "Customer Courtesy Coalition." "Well no," she said. "It's more like, well you see…" She ran her hands through her hair, racking her brains. I almost felt sorry for her, almost. "You see, it's nicer than that." I tried really hard to conjure up a sympathetic smile.

"Like a Mail Boxes Etc or a downtown Purolator Centre?" "Exactly!" She perked up, hoping now I'd know enough to back off. But all I could see was a red light, highlighting her grin. (Rule #3: Perseverance. You can be a politically correct bigot if you try.) "So," she continued, looking over the application. "You may be called in for a second interview, for a driver's job that is."

"Because you don't hire bull-dykes?" I blurted. "Or any other visible minorities in positions where they might have to interact with the upstanding Bay Street crowd?"

She was stunned. Rule #4: If all else fails, pretend you don't know what they're talking about. (Special side note: This is especially effective with those who don't have Anglo accents.) After that she responded mechanically. "I'm not sure what you're talking about, our procedure ensures we always hire the most qualified applicants." But I was ready for that one.

"Oh, I'm sorry," I said, rather mechanically myself. "I don't fit into the poster-personnel diagram you've got hidden behind your smile. And even if I did, you've already hired your token minority this year?" I could see her searching her brain for Emergency Rule #5: Bring out the token employee. Flustered, she opened her desk drawer and pulled out a red envelope and started waving it around.

"I don't know what you're talking about. Here, I've got it right here, our discrimination — uh — anti-discrimination policy. It says we cannot discriminate on the basis of race, ethnicity, religion, etc…" She was searching through the coveted text when I shook my head and got up to leave. "See? It's right here," she insisted, almost out of breath. "We don't discriminate against sexual orientation!" Because of course she had not once noticed I was queer during the interview. Before she dug herself any deeper — as pleasurable as that would have been — I grabbed the piece of paper I had signed, tore it up and walked out.

Although I didn't get the rent or groceries I needed, I kept my dignity. I held my head up high while making a fabulous diva-boy exit. You know, there are a lot of reasons why I'm stone. There are the angry and justifiable reasons I could have used to pummel her, but the reality was I just slipped back under my stone — where years of violence, hateful words and violations don't hurt. It protects me from thinking, "I'm sorry I'm here" while I secretly scream, "Fuck you!" in my head. Eyes cold and unmoved, back straight, I just walked out of that UPS building and moved down the pavement to my next interview.

↩ **VLAD ELIZABETH WOLANYK** makes his way through the everyday as a writer, filmmaker, performer and cowboy social worker. Other times you can probably find him working on community-based projects. Vlad's films *Untitled* and *Farshot* have been shown at many festivals across North America. His alter ego, Big John, can occasionally be found performing at the Femme Cabaret, the Sexin' Change Cabaret and as a member of the Drag Kings of the Iron Curtain. Vlad is currently working on his next film, a musical comedy about self-harm.

☙ LEAH LAKSHMI PIEPZNA-SAMARASINHA

I WAS GOING TO A READING for the first time in a long time. I was way too skinny and doing a passable job of looking like everything was fine. Yeah. Sure. I was walking down the street with the boy, the one who had been the queer '90s version of the Young Lords three years earlier but had mutated into a straight, scary Nation of Islam member doing the "I'm-Oppressed-So-I-Can-Get-Scary-And-Fucked-Up-Whenever-I-Want" number. I was kicking myself in the ass, asking myself why the fuck I had left New York in '96 to come to this little backwater of a city, cuz, I mean, if I had been less freaked out I coulda been a contender. Like at the Nuyorican. But instead here I was going to what was probably going to be some lame-ass white girls' lezzzbian folk song gig that was the only game in town in a town with no spoken-word scene except for occasional pole-assed "cabarets" where people *clapped*, politely, after every poem.

So we walked in, me with him and his older, adopted bro. Lots of white girls, lots of white queer freaks. But lots o' girls who didn't seem to have a lot of money, either. Not just shaven-head neo-Nazi lookalike bleached-headed chicks on a trust fund. And yes, there were three earnest muffin girls doing some kind of folk song. And then I got up. When I got onstage and did "mestiza rapechile love story," I had that feeling I hadn't had in a while, that sense of grabbing the mic and feeling waves of power come up the stage through my cunt, my hips and stream out my mouth. I wrapped both hands around the mic and felt that beautiful thing of doing the piece, saying every word like it was the first time words were said, stopping at the right moment, editing onstage, feeling huge waves of sex and crying and shit crashing back and forth between me and the audience. I love to perform. I love to be in that moment where people get what they want and every-thing changes. I fuck like I perform. Present. Conscious and fully responsive. Back before I started fucking again, performance *was* sex to me.

Not long after I went to every queer-women-of-colour night in town, which blooms and blooms even through monumental pain, betrayal and bullshit. I got a gig at Desh, at Mayworks, at Desi-Q in San Francisco for Pride, 2000. I get lots of chances to blow folks' minds open. I'm grateful. For queercolouredwordgirls Toronto is a kaleidoscope where no one place is home. There are brown straight nights where conscious means dyke jokes, whiteboy academic nights where you could die and nobody would notice, & this. Clit Lit. Where queer freak girls get up onstage, open their mouths and shut everybody up.

149

mestiza rapechile love story

thank you for showing me what ecstatic sex was like   sex without rape, contempt
or exploitation
even before I remembered my colour. or my rapes.

your sweetness lingers
the secret place high in my womb   that spot
buds & swells at tha thought of you
still makes that river of honey flow
outta my azure brimming cup   bursting from musky plum nipples   coconut cream
flowin down rivers of honeefunkin thighs
leaves me with every cell shining
leaves me drenched   satiated
in sweetness

1998: I hated you for years for leaving me without a forwarding address, I hated you for years
for busting my cool then walking away   & then when I open the magazine
& yr photo jumps out the page and this happens I hate myself, think i'm stupid, a fool.
You were nothing, it's been four years, i'm an idiot for still letting you honey me up...

1994/losaida nyc

your skin is my colour, maybe a little darker   it's June, the season of brownness, the mestiza's favourite season cus it's when we look like who we are & my skin is honey bronze my hair is napping chestnut in a million locks standin up shot through with bronze flaming deep mahogany red like some kinda lavender apple tree bloomin in NYC   N-Y-C NYC of sweetly stinkin wet air   plum skies, swift rainfalls little green trees & rottin garbage in the courtyard   sidewalk piss and rat carcasses boilin make you gasp in flesh as it all sticks to you   & humidity makes a layer of moist cream on the top layer of your skin

& my little faded black thin strapped tank top is fallin low over my honey peach suckable breasts w/long kinkin coarse nipple hairs   cut-offs bleached to pale white and ice blue are tight over my brown legs with their fat thighs   sistah ass & little golden shining hairs curling above my ankles purple toenails are curled inside beaten combat boots

& you got them deep set black eyes dark bronze copper skin & cut cheekbones   black bristle hair, separate each strand & thick, cut short to your head   would it nap if ya let it grow?   When you walk into the living room and say hello our eyes meet and stay when I ask you what you are you say w/one blink "corsican"

if you'd asked me back then what i was i woulda said w/a wide smile "polish, irish, portuguese, and a little bit of malaysian"   (since that was where my father grew up i didn't even know the names Tamil or Sinhala)

corsica's pretty close to algeria last time i looked

well there are a lot of dark folk in europe hunh

you silently throw over your blond plump assed blue eyed gringa girlfriend who's travelled across the country to meet you at stonewall 25 & see you for the first time in 4 months   we both feel pretty bad about how things are unfolding but we can't help it   there's something here neither of us can name we both need

i'm 19   48 inside   you're 25 what i'll be when i get there   I don't got no words for what makes me feel so young so old yet   we don't got no words for what we

are   so we meet in the palace of touch silent
                              but eye to eye

being possessed isn't erotic to me   being known is   it's rare anyone does
                                                    you know what i
you take me brimming in waves crashing over fully
want without me having to labour to explain   because you know who i am you
cherish it man you cherish it   you wrap my hair in your fist jerk my head back
so you can suck my neck in washington square park surrounded by rasta dime baggers
on a long walk home to avenue b   where you suck my clit flicking your tongue faster
than the speed of light over her   pump my vulva w/four fingers makin sure to
rub my plug with that tips   & right at the exact right moment   as i'm
giving you all of me moving up & down on your hand & letting everyone in the whole
tenement know just exactly how much i'm feelin it you thrust a thumb up my ass & i
gather up surge spit pulse   make jungle bird song cries that come from my womb
                aiiiiiiijeeesus

& am satisfied
for the first and only time in my life

you're leaving town in four days   that makes it safe for me to do this

'cause babygirl didn't make it
outta childhood that is
be a girl tryin to fuck fingers came too young outta her
any other fingers be willing
be a girl/all her walls babyfucked outta her
be a girl/only time she feel good is from fingers erasing her
be a girl/looking 6 and 86 w/no in between
be a girl/had the courage to heal at 16
still too late
be a girlhole suckin everything in/to/love me?/fix me?/heal me?/fill me up
even though i'm desperate/crazy/desperate/crazy   fill me up
like 48 twinkies or a whole tiramisu cake   3 packs of cigarettes and 8 cups of coffee

fill me up like money pulled outta tha atm
fill me up like crack pulled up a stem
fill me up
be a girl don't know the inherent aqua spangle hipped railroad track walkin loveliness/
treasure/is herself

never seen it in any mirror/in any woman of her blood/kept carefully away
be a girl all she knows how to be tha erotic exotic/eurasian/anais nin/that cinnamon
skin/spices & gold is taken from by white skinned men with brown & blond hair
out for what they can get   surrounded always by walls of white

& meet you
who don't take anything from me
who gives me what you can
which is what we are

1998/i am feeling lost/of a year of not only celibacy but absolutely no desire for sex/
after 7 years of frantic spastic fucking because it was the one thing i was good at/after 2
years since memory burst outta her pen 900 miles away from her mother/1 year since i
stopped fucking because i realized nowhere in my bones did i know that i cld say no &
not be killed/because i realized i didn't know how to fuck w/out becoming the
servant of servants in the middle/watching my body go through the motions from the
ceiling/after 1 year and 2 months of incest survivor celibacy i feel desire again/it's you/
i don't understand why

1994: we try to fuck a couple times but for the first time i can't hypnotize myself out of
having severe vaginismus so that everything looks Normal & the show goes on   i am
terrified and lost because every time you try and put your cock inside me my cowrie feels
somebody trustworthy for once & refuses to lie for me   she slams her door
shuts and bleeds   oh well   you still make me come like none other before
or since   like not an itch bein scratched or a muscle spasm but with no
limits brimming in rainbow waves i can see moving through my body   same way you
can watch pressure waves moving the land in thick ripples during an earthquake

when i try and do my usual i-give-the-best-head-n-town thing (which i do by psychically figurin out what the other person wants and hypnotizing myself so i can do it) so i can get love and get it over with you say it's all right, don't worry about it   your eyes are a wall i don't understand   you are smart enuf not to go further into it   i've never met anyone who turned down my offer of serving before   i don't understand what yr doing

1998: thank you for knowing your limits and not violating them thank you for walking away from my gaping holes   my desperation for someone to lay on their hands & fix me

1994: the last day we were together you slept over at my house & i could feel your body leaving me already in the ways you curled away from me holding you   you knew what you wanted and it was not my confusion about ecstasy and need meaning salvation   you showed me how to do that

but that last morning you walked me to my shit job   up avenue a and down east 4 then   around 10 minutes into the walk the thunderheads began to mist down five minutes more the water was pouring down thick in a green jasmine steaming river around our ankles   ten minutes more lightning was flashing in sparking lavender charcoal and the thunder was splitting the sky   i was soaked to my skin & i had a hard time breathing because the air was so full of water   five steps away from my shit job   i grabbed your wet waist you grabbed mine and our bodies clung lips to nipples to belly   kissing with all the passion muscles in our bodies flowering in our tongues as Kali, Oya & Shango applauded our union with their dance   my real Mother blew her conch shell the wind that blasts away all that no longer serves us

you kissed me good bye then walked off to harlem before you started hitchin back home

LEAH LAKSHMI PIEPZNA-SAMARASINHA is a bi-queer femme "breed" Sri Lankan writer, spoken-word gal and multitasking revolutionary diva. She is proud to be continuing the tradition of her grand-mother and great-aunties, mixed femme slut girls who were kicking ass against colonialism and war in 1930s Sri Lanka. She has performed her work widely and has been published in *Fireweed, Anything That Moves, Bamboo Girl* and the anthologies *A Girl's Guide to Taking Over the World, Femme, Brazen, Colonise This!, Dangerous Families* and *Planting A Tree: Mixed Queers Speak.*

❧ LARA VLACH

I WASN'T NERVOUS about reading until my cousin Amanda turned our truck onto Church Street. Then my throat tightened and I began to fidget, straightening my sweater, my hair. In my nervousness I kept looking out the window. Having come from out of town and never having been to the Church and Wellesley area before, I was thrilled to see openly gay people. My home city, London, isn't exactly the best place to see two girls holding hands on the street. I started to relax a bit, it's hard to be tense and to grin at the same time. I didn't relax enough though; after we parked it took me two blocks to realize I had left my story in the car. Oops.

Inside I met up with friends. Then I went to get a drink of Coke; I'm seventeen, among the youngest to read at Clit Lit. Sitting in the audience I was thinking that my story wouldn't be nearly on par with the other ones. I made myself remember that everyone had probably started off just like me. Elizabeth Ruth introduced me by reading my bio and then telling a story I had relayed to her about my first day in a new high-school class: "Lara's English teacher thought it would be fun to break the ice on the first day of school by playing an alliteration game based on the first letter of your name. Going around in a circle everyone had to make up something revealing about themselves. When they finally got to Lara, she realized that 'lovable' and 'likeable' had already been taken, so she bravely stated, 'Lesbian. Lesbian Lara.'" Kind of a big deal. I was suddenly out to my classmates.

After the readings were finished, my cousin and I said a few quick good-byes and made our exit. We walked back to the truck, changed out of our "dressy" clothes and into our pyjamas and started the ride home to a completely different planet. Because of the fabulous reception my story got, both at Clit Lit and later amongst my friends, family and teachers, I have decided to expand my characters and have begun writing more.

Seeing Angel Fly

I have two mothers. I always have. My father was a number in some sperm bank. Number 68C4529N. The only other information I have about my biological father is that he was of Native American descent (I don't even know what nation), he was twenty-eight at the time of his "donation" and he was a carpenter. That's my Dad. I am twelve now and I live with Angel and her new partner, Sara. Angel is my non-biological mother; she and my other mother were together three years before I was born, and Angel and I moved out when I was nine. It's weird, but when you think of it their relationship was only as long as I am old. Twelve years, and only now are we beginning to really live. Being able to live with Angel wasn't easy; she fought for custody of me for five months and during those months I had to stay in a foster home. It was weird living with men. It's different having a "father." I wouldn't trade Angel for anything in the world. She loves me best.

My foster parents were all right, they treated me well and I like that they didn't look at me as if I were a fine china bowl waiting to be dropped, the way the workers at Children's Aid did. I guess *they* don't realize that being through what I have has made me stronger (hey, I didn't even realize it for a while...). If anything, I am like Tupperware — strong, protective and flexible. During my months at the foster home I saw Angel eight times and I saw Momma only twice. She cried and tried to hug me and talked about how she was getting help — group therapy. I love my Momma, and I don't want her to cry, but it still scares me to be near her. The man supervising our visits was off his chair as soon as he realized she was going to try to touch me. He watched the whole time. That makes me feel safer. I really want Momma to get better. She wasn't always so scary.

Angel moved into a big two-bedroom loft while she was preparing for our court date. Now we share a pool with the woman downstairs and we have a big bathroom with a hot tub. Angel was so sure that I would get to live with her that she decorated my room exactly as she thought I'd like. I have a big bay window with purple sheer drapes, and hardwood floors. My walls are pale yellow and I have a canopy bed made from the same light purple fabric as my curtains. Angel knows exactly how I feel, too. She put a picture of Momma in my room, one where she is young and laughing and I'm on her knee, about four years old. I like the picture because the frame opens and closes so I can look whenever I want to. I always close it before I fall asleep.

Angel went back to work. She hadn't worked in nine years; Momma wouldn't let her. Angel is a paralegal, and she spends a lot of time working on her cases. She represented herself at our trial, that's how smart she is. There is a lot about Angel that I didn't know when I was growing up. Momma worked at the police station, where she was a narcotics officer. She lost that job when Angel and I moved away because you can't be a cop if you've hurt people. I am glad that Angel and I left Momma even though she was probably mad at us. The last time Momma hurt Angel we had to tell the people at the hospital that Angel fell down the stairs.

In court, Angel told the judge that the last straw was when Momma hit me. She said she would sooner die than see *me* hurt. I heard Sara tell Angel that she likely *would've* died if we'd stayed any longer. It makes me sad to hear Sara talk about Momma that way. I like Sara a lot but she never got to know the person my Momma really was; she only knows what Angel and I tell her, what the papers say about the cigarette burns on Angel's arms and back that make her ashamed to wear sleeveless or backless dresses any more.

After Angel got me back she enrolled me in school. I'm in grade seven now and I like school, but it was really hard to make friends at first. Everyone knew who I was because of the newspapers. My grade four teacher only made it worse by having me introduce myself to the class on the first day. I told them that I live with Angel and that we moved here for a new start. Then the teacher asked if anyone had questions. A boy in the front row asked me what it was like to have two moms, and it hadn't hit me until just then how many people knew my story. I looked right at him and asked what it was like to have a father, because having two moms isn't really all that different from having a mom and a dad. He said sorry for asking, and then the teacher let me sit back down.

I have some really good friends now and it feels good to have friends that treat you normally, who want to go to the movies and the mall. Friends that don't stare at Angel's arms, and who don't ask how Sara and Angel know that they are really gay. My best friend now is Pieter — the boy who asked me what it was like to have two moms. I found out that he didn't have any mom at all, and so I told him he could come over whenever it was all right with Angel. In a way I have three parents, Angel, Momma and Sara — so it's okay with me if Sara and Angel treat Pieter kind of like another one of their children.

Angel met Sara at the law firm three months after I moved in but Angel was really scared to go out with her. I know because Angel and I talk about everything. Sara knew that Angel and I had been through a lot, and they decided to go really slowly. Sara only moved in two months ago. That is pretty slow; Angel and Momma moved in together only six weeks after they'd met. I see Angel flinch sometimes still when Sara goes to touch her, and in those moments Sara's lips get tight and she looks as if she's going to cry. When that happens Angel always turns around and kisses and hugs Sara, and they tell each other that it's only a matter of time before things change.

Sara and I make breakfast together, except on Sunday when Angel makes breakfast for the three us. After breakfast on weekdays Sara and Angel drop me off at school and then they go on to work. I walk home after school, unless it's Monday when Angel or Sara picks me up and takes me to see my social worker. The social worker always asks how I'm feeling, if I am still having nightmares, how school is going? Things like that. On Thursdays she takes me to see Momma at the halfway house for an hour. Momma says she's feeling a lot better these days. She says she knows how much she hurt us, but she hopes one day we can be friends again. I don't know about that, but I do know that I don't always back away when Momma tries to hug me now.

Angel and Sara are getting married in six months and I'm really excited. My friends don't understand how they can get married, and I had to explain how marriage is more than just a slip of paper from the government (although that would be nice). But that Sara and Angel are really happy to love each other and love me, so their marriage is a celebration of their commitment to each other and the love between all three of us. It is only going to be a small ceremony, just close friends, Sara's brothers and sisters, my three closest friends, Pieter, Taurie and Vanessa and of course, me. Angel will wear a long white dress with no sleeves and a low-cut back. She decided on that outfit because Sara told her that she can't really see the scars any more, and that she loves the graceful slope of Angel's back.

➻ **LARA VLACH** says there are three things she really loves to do, in no particular order. The first only sounds great in the shower (singing)… and the second (camping) can't really be done in the winter. The third is to write. It would be difficult to do this in the shower, but at least it can be done all year round. Lara mostly writes poetry, unless a story pops into her head and demands to be written. Among the youngest writers to have read at Clit Lit, Lara is also out to her high-school classmates.

✒ MARGARET ROBINSON

I SIGNED UP TO READ at Clit Lit before I had any material, so the looming deadline gave me a good kick in the ass to get the work done. It was challenging to read work that outed me as bisexual to a crowd that, unless one knows otherwise, is always assumed to be lesbian. Because this was scary I decided not to distance myself from the piece by the creation of a fictional narrator. I was relieved to get laughter rather than booing.

Three Dates

July
She was tall and flat
with a mop of black hair she kept pushing back out of her face
She had a thin nose and high cheekbones freckled by the sun
She wore no make-up
Her thin fingers pressed my hand in a firm handshake
She started talking about her ex during coffee
Her ex had worn make-up and had long hair
Her ex was bi, which she said proved she wasn't serious
Her ex used to cry after sex
Her ex had been abused

I ordered chicken
and she reminded me meat was murder
She said she was a strict vegetarian
I confessed that I used all my teeth
Over the entree
I learned that true love waits
"Celibacy has been great," she said
"It's taught me so much about me."

September
She was small all over, like a pixie
At the women's-only dance at the Civic Workers' Club
she wore combat boots and a black prom gown
When she danced her hands were like butterflies
circling her body for a place to land
When they twirled above her head I knew she didn't shave

We drank margaritas
and talked about building bi community
we slow danced while Patsy Cline sang Crazy
When I got home that night I wasn't surprised
I had soaked through my underwear and my jeans

Breaking up with me on the phone
she apologized
"I'm sorry, honey," she began
"But open relationships take all the fun out of cheating."

February
She was round and soft
and moved like she knew she was beautiful
Her hair was a dark, false red
And she wore blues and greens and whites
The colours of the ocean
At a lecture on Women's History
she leaned over and whispered to me
"The great thing about this top," she said,
"is that it has so few buttons."
Later, drinking burnt coffee out of Styrofoam
I revealed myself in layers like a striptease
bisexual, polyamorous, sm dyke
Waiting for the light behind those green eyes to flicker and fade
"What about you?"
She licked her lips and tucked a red curl behind a seashell ear
"I choose not to label my sexuality."
She leaned forward and placed a hand on my arm
"Is that going to be a problem?"
Later, lying naked like a piece of wood tossed ashore by the ocean,
Covered in her wetness and my wetness
With fingers waterlogged and wrinkled
I finally understood what people meant
when they said sexuality is fluid.

The Ballad of Little Billy

My uncle Bill came from that generation
that named their kids after themselves
Roberts sired Bobbies and Pauls made Baby Pauls
My Uncle Bill had Little Billy Robinson

Little Billy was a problem from the get-go.
Started smoking when he was nine
Started drinking at thirteen
Wore a jean jacket and didn't want to cut his hair

One time, or so I've heard,
Playing hockey with a few of the guys,
Little Billy had a breakaway
Flying headlong down the ice
His hair streaming back like dirty ribbons
No one could stop him
Of course he scored on his own net
And Little Billy was transformed into
"Wrong Way Robinson."

By the time I became a person
in the eyes of my family
(Seven is supposed to be The Age of Reason)
Little Billy was 22 years old.
Little Billy looked like Bryan Adams
and always smelled like old beer.

He had married a woman named Debbie.

Debbie wasn't very bright
In their infinite sensitivity,
My family called her Poor Stupid Debbie

One night
after drinking in my aunt's kitchen
Little Billy hit Poor Stupid Debbie
in the head with a beer bottle

When he went to pick her up at the hospital
Unshaven and smoking home-rolled cigarettes
made from the butts of the night before
Poor Stupid Debbie wasn't there.
For about a month afterwards everyone called him
Beer Bottle Billy
And Poor Stupid Debbie
Who no one ever saw again
Is now just Debbie

165

MARGARET ROBINSON is a bisexual Micmac
from Nova Scotia. She is currently finishing graduate
work in theology at the University of Toronto.
Margaret is also active in the local bisexual community and is currently co-chair of the Toronto Dyke
March Committee. Since reading at Clit Lit,
Margaret has been slowly building up a mystery
novel of the cozy variety.

MARGARET ROBINSON

●◆ TANIA ANDERSON

CLIT LIT CHANGED MY SELF-PERCEPTION. I had always thought of myself as a working person with a mostly forgotten visual-art background. Always an avid reader, I would never have referred to myself as any kind of writer and couldn't imagine that I would ever write anything of interest. I had always kept a notebook, but had never liked anything I wrote. Wonderful ideas would come into my head while I was riding my bike to and from work and that was where it stopped. About two years ago I began to take my writing more seriously and was beginning to find my voice. I started coming regularly to Clit Lit. The event gave me the confidence to take my writing to a context outside of my notebook.

Untitled

They paved over the park today
Specifically, they put asphalt
over the gravel path
They left the inner circle path gravel
for 2 weeks
and then it got paved too
No more bare earth to touch
effectively sealed
after another shouting fight
2 weeks went by
and then, enraged you threw
your bicycle off the porch
I turned away from you then
and felt the pain of this withdrawal
too
I went behind myself for awhile
put my passion
my compassion
on hold
sealed, like the path
hoping that some powerful solvent
could melt the black
penetrate the landmine that is
my body
and shout for something better.

TANIA ANDERSON

TANIA ANDERSON is a social worker, book artist and occasional writer who likes to remember, on paper, particular life experiences. She doesn't mince words and is known for her *brief* Clit Lit appearances. So far, Tania's published works are comprised of books she has made entirely from scratch.

SUE GOLDSTEIN

Deconstructing Daddy

(After "Daddy" by Sylvia Plath)

You do not do   you do do.
The thinning heel of your foot longs
To stop out my wavering path
My veering off of you.
Nature is suddenly your friend, city boy
And I, your natural enemy
Against your nature, your trail.

I do not do   I won't do
But you'll have to crack our mirror
And still I'll reflect in shards of your everyday.
Seven years costly luck
or perhaps seven millennia
of trying to fit the wrong peg into the wrong hole;
But the peg will not do
What it is supposed to do
It has a mind of its own
and will not mind you
Daddy.

I've been dreaming about you lately
You say you'll never change, you are
Who you are: a man treading
Heavy, in a rut
And now I am one of your targets.
I'm not content to crawl home to you
Periodically coming in for a bruising
Having to pull myself
Belly down in the dust
Back up to my comfort
And the sores are accumulating
But they're not getting enough time to heal,
Daddy.

Daddy, I think of you every time
I see World War Two.
You miss your European roots
If only in times of war;
Late at night you rejoice
Celluloid rituals and purple hearts.
You identify with the aggressor you prefer
Never with the Jew that you are.

But my tongue got stuck in your wires
Historical snares gave you
Hysterical fits,
Your battleground unproven
I make you run from your womanhood
Back to boot camp
Back to kick, kick, kick.
Heel, you say
Heel, to the dog!

Give me just one more bruise, Daddy
Allow me just one more open wound:
Shut me off for good, yes

let's say "good-bye" and mean it, Daddy
Take your will, take your money
Lavish it on some other girl who will take
Your loathing of all who won't suit you
Some other girl who won't challenge
Your manner, your carefully placed barbs
against skin belief dress behaviour sex.
Some one who will love you
Just the way you are
There is no choice
You place your feet into cement
Knowing it will be harder and harder
To break out of place.

No. Daddy
I'll be okay
I'll sit Shiva for us
Who no longer fit
The ones that don't do.
Don't worry Daddy
I can sit Shiva all by myself.

SUE GOLDSTEIN

➜ SUE GOLDSTEIN was born in New York but seems destined to live everywhere but there. She currently attempts to make her way by dividing her time between writing, making art and waiting tables in Toronto. A graduate in fine arts from the Concoran School of Art in Washington, D.C., Sue is also working on a second degree in design and illustration at the Ontario College of Art and Design. Sue's artwork has appeared in *Fireweed* and *Canadian Women's Studies*, but her writing has never before been published.

•⟡ DEBRA ANDERSON

CLIT LIT HAS HELPED ME write through my writer's block and this is a huge gift, because without a public forum and without the pressure of deadlines, my desk drawer sometimes stays empty for a while. My second time there, I read from a novel-in-progress entitled *Code White* — a book about a twentysomething dyke who has her first manic episode and is involuntarily hospitalized at the Clarke Institute of Psychiatry. In the novel my protagonist has to deal with the fact that having a marginalized gender or sexual identity added onto the already stigmatized identity of "mentally ill" can be both disempowering *and* liberating.

FROM

Code White

September 5, 1999

This is the truth. Honest. When I smell my armpits, each smells different. One reeks real strong of raunchy male sweat and the other smells of dainty female perspiration. No one will believe me, but it's true. I keep checking every day and every day the left is male and the right is female. I put anti-perspirant on both sides so I don't know what gives. I tried to tell the nurses but they just looked at me like I'm crazy.

I discovered my bi-gendered sweat two days before Jamie arrived. I was in the kitchen when I first saw her come in the ward door with two nurses and then three others swarmed her. I was wearing my checkered old-man pants, my pink plastic soapbox stuffed down the front to represent the dick I thought I should have and a Metallica T-shirt I had slept in. My hair was all dread-locked in the back 'cause I'd forgotten to brush it for a few weeks. And even though all my instincts were now telling me the most unfamiliar fact that I was a boy, I still couldn't give up some of my old femme habits, thus the eye make-up from the day before, which I'd been too tired to wash off, and which was by then riding a much wider surface area than when I'd first applied it. I sat watching the nurses explain some of the ground rules to Jamie, whose name I already knew, it being such a small community. I didn't know Jamie personally though, and she didn't know me, but I'd seen her around. I wondered if she was nice. I wondered if we'd get along. I wondered what she was in here for and what was wrong with her.

And then I crammed more catsup-flavoured potato chips into my mouth and licked my fingers, which were stained a salty red. Every time I came to a break I would whip out my compact and reapply my bloody red lipstick, only to smear it off in the very near future while I jammed my mouth with more chips. I crunched extra hard, as loud as I could that

173

DEBRA ANDERSON

time, and Andrea, this bitchy anorexic girl who always got dressed and never wore her PJ's during the day, well, she was trying to watch *Oprah* in the open-concept lounge and she kept turning around to glare at me. I didn't care. I wasn't at the Clarke to win a popularity contest.

The gaggle of nurses blocked my view. Is there ever a time when they don't get in the fucking way, I thought, just as they separated. Just like the Red Sea splitting and then there was Jamie again, resplendent in all her butch glory. I hoovered in her image: man's white dress shirt, tie, sweater vest, black pants and jaunty black cap on her head. It felt like it had been forever since I'd seen a dyke, never mind a hot and classy butch. I wondered how she smelled. I looked a mess. I checked my lipstick in the compact and felt that the soapbox was in place with my other hand. Jamie looked at me just after I'd decided I needed to go hide in my room. (I stood up too fast and tripped. I'd forgotten I'd taken off one of my flip-flops and it's hard to keep your balance in only one platform shoe.) By the time I put on my shoe and stood up again properly I could tell my face was bright red and my hand was shaking. Andrea laughed at me — *Oprah* was on commercial so she had the time. But Jamie was still looking. I made my way past her and that's when she winked. She winked at me. And then mouthed one word: "Later."

In my room that night, in between the night nurses doing their checks every fifteen minutes, which involves them noisily opening your door and shining a flashlight in your fucking face, real good for people with sleeping problems, eh? Well, in the middle of all that shit, I tried to time the length of relative privacy I had until the next one came back and I jerked off hard while thinking about Jamie's handsome face and small hands. I already assumed she packed; it was just a question of what her dick looked like. I came in thirteen-minute intervals that night for hours, until the sleeping pill, exhaustion and bliss made me pass out.

October 7, 1999
I've finished my zombie walk around the gym, which involves me rhythm-ically dribbling a basketball around the gym's perimeter. Each time I slap the ball I pretend its orange bumpy surface is a girl's ass that I'm spanking. By the time I spank the girl or the ball around the gym thirty times, my hand is pink and sometimes kinda swollen. It's a good thing the Clarke doesn't

174

BENT ON WRITING

allow therapy, because if I told a shrink what I'm pretending with the basket-ball they'd keep me in here even longer and worse, they'd take away my gym privileges.

After I'm done my little "scene," and I know how pathetic it must seem to those of you who are not in-patients, I sit on the wooden bench in the hall by the gym. A bunch of male patients storm past me with two attendants. This one guy lags a little and cases me out. I've seen him in the elevator before. Today he's wearing the same PJs I wear up on the ward. The blue wide-legged bottoms that have Hospital Property stamped all over them. My eyes narrow. I'm about the only one who wears them on my floor and I feel like they're mine. It's as if it's the prom and we've shown up wearing the same dress. But it's not the same dress, it's *my* dress. Those are *my* PJs goddamnit! And boy does he smell good.

He's in the gym now but I can still smell him, fresh and clean. No cologne, just pure boy smell. I'd forgotten what that smells like. And I feel guilty for liking it. The boys are exploding in the gym, as if on fast forward. They are firecrackers going off, filling up the place with their frustration at being cooped up on a ward. I watch one guy wrap himself in the volleyball net as the attendant approaches him.

I remember coming to the gym with two attendants a couple of months ago, when I was still manic. I spazzed out with a basketball, throwing it roughly around everywhere, not even keeping track of where the nets were. There were other patients in the gym too, from a different floor, with their own attendants. This one patient was older than me and had a black fingernail so I asked him if he'd painted it that colour or slammed it in a door and he said he'd hurt himself. Then I got on my high gender-revolutionary horse and told him I wished he'd painted all of his fingernails and he should try it. That day I had either an orange stuffed down my underwear or my trusty pink soapbox so I was packing and he stared at my bulge. At the time I thought he was envious, now I know he was just weirded out. He hollered and the psych assistants all came running. Pat and Ralph took me back upstairs even though the other patients said they hoped they'd see me soon, that I was so much fun. My gym privi-leges were revoked for a long time.

Those guys in the gym are still fizzing all over the place, bouncing balls off walls, dunking balls into basketball nets, scooping plastic pucks

175

with hockey sticks, running in crazy circles, expelling all this energy I don't have, or remember ever having. The PJ bottom guy runs out the door after this sponge ball that's all rusted. He throws the sorry-looking thing against the wall a few times and doesn't look at me. I don't look either but I can tell when he's gone back inside. The bottoms of my feet are burning and my hand is shaking. The left one again. He comes out and sits on the stairs, spits into the garbage can without getting up. I think, gross, what if he missed. But he doesn't. He scratches his back and the top of his underwear shows. They're grey and remind me of Jamie. Then he sits in a chair by the fountain. His head is shaved and I think wistfully about when was the last time I saw a dyke with that haircut? I think about how good a shaved head feels under my hands, against my thighs, between my legs...and I blush when he speaks. "I know you," he says. "You went to my school. Did you go to Northern?"

I look him firmly in his eyes. They are grey like his underwear, and he seems crazy, whatever that is. I want to stop this before it starts, even if he does smell good. He's a boy. I'm a dyke. We're both locked up in here and I hate it that part of me wants to take him to the water fountain where the assistants won't see and kiss him. I hate it even more that he is here and Jamie is not. "You don't know me," I say. "I didn't go to your school. I'm a lot older than you."

"No, you're not. I'm twenty-four, how old are you?" I'm actually twenty-four too and I know he somehow knows this, but I don't want to answer him. And then he starts doing this musical thing with his mouth — dadadatadada — over and over, punctuated with squelching noises too. We stare at each other while his mouth makes musical accompaniment. I don't know why, when I stare at him, all I can think of is Jamie adjusting her tie. Of Jamie underneath me on the floor beside my bed, on the side furthest from the door so we're hidden from a nurse. I look at him and I think of Jamie lying on the cold floor and of me shoving my/this guy/our hospital PJs down around my thighs. I look at his hands and somehow they're Jamie's hands on my ass while I'm straddling her and sliding her big cock inside me after I'd ordered her to lube it. I look at his fearless eyes and remember how afraid I was that day when Jamie and I had miscalculated time and that a nurse would be by any second, and how I'd get caught with that boygrrl's dick inside me. I remember how afraid I was that I was letting her fuck me, then afraid I'd never get to be fucked by her again. Mostly I remember being afraid that I'd never get to have her. And I didn't. Jamie's a bit of stone, a bit of a trannie boy and I didn't have enough time or space in between those precarious room checks to flip her. It wasn't the right place for that.

The boy in the gym winks at me. I don't know why I don't just leave, or why I'm wet, or why I wish he was closer so I could smell him better. Then the psych assistant comes out and asks me if I'm staff. PJ bottoms smirks. I should have said "yes" but I say, "No, I'm a patient." They both leave. I picture PJ bottoms blowing me a fruity, flouncy kiss over his shoulder, but of course he doesn't.

I go back into the empty gym and stand in the spot I first saw him throw a basket. I aim for the basket and shoot. The ball doesn't even hit the board. My throw was too low and my arm sockets hurt from the effort. I sit on the ball. My ass bones hurt against its bright, tight orange. I think about the picture I wanted to draw for Jamie, how if I was an artist I would've. But I'm not, so Jamie will never get this painting with her legs spread and both my hands inside her cunt. Coming out of my hand would be a bouquet of girly items, all pink. Stuff like ribbons, lipstick, garter belt, a pair of high heels and, of course, flowers. Her hands would be cupped around my hands. It'd appear that we were both holding the bouquet, both offering the bouquet to the other. Underneath it would say, "One day Jamie, I'm gonna get your girl and give her to you."

I go to the opposite basket, closer, to the left this time. Then I zero in, aim at a spot on the board and release. The ball smacks the board and falls effortlessly through the net and hits the floor. My arm sockets are fine. I hear clapping and turn to the door. At first I think it is Jamie standing there and then I think it is PJ bottoms, but it's just Ralph saying it's almost dinner and they want me back up on the floor. I've been gone too long.

October 15, 1999

In the smoke room Mary said she's being discharged this Friday. She's supposed to go and live with her brother for I don't know how long. A while? The rest of her life? She said she doesn't want to. Doesn't want anything she's so depressed — except a smoke, a coffee (triple-triple if it's jumbo, double-double if it's just a large, and always with cream and not

177

milk) and to kill herself. What about her apartment that she pays rent on with her ex's alimony payments? It's been empty so long and it'll still be empty. I wonder how it looks, how Mary would decorate her space, but I can't ask. And if I asked her, well, she already thinks I'm weird, but it seems an unsightly question. I don't want to pry. I know what her left inner forearm looks like — the old cut that reads, "Help Me" and round bumpy burns, as if butts had been poked into her skin like you'd dab a napkin at the corner of your mouth if you were trying to be well-mannered. There are layers of cuttings and scars on her arm. The newest one is cross-hatched to look like Frankenstein stitches.

I remember a few weeks ago when she was sprawled in her white bathrobe, holding the coffee I'd brought her 'cause she isn't allowed off the ward. How nonchalantly she'd talked about cutting, answering Nicole's question by saying, "Everyone has their hobbies." And I picture Mary applying for a job (although in reality I know she's too sick for that even though she's being discharged) and her filling in "cutting" on the part of the form where they ask you to list your hobbies. Apparently she's ready to leave here, even though she never got full privileges and made two suicide attempts. But her burns have stopped oozing pus and are now only scabs. Maybe that's how Dr. Dorbo measures progress.

November 5, 1999
Today at lunch I sat with the new girl, Ann. Janice came over to our table and asked Ann if she was on assignment. Ann looked scared and asked what Janice meant.

"Are you helping someone, assigned to help someone?"

"No, I'm just a patient," Ann answered.

"So am I," Janice said, as if there was any doubt. "But it seems like such a waste of time to be only that."

And the crazy thing is, I agree with her.

November 6, 1999
I lost my job today. Well, I probably lost it before. I bet they were just waiting until I was well enough to hear the news that they were letting me go. I called the store to check in and tell them I'm supposed to be discharged next week. My luck it was Bob who answered and not Donald.

So Bob hems and haws and then tells me they hired two people in the interim since I've been "away" (as he so politely put it) and blah blah, they didn't know how much longer I would take, I'd been away for so long, blah blah (as if that was my fault, like if I was being a good patient and working harder I would have gotten better and gotten out sooner). Then Bob tells me the new people were really working out well (as if I didn't, I worked my ass off there for years). I ask him what about me, and he got all nervous and I knew what was coming and I just wanted to slam down the phone but then I saw bitchface, Nurse Susan, accompanying Janice to her room and I got distracted. I heard Bob say how they have a commitment to the new people, that they hired them and can't just let them go. And I'm thinking, well, isn't that what you just did to me? I'm furious and scared and wondering what about the unfinished pieces of furniture I never got done restoring at the store before I got sick, but I guess the new uber-employees finished them. And I'm pissed off but then I was always labelled "temporary labour." I mean they never even gave me a T4 slip and there's no way I can get that job back. So now that I'm going to be discharged soon, I have no job. Bob made pathetic small talk on the phone to cover up his discomfort with talking to me. He had originally told me that I could come back when I was better, and now he'd given my job away. For once, I don't cry and I'm so glad. Instead, I mumble some shit about how if they need help anytime to give me a call and he says, "Sure sure," which I know means, no way.

He told me they'd had to cut down on everyone's hours. So why did they hire two more people? He told me they're finally going online with the rare stock. He told me everything I wanted to hear, except that I had a job to come back to. He had lent me some books before I got sick and so then he asked how I liked them and I explained I hadn't read any because I'd been too depressed and had trouble concentrating and that when I did occasionally read, it was books about manic depression. He didn't really have too much to say after that so we ended the conversation.

I went to my room and cried. And then after to the smoke room for a butt to calm me down. But I cried there too and Barb and the lady with the white slippers and fuzzy pink house dress (who did up the zipper on the back of my dress for me yesterday) tried to make me feel better. They gave me the old "one door closing is another door opening" speech. I appreciated their efforts but it didn't give me my job back. White slippers even got some Kleenex from her room and gave it to me to sop up my crying fit. That was truly sweet and generous, because patients have to provide their own snot rags unless they use t.p. (toilet paper). Can you imagine? A psych ward that provides restraints on every bed, but no boxes of Kleenex?

November 7, 1999
I spent the rest of yesterday lying on my bed curled around the pile of clothes that I can't seem to put away and my housecoat and shower stuff. I got really stiff after a while but I couldn't change positions because of all the shit on my bed. So I just stayed in that half-moon curve, curled up like the letter "c," spelling out "crisis" in bold blazing letters, trying to summon the courage to take the shower I'd avoided for days. But I was too afraid of the water and of someone walking in on me in the washroom. Of course it has no locks.

November 10, 1999
"I'm sorry to always make you cry," the woman with the fabulously fierce and sharply perfect eyebrows says to me. How can I ever hope to get better and have eyebrows as precise as hers? She's Mona Camu, the community care Wworker. She hands me the green packet with a drug card inside. The card looks more like a file folder than a card and there's no laminate officiating anything. I could drop it in the sink by accident and it would melt. Except the taps on the sink in my room don't work. I can't help but keep crying as she explains how when I get discharged a homeworker will come to see me every week and help me with things. She doesn't get that I don't want help. I want to be better. I want to work. I want my job. I want to be able to pay for my own drugs. I don't even want to have to take these fucking drugs, but I need them and I don't feel ready to leave this place even though I hate it. I'm not well enough to take care of myself on the outside.

In the last few months before I got sick I was irritated with my job and thought it might be time to find a new one but now I know how lucky I was, being able to work at all. I'm scared I won't ever be able to do that again. And Mona, gracious as ever with her social-worker phony friendliness and fear of unpleasantries, excuses herself. "Well, I really must be going. Good luck, Alex." And then she and those perfect eyebrows walk out of my room and they don't close the door shut all the way, which I hate.

November 12, 1999

So I've been discharged. And it's like I can't sit still at this part of my life. It sucks so bad I want to fast-forward to the "good parts" as if I was a little kid. It scares me how nothing is set in place except that damn home-worker. I don't have a job and I don't remember how to find one and I don't even know what kind of job to look for. Will Bob and Donald even give me a good reference letter? What do I say on my resume about the huge gap of time when I was in the hospital? What would I fill out under "hobbies"? Sleeping. Smoking. Staring off into space? And I guess to account for when I've been manic I could put: spending sprees. Grandiose notions. Indiscriminate sexual activity. I have no clue. I can't even wake up in the mornings, never mind go to work. I just keep hearing that metal-and-lavender ward door heavily click shut from the out-patient side for the last time. I left for good and all I can see is how Barb was collapsed (she was definitely not lounging) in one of the TV chairs and white slippers waving good-bye good-bye good-bye to me through the window.

November 17, 1999

One of the worst things about getting sick is that I can't make conversation anymore. Not with people I know and not with people I don't know. Because one of the first things people ask is, "What do you do? Where do you work?" It's awkward because I do nothing and I don't work anywhere and then people want to know why. It doesn't make a very good impression to explain to someone you've just met, "Oh, I don't work because I had a mental breakdown and had to be hospitalized for a long time and lost my job and I'm still too sick to find a new one. Want to be my friend? So, what do you do?" It's just easier to stay at home and hide.

November 18, 1999

I used to think it was noisy on the ward, with the TV always on and someone playing the piano or ping-pong or both, and my room across from the pay phone where patients would plead into the receiver, cry or yell and slam it down in anger. Then there was all the slipper shufflings down the hallways. The fights. The crying. But now that I'm out, it's truly noisy. Everywhere. Bright colours and people and it always seems like rush hour. I don't want to do anything but sleep and I feel guilty for my laziness. "What did I do today?" I ask myself, but just like on the ward, I'm not sure. I'm not ready to find a job or start a course yet. I feel too stupid and out of it. When I'm on the bus I look at people who are resting, their eyes closed in complete exhaustion, and I'm ashamed that I no longer know what it feels like to be tired after a full day of work. Ashamed that I'm just tired all the time, after doing nothing, for no good reason.

↦ **DEBRA ANDERSON** is a four-eyed femme word-slut who has been published in *Tessera*, *Fireweed*, the *Church-Wellesley Review*, *Periwinkle* and *Acta Victoriana*. Her short animated film *Don't Touch Me* screened internationally. Debra has work forthcoming in *Brazen* (Arsenal Pulp Press, 2002).

✒ MONIQUE WEIR

GO

On the GO
to Oshawa
the City rolls away from me.

It deftly sheds
its concrete and girders
undulates into
a motley, softer
version of itself.

It gently morphs
into embankments
of clover and Queen Anne's lace
amongst the spasms
and pangs of graffiti tags.

When I arrive
the City does not recall itself
its echoes are empty,
language is different
and I cannot converse across the distance.

Requies

News! News!
Death of the muse!

thrilling cry
from a dark bird
clamped to my ribs

even in half sleep
happiness haemorrhaged through me

↝ **MONIQUE WEIR** shares her birthday with the anniversary of the French Revolution's storming of the Bastille. She has been co-chair of the Lesbian, Gay, Bisexual, Transsexual, Transgender Pride Committee — the group that provides Toronto's annual parade and celebration. She has also worked with the Lesbian/Gay/Bi Youthline, Equality for Gays and Lesbians Everywhere, and the HIV and AIDS Legal Clinic. Monique produces and hosts The SALON — a queer women's arts and culture program for CIUT Radio in Toronto. The show also airs worldwide on the Internet. Monique's first written publication was in the *Literary Review of Canada*.

☙ JULIA GONSALVES

THERE IS AN IGNITION that happens when you meet someone and she says she's a writer. and you find her sitting against a wall in the subway with her recycled sketch pad creased open and you can physically feel the poem between you. and you read her work, her descriptions of other bodies and voices and episodes of sex, and wonder about the way she'll write you in, about the shape that might be formed by the ends of small, stacked-up sentences. and you wonder about how she'll read about you, if she'll look up, the progression of ideas memorized and ready, if she'll shake a little, get louder or softer or shift her weight when she says your name.

and i stood up on the sticky step of a stage and joked about my parents not being there, made a punchline of my hometown and the religion i was raised on. and i threw out all these hard ugly things and put them on a pile with her hard ugly things. and she added a memory, old bruises new cuts and she added a warning and a lesson learned the hard way, and she added pepper and lime and cumin and we stirred. and the talking in circles began to swirl. it was about collecting histories of running from ignorance and abuse into open-concept spaces where being open is just a concept. it was about tearing up patents on the gay community and the women's community. how it hurts, this belonging to something that doesn't belong to you. how we hate it but can't help it, this needing to belong.

i used to play the big current with my friends in pools when we were kids. we'd hold hands and move around in a big ring, walking then swimming then faster and faster until 1, 2 and we'd let go 3 and the undertow we created would carry us along and we'd grab at the smooth tiled sides trying to keep ourselves from slipping through the drain and out to sea. Clit Lit is a pool where the water, like all water, is thick and difficult but trudging through in this unmatched mass we'll make a current so the kickers won't always have to kick and the floaters will have to do more than just float by. take a deep breath. steady yourself. say something to introduce the microphone to your mouth.

Moving Day

so yeah I'm from Scarborough and for those of you who haven't been
there
Scarborough is this big church surrounded by a sturdy fence and a well-
behaved dog
three clean non-sexual perpetual children and the friendly smell
of downy across a green backyard
no smokers no drinkers no porn makers and definitely
definitely even on a bad day
no queer
but I feel well-loved in Scarborough though really
this is my no place like home only auntie emm never stops screaming
toto bites people and there are too many witches getting squished under

houses
and not enough wizards
wearing striped stockings

what scares me is the memory of marching in anti-abortion rallies as a
kid
clutching some god damn-made sign in my 11-year-old fist and
clapping
each time a car honked
local priest police taught me that the baby is punishment for sex
my 11-year-old womb was never told she had choices

then they said choices are only temptation in disguise well they
should've called me eve cause i'm broke till you say you're thirsty girl
and i'm not hungry
till you open your legs

and they said
sex is procreation
that adoration is not enough and they would rather
i take Christmas portraits beside a man who beats me
instead of a woman
because at least they think
the man can be cured

and i wonder if i'm who you want me to be yet if i should stop trying
if i'll even come close

at this point
i have two ways to go
i can decide that 1. masturbation is not a sin or 2. that i enjoy sinning
sin being a term invented for things that
make you feel good

at this point
separatism and reverse discrimination sound like a fucking good idea

at this point
i find myself crying way more often than a good butch should
but i cling to the knowledge that on at least one day in these 21 years
they looked at me
and thought i was beautiful and on at least
one day i was worth
something more than the write-off on a tax return
so if they look at me now and think i'm sick
i've got another five years to go before it becomes the majority of my
life

and if she commits suicide they're all gonna blame me whether or not i
blame myself
they'll forget of course that suicide is also on the list
hell of a long list isn't it those Catholics and their sinning a mile long
and room for crossover
i could break upwards of eighty in a day if i was really being myself

cause they say i should grow my hair out buy a padded bra or for fuck's
sake
at least wear a bra shave my legs more often shave my pits more often
cut my nails less often
they say it isn't right to moisten the pew with your cunt or chew on a
rosary bead
while you think about fucking someone

yes i am what you'd call a sexual perversion
but don't blame my parents they taught me well
taught me to hate myself taught me to fear god in houses streets
churches

bedrooms bathrooms changerooms closets

they taught me how to say my prayers too
only now i just forget the words
and get on my knees
for a different kind of worship.

My Dirty Side

you were polite and insulting at the same time
kissed my hand
and asked if i was a Latina girl
you didn't know where Guyana was
but knew where to stare
at dykes who don't wear bras under their tank tops

she called me her olive baby her coffee and cream and i can't say i
didn't
like it but i always wanted to be blond hair and blue eyes
and she always wanted to fuck blond hair and blue eyes
and i didn't think i was
good enough for goldielocks

i think i hated my hair first the hair on my body
i begged my father not to cook and decided i hated curry because i
didn't
want the scent to surface at school or see her nose wrinkle up
her mouth make excuses to go home early
I felt like shit but then
my Guyanese side did use to be my dirty side

it must have been three years ago that the white got stuck in my throat
and i know it's easier for me
because if i'm thinking Guyanese my accent is English
but i notice when there are only flashes of brown and i see my skin
a shade darker than it is

my head turns when i hear West Indian motion in the ring
break my neck to find her because i hear my family
and because it's rare as hell
when your family doesn't let you be queer
you look for something queer to be your family
and when you don't find it you start
to eroticize Guyanese you become an olive baby

i want to have grown up my father's pickney
loud and hungry and always singing about some girl in Kingston town
can you call a place you've never been to home
and what does it mean when you start to eroticize the stuff you are?

↝ JULIA GONSALVES is currently writing and performing spoken-word. Her work has been published in the anthologies *YorkStories: Women in Higher Education* and *Now See Here!* as well as various local periodicals. She is also involved with visual art, music and video. Her video *Sabrina We Broke Up* screened at the 2001 Inside Out Lesbian and Gay Film and Video Festival. Julia hopes to skirt the queer-starving-artist trend by keeping her fingers in many artistic pots.

☙ HILARY CELLINI COOK

I HAD BEEN to the venue before. Latina drag queens were there. It was a time when my lover and I were happy for every moment we could get away together, but crazy all the time too, with one kind of jealousy or another. She had been with a group of friends I hardly knew. My life was so tied up with children and my children's father — my primary partner at the time, flying in and out of the city. I had just moved back. Didn't have a baby-sitter yet, and was barely coping with heaving cardboard boxes around trying to find the right one, the necessities of life like keeping the kitchen cupboards stocked in cereal and puréed Roma tomatoes. Basil in tall jars from the corner store. But then this thing came to the Red Spot. This flyer about an event called Clit Lit. "Let's call," said my lover. "Let's read." I had read before once, at San Diego Pride for a femme event at a bookstore. There were maybe twelve dykes there, no microphone, a very loud air conditioner right over my head, but it had gone okay. I had enjoyed the nods of recognition, the solidarity.

The theme of the first Clit Lit I read at was "Erotica." My mother wanted to know where I was going. "I'm giving a reading," I said. There was no way I could tell her the name of the event. It wasn't even clitoris, just "clit" — like you were so familiar with the thing, said it so often you had to give it a nickname. She looked interested, like she might want to come. I thought of the piece I was planning to read, a tender six hundred words about fucking my girlfriend in the ass with a red dildo. "It's a lesbian event," I said. Mom still looked like she might be willing to brave it. I was reading, for God's sake, and she wanted to come just like it was my graduation. I played my trump card. "It's called, uh, Clit Lit." That did the trick.

When it was my turn to read I began to understand something that musicians and actors are always saying, about good crowds and bad crowds. This was a good crowd. And I, who started out nervous, got funnier, got better timing, became a better reader. Found myself adjusting the words to improve the rhythm even though I had already tested my pieces aloud at home. After the reading I made notes on my page to remind myself of changes still to be made. I was totally hooked. I read about the red dildo. The audience members held their breath and squirmed on their seats — a hunger to hear about our own lives was being, in part, satisfied. Clit Lit is what a reading series should be. The literary soiree: readers, microphone, lights, cash register and the crowd when gripped, laughing out, slapping each other on the arm, calling out "Yeah, baby!" And when she's really good, the reader comes offstage like she's Michael Jordan, everyone touching her as she passes, nodding, hugging, telling her what a good job she did.

Photography

I was a double agent. I reported back to her. It works like that. She has a dick. She moves as if she does but she's not sure about the technicalities, about how it functions. Or about how it feels for me. Some straight girl told her that it would never feel the same as a real one and she believed…

I had to hold back from photographing my lover. Finally I mentioned it, casually. Like photographers do; I was playing hard to get. She took me up on the offer. Came over one day for coffee and said, "You wanted to take my picture. With my clothes or…?"

That wasn't what I meant. I wanted to photograph the white skin shining through her hair on the back of her neck, trimmed short with barber's clippers. Her stance. Her jeans and white T-shirt. Her Doc Marten boots. Show how you could see her eyes through the light reflected off her glasses. She started out defiant and tense, head tilted back. She lay face down on my white sheet with her head propped up on her hands, bobbing her feet in the air. I lay on the floor to photograph her. It was bright in the room, a white sheet on the floor. Then I climbed on a chair and tilted her head around. Looking at her. Taking pictures. Reloading.

"Is that what I look like?" she said when she saw the pictures later. She was luminous, intent, beautiful. There was no trick. Just a white sheet on a folding screen, the vertical blinds pulled back and the light pouring over her. I wanted to show her what I could see.

Occasionally, as a child, I would be handed a camera, given an Instamatic. When I got the prints I never knew what had gone wrong. A head would be cut off. A church looked as if it was falling over. I would wonder if I had even looked through the viewfinder. Maybe I was jerking the camera when it came time to push the button. But when I was fifteen I spent a summer holiday with my father and he loaned me a camera without my asking. An Olympus. "Here's the f-stop," he explained. "Here's the speed. Set it on manual and use the hand-held light meter until you get the feel of it." We shot roll after roll. He left me to print our contact sheets while he took a nap. When he got up, we looked at what we had done, then went out and shot some more.

It seemed natural to graduate from being photographed to being the photographer. Having my picture taken was serious business when I was small. I remember my father's hand brushing my cheek as he took a reading, the light meter resting in its leather case, the smell of cigarettes and Eau Sauvage. I remember being in the beam of his attention, his brushing back my bangs or adjusting the turn of my head. Now when I am out with my camera I am pulled back from a scene, detached. I cruise for a shot like gay boys cruise for sex. I see something in a doorway. I pass by. Stop. Go back. The house's number, old-fashioned on a cracked enamel plaque. The door-knocker is a woman's hand holding an iron ball. Yes, that's what I thought. Look how the light is falling, the texture of the paint, I think. Or I see nothing of interest and walk on. I cruise the other way too — not for sex but more like window shopping. I turn to look at a handsome girl, the way she walks. Or a pretty boy fixing his collar in the reflection of a street-car window at night. I lean forward from my balcony seat to watch that one in the orchestra shrug her coat off and settle into her seat, run fingers through her brush cut as if it used to be a bit longer. I wish I could keep that moment like a photograph.

I like the stern-faced butches, the don't-fuck-with-me butches who scare the general public. I like the soft butches, the ones that people try to compliment when they say, "Well, you're not *really* butch." I want to show the black dress shoes, the broken-in boots, the red cotton high-tops, the police academy shoes. Look here, at the velvet on the back of her neck, I think. Look at her hands, her long fingers with the knuckles prominent. Look at the way she puts her hands in her pockets and slouches to hide her breasts. Look at this boy-dyke professor; look at the trouble she's causing, holding her office hours at an Italian coffee shop. Look at this silver-haired streetcar driver, she almost missed the light because some girl was grinning at her from across the way. See the Fed Ex girl who never cracks a smile. I swear I saw a gleam in her eye the day I got that plainly wrapped package from the nasty store in San Francisco.

When I was younger I waited for a girl to look at me and *know*, ask me out. But it was like a high-school dance all over again, where everyone stands along the walls hoping to dance, too cool to do anything about it. Finally I took matters in hand and told a girl that *I* wanted to kiss *her*. Immediately my friends wanted to know how I had pulled it off. "I just asked," I told them. Butch women rarely make the first move. Why should they, when if they just hang around long enough looking incredibly lesbian, someone will take them up on it?

I enjoy being the object of my lover's gaze, of her lust. I am the body on the roller-coaster and she is the builder, astounded by what she has wrought. At first I am outside too, sometimes outside myself, sometimes looking down at my body, my breasts, trying to see the girl that she sees. I know the roller-coaster is going to go over the top, I want her to see it. I want her breathing to change. I want her to lose her composure so I lose mine, completely letting go of self-consciousness. I want to moan or yell or curl my hands into fists so tightly that I can hardly get them open afterwards.

I always wanted to be like my mother — boyish, flat-chested, so beautiful that everyone wanted to be around her. It was just natural that we should love her, my brother and I. Everyone else did. Instead, I grew up looking like my father, like his sister: luscious. Her favourite colour was red. And she was a tart like me.

For my lover I buy stockings with a band of lace around the tops. I go out dancing in a velvet dress that shows my knees. I wear pretty earrings and hold her hand at a play. Walking home with her late at night in heels I think, "If I had to run I'd be in trouble now." For work, for conferences, for taking my kids to the park, I wear twill pants, boy's shoes, and sit with my knees apart. I establish my credibility in the camera store by taking out my Leica, talking technical and pricing second-hand lenses. I hold the door for women, sing alto in the choir, own power tools and know how to use them. My lover tells me I'm butch when I pick up a camera, and I guess it's true; taking pictures is like fucking: you have to know what you want. You have to take what you want in order to be good at it.

I take a picture of my son. He is three years old. He is naked and sitting on a dark green plastic stool on my terrace in San Diego, but you can't tell if he is a boy or a girl. He is wearing every necklace, every string of beads that I own, and a few of his own. He pushed up a chair and has taken

195

them down from the brass hooks where I hang them, passing each one over his head. I wanted to put them away, as he had broken several already. There were blue glass beads that tended to chip off, a worn string of baroque pearls that belonged to my long-faced but flirtatious grand-mother. He is leaning forward to show me how he looks wearing so many necklaces. They cover him like a shirt. I love that he enjoys being pretty and that it is still uncomplicated for him. I knew then that I was catching something that would be gone by the end of the year.

My lover and I pick out women at parties and pay attention to them. At some point we'll take one of them to bed, but in the meantime it's just window shopping. We pick out the tall butch one in the short Catholic-girl kilt at the Halloween party. Or one of the day-care mothers. She catches us looking. We're objectifying you, we say. My lover tells me it's okay. It's okay to dress in a skirt and heels to please her, to let her touch me and kiss me in public, to ask her to fuck me, to suck her dick. Things I didn't do, games I never played for men. Concessions. (I was kind of straightforward. Not silly. Kind of like a boy. And men liked that in me.) Now I enjoy my femininity in part because I can see that my lover does too. She gets a contented look when I stop again to look in the window of a shoe store. She genuinely loves the flesh that makes me curvy in a dress. I become aware, when I walk, of how my knees swish past each other, the way I hold out my fingers when I pull on my gloves. Society assumes I owe this to a man, even when he doesn't. But what's the fun in that? It's like paying taxes. To give it to her instead feels like subverting the sexual economy.

My first girlfriend was femme. And my fourth. I made them sad. With each of them I felt like a boy. Like a shy boy being vamped by some woman. Or I searched them for some sign of butchness. The way Becky's hair was cut short at the neck, or the way that Genevieve danced in her faded blue jeans, knees bent and apart. So sexy. The first time I lay down with a butch, with her James Dean haircut and her rounded woman's body, I was overwhelmed by the urge to fuck her, to do something, take her — make her lose control. I still want to pin her down and force my way in. I want to put her on her knees and pull her on and off my dick. Devour her. Why is it so much easier to write about myself as an agent, and so hard to write as the one acted upon? Why are there so few women photographers? Why do both men and women spend their money buying magazines filled with pictures of beautiful women? Why is it so hard to photograph straight men? Why Cindy Sherman? Why Frida Kahlo? Why do women artists make themselves the object of their own gaze?

I photograph myself from time to time. Usually in the washroom mirror on airplanes. I am deadpan, holding the camera so you know who's in control. I photographed myself naked when I was pregnant because it felt as if such an extreme state had to be documented and I didn't trust anyone else to do it. I move between *being* myself and *seeing* myself. I think many women do. I caught sight of my hands low in a mirror one day and suddenly saw what my lover saw, my blunt fingers, my capable hands, were *sexy*. Made to fuck.

I used to photograph the fey ones. My boyfriends, or pretty Erik from high school, and the dancers in his class. I wanted to take them, possess them in the same way that I want to possess women. (To be fuckable and to be photographable both involve a kind of feminine generosity, availability.) I couldn't always get what I wanted. I needed that intimacy, that access you get with a lover, but it's not my taking it that makes it exist. It's something that's given. I also want to see myself as the beloved, as the photographed, so I am grateful that my lover has an imagination like mine. Slides my skirt up, then pulls my underpants down just enough, wets her fingers in her mouth and slips them inside me. She bites my neck, digs her nails into my thighs, slaps my ass, gets out the crop. She calls me her good girl, her dirty girl, her whore, her bitch. She can be so rough, so goddamn rough. Each incursion not shocking, but like coming home. Holding myself up for her, the sense that it's almost too much, brings *me* clearly into focus.

197

HILARY CELLINI COOK

➻ **HILARY CELLINI COOK** is a photographer lawyer pervert writer. Her latest story can be found in *Faster Pussycats: Live Girls After Hours* (Alyson Books).

•◦ MONICA NOY

CLIT LIT IS POETRY AND PROSE in a dark, smoky room with shadowy listeners covered in the haze of lit cigarettes. In winter it's my very own beatnik community, where politics and literature are sometimes the same thing. In summer the smoke mixes with sweat and even I long for a cold beer from the bar. It's where I see so much of my community come together, just to be divided. It's a place to watch people and let people watch you, a place to talk, but mostly it's a place to listen.

When the lights are on we look like such a rowdy bunch; tough too. There's a lot of black, some chains, tattoos, muscle Ts, cleavage. A lot of broody scowls, spiked hair, shaved heads, searching eyes. Everyone is constantly looking, watching to see who is watching, checking out the first-timers. Sometimes it scares me and I go away feeling like I don't belong. Other times it inspires me that so many different people have so much in common.

Clit Lit began around the same time I was coming out, and for me it was like food for the hungry. I'd sit amongst all those queer folk, I'd even read to them, and wonder just how I got to be in the middle of it all. I still think of myself as small-town. I mean Melbourne, Australia isn't all that small, but I never got to know it the way I know Toronto, and no one ever asked me to speak just because they liked the sound of my voice and no one ever invited me into the secret parts of their lives quite like the readers at Clit Lit. There I've shared laughter, tears, anger, frustration, sadness, joy, sometimes all in the same night. I've learned things about politics, culture, oppression and expression and about myself.

The Lady Vanishes

Then there is the pale, pale blonde, with anaemia of some non-fatal but incurable type. She is very languid and very shadowy and she speaks softly out of nowhere and you can't lay a finger on her because in the first place you don't want to and in the second place she is reading The Waste Land or Dante in the original, or Kafka or Kierkegaard or studying Provençal…
— Raymond Chandler, *The Long Goodbye*

"Smooth," I said to my reflection, hat dipped rakishly over one grey eye. The suit, dark pants and double-breasted jacket still had a faint smell of honeysuckle perfume drifting up from the lapel. Suddenly a ghost appeared in the mirror beyond me. A kiss of red in a shimmering white body that vanished quickly. "Detective Kelly?" A voice like the morning's first bourbon slid into me. The ghost in the mirror was standing in front of my desk, peeling off a netted white sun-hat, letting pure gold hair fall down the back of her white dress suit. She took me by surprise, no doubt because my nicely stacked, nicely drunk secretary didn't bother to buzz me.

"Ms. Wonderly?" I offered my hand and looked her up and down while I composed myself. I had been expecting a client, I hadn't been expecting such a client.

"Please, call me Christine," she said.

"Christine," I repeated, motioning for her to take a seat. "Christine Wonderly," I said, tasting bittersweet familiarity. We sat across the desk from each other and I took her in. She had everything anyone could want in a woman. Astounding beauty, soft, pouty lips, high cheek bones, deep cleavage and long, slender legs. "How can I help you?" I said, finally. She put a cigarette in her mouth and I rose from my seat, match at the ready.

"Thank you," she breathed, smoke rising from her mouth in languorous tendrils. "I need you to find something very rare for me, Detective

Kelly." She sat forward in the large chair, knees together, back straight, hands in her lap. The split of her skirt travelled all the way up one milky thigh. A thin silver chain danced at the edge of her slim ankle.

"Do I get any more clues?" I asked. She smiled and took another drag from her cigarette, her blue eyes sparkling through the cloud she exhaled.

"You do know your reputation precedes you?" she asked, neat brows arching.

"I pass as a detective, Ms. Wonderly. I find things, I find people. I do it for a price. I carry a gun and I pack. Apart from that, there's not much variation in private dicks around here." The fire of her lips spread across her face in a grin.

"Oh but there is. What I'm looking for could be badly mistreated in the wrong hands. In fact it already has been and I don't know if it's even recognizable any more. But I think you would complement it, rather than compete with it. If you can find it."

I scoffed. "You just leave that to me. Now let's get down to brass tacks. What is it I'm looking for?" Christine threw her head back and let out a crisp laugh. She sat upright again, breasts straining against her fitted jacket.

"I am hesitant to put a definition to what I am searching for. I'm afraid it's somewhat intangible and I'm not sure detectives such as yourself consciously search for the intangible."

"You'll have to run that one by me again, doll. I'm not getting it," I said, getting a little tired of the circles she was running around in, wanting to chase her anyway. She shook her head slightly and her hair rolled over one shoulder, then the other. If it had been the silk of a spider's web it could not have been more effective in entrapping me.

"Perhaps," she said, "it's all a bit too ambiguous."

I stood, arms out, grinning. "But wouldn't that make me the perfect person for the job?" She laughed again and it sounded like a row of crystal glasses being tapped simultaneously.

"Well, Detective Kelly, since you insist. I seem to have lost my point of view."

"You lost your point of view," I repeated, a little incredulous. I reached for the bottle kept in the top drawer and poured us both a drink.

"In truth, it has been appropriated away from me," she said. I looked at her long and hard, but there was no wry smile on her lips, no humour in her eyes. Her face, serene as it was beautiful, held only sincerity. Either she was going to convince me to call someone to take her away, or I had just diversified my practice. I decided to proceed in the usual manner.

"When was the last time you saw it?"

"Oh, I've never seen it. Well, maybe glimpsed it once or twice. A phantom woman, a ghost out of the past, with an angel face. Though mostly these were inversions, not true perspective. Sort of like inventive fakes." She took a sip of her drink.

"Um, well, what does it look like?"

"Hard to say really. I know what it's *supposed* to look like, but I don't think it's looked like that for a good, long time."

"It's in disguise?" I threw the bourbon down my throat and poured another.

"No. Well, yes, but not one of its own choosing." Christine sighed and downed her own drink as though she'd done it many times before. "This is all a bit strange, isn't it, Detective?"

"This is somewhat unusual," I agreed, putting it mildly. "Do you know who took your point of view?"

"Not precisely. It was appropriated a long time ago but it's changed hands many times. I can tell you that those who have had it, or have it now, are mostly men." The soft afternoon sunlight streaming through the wooden slats over the windows lit her like the moon on a dark night.

"What type of men?" I asked, enchanted.

"All types," she said. "Except they usually have money, or influence of some sort."

"I see."

"Do you, really?" she replied, standing up, fresh drink in hand. "Because so far what you've seen is somewhat typical. But what you see is not what they see."

"Who?"

"The audience, the reader, the watcher — whoever's gaze is upon us."

"We're being watched?" I asked. My hand fell immediately to the gun in my holster. "Are you in danger?"

"I am always in danger," she said matter-of-factly. "After all, I've come looking for my perspective in a first-person narrative that negates it entirely. That's dangerous, wouldn't you say?" She raised her head, as though to challenge me.

"I don't see how. I've described you favourably," I told her, a little indignantly.

"Oh yes, I'm beautiful, sexy, all in white, somewhat ethereal because of my ghostly appearance and striped with shadow and light. Your description is a split perspective. It's steeped in suspicion and textual clues as to what really lies beneath this skin." Christine sashayed across the room to the window, hips swivelling, heels tapping the floor with each soft step. "I am a reflection," she continued. "You see me as a sexual being, a woman of intrigue and mystery, but a woman you could possibly love if you could ever trust her. The reader of this genre sees the femme fatale you paint. Am I good girl or bad woman? What are the clues? The dress, the toss of my hair or the fullness of my breasts? Good girls are just a little homelier, don't you think, not quite as exotic? And they would never sashay." She turned and grinned knowingly. "Here, my point of view is your gaze. I thought you might be different, given your own...ambiguities, but it seems the sexually confused hero is built right in."

"Are you trying to tell me I've forgotten where I came from?" I stood, pounding my fist on my desk. Christine smiled, her lips glistening like she'd just eaten something ripe and juicy.

"Not at all. You just see differently now. If you didn't, you couldn't pass as a detective, and I couldn't be an archetypal femme," she said, something in her eyes making her grin malignant. It took me a moment to realize it was anger.

"My point of view isn't the question here," I said, sitting back down, pouring another drink.

"A standard measure is rarely questioned, Detective Kelly. You of all people should know that."

"That is not to say it isn't transgressed." I thought I had her there, after all, we'd both mastered the art.

"And has been, many times, but for what end? It's a plot device, that's all. A symptom of my motivation."

"What is your motivation?" I asked.

"Money, love, power, revenge. Take your pick, it doesn't matter. The point is the motivation is there, it has to be, or I wouldn't exist."

"And now?"

"The Last Seduction?" Her smile dripped irony and I caught it full in the gut.

"I'll take the case, Christine," I said, decidedly. "I'll find your point of view." She walked back toward me, smiling.

"I knew you would, Detective Kelly," she said, rummaging in her purse. A wad of cash landed on my desk. "That should cover your expenses."

"And when I find it?" I asked. "Because I will find it," I assured her, full confidence in my ability.

"I've no doubt you will, Detective Kelly, but it's a good thing I'm already a rich woman, because it will take some time, and considerable expense. It will also be a dangerous journey, and one hell of a ride, so you better pack, if you know what I mean." Christine caught my eye before it became hard to read behind the netting of her hat.

"I always carry a gun," I said, a churlish grin on my face.

"When you eventually find my perspective," she began, ready to leave, "I'll know it. I'll contact you then." I raised a disbelieving eyebrow.

"Give me one week," I told her, as she moved gracefully to the door. She turned and peered intently through the netting.

"Always so cocky, and with so much to learn."

My mouth dropped open as she shut the door, blood boiling with snappy comebacks she could not hear. She'd left more than enough money for the week it would take me to find what she'd lost and when I found it, when it was in my hands, then I'd have the last word. I sat down and picked up the phone. "Doll, Get Marlowe on the horn, will you? Oh, and when you've done that come in here, I want to ask your opinion about something."

203

MONICA NOY

◦ **MONICA NOY** is an expatriate Australian who has been living, studying and writing in Canada for the best part of six years, though she mostly finds herself writing about the not-so-romantic version of Australia that resides in her head. She has been published in *She's Gonna Be* (McGilligan Press, 2000). Monica has been working on her first novel, *The Meadowlea Mum*, for a long time, and hopes to have it published sometime before she dies. She is currently studying in a field unrelated to writing, with the long-term goal of having lots of time to write, and lots more to write about.

●◦ MEREDITH ADOLPH

THE FIRST TIME I READ my work in public I was seventeen. The university in my hometown was hosting a poetry evening with an open mic, so I gathered together some of my more bohemian friends and signed myself up. The evening filled my criteria for what I thought a poetry reading should be: funky-looking academics, wine and candles on the tables. I sat through the performances thoroughly enthralled but growing more and more nervous. Having been onstage many times before in piano recitals and high-school plays, I thought I'd be fine, but when my turn came I was terrified. At the mic, my legs shook uncontrollably. If I tried to steady them my voice and hands took up the slack. I silently thanked my long skirt and let my legs shake, unseen. The difference between acting and reading your own work became abundantly clear to me that night: theatre is the art of representing someone else's feelings, but reading your own work means exposing your core.

When I was eighteen I moved to Montreal so I could become a writer. Montreal, the city where everyone is beautiful and no one owns jogging pants. I went to readings all the time but was filled with a sense of alienation. The people there were all better writers than I was. But it wasn't just that. I could never be that hip, that sexy, or that weird — no matter how miserable I looked, how wildly I dressed, or how much I smoked. I felt like an impostor. I wanted to be a writer but I was not like them. I used to bring a cigarette up onstage with me so I'd have an excuse to breathe. I see now the only things I lacked were confidence and a more supportive venue. What I wanted most at the time was to get down into the gritty stuff but to my mind then, anything was worthy material — except me. I stopped writing.

I've found a wonderfully welcoming and supportive venue at Clit Lit. I enjoy it because the writers are of varying abilities and at different stages of development. I took a big leap there once: I read one of the first sexy pieces I'd ever written, one that made me feel naked and scared all over again. The act of reading it out loud to a roomful of listeners made it real, made it funny, even. Now while I write, my back is straight and I can feel my feet flat on the ground. I breathe. When I go onstage I just step up, plant my feet down, and nothing can knock me over.

205

hawkeye

I always wanted to be hawkeye pierce the way
alan alda played him, so suave and flip
we all know that's how he survived Korea:
made bathtub martinis
his world was all women & smarm

not like klinger, with hook nose & hoop earrings
didn't make a pretty one but lord knows
he grew to like it after a time,
picking up muumuus
on leave in the city.
marching with a purse over his arm
a caricature, thinking
this'll make them do it this'll get me home

hawkeye knew that women were the way home.
knew that soft flesh would muscle him through to war's other side;
after the war he could be himself again,
wipe the smirk off.

•• **MEREDITH ADOLPH** is a hardworking writer who cooks for a living and studies shiatsu massage in Toronto. When she's not playing Supergirl she takes long walks in High Park.

✒ ROBERTA BEST

I ATTENDED CLIT LIT one night, as I did every month, and as the event ended I was sitting on the couch thinking about how brave it was of these writers, many of whom were reading in public for the first time, to share. I'd always been a bit of a closet writer myself, one of the angst-ridden poetry types who used writing as a way to work things out, things that doubtless would have cost me a fortune in therapy. I had published a few pieces but had never actually read anything in public — too shy, too reluctant to be the centre of attention. So there I sat yet again, contemplating my own scribblings and navel-gazing, when Elizabeth Ruth came by to say hi. She leaned over the couch towards me and casually added, "Oh, by the way, you're reading next month. I've already got you down on the schedule."

"Whaaat?!" I sputtered. "But I don't have anything written. I don't even know the topic!" She smiled. "It's 'Spunky: Gay Men's Writing.' You'll be great, don't worry."

I worried. I worried about my performance anxiety and penis envy. I worried about looking foolish and out of place. I worried for three weeks and three days and then I finally sat down to write. "But I'm not a gay man," I kept insisting to friends as I struggled to put down even the first word. "They'll hate me. I'll look like a fraud!" One of my less tactful companions quickly set my mind at ease: "Oh, shut up," she said. "You're faggier than most gay men I know."

I could hardly argue. A proverbial fag trapped in a dyke's body, I've always identified closely with my gay male brothers. On those rare occasions when I'm feeling at all effeminate I never think of myself as feeling "girly," but rather as getting in touch with my inner fag. I came out and spent my early homo-formative years amongst fags, and from them I've always taken my cues: how to dress, how to dance, the porn collection, the cruise (still working on that one).

Ah yes, the gay male cruise. Is there any dyke who has not lamented the ease with which fags pick each other up? I love the blatancy of the fag cruise, envy its ease and (seeming) lack of a fear of rejection. I'm sure it's not quite all that, but compared to the foot-shuffling, eye-averting, innuendo-filled agony that is the lesbian mating dance, it seems to be a walk in the park (with a side trip into the bushes, and then...). Like many boyish girls I've experienced various degrees of being "picked up" by fags — ranging from a rakish up-and-down leer to a full-on come-on and grope. So in some ways I wrote from what I know.

Given many dykes' well-known love of fag porn I was surprised to be the only girl reading that night, and was therefore more than just a little intimidated. I needn't have been so worried, though. A quickly slung-back drink and the glare of the lights obscuring a house filled mainly with smiling guys quickly put me at ease. The fags swooned, the dykes cheered and I was very glad that I had changed the ending of my story. The original version had the protagonist getting caught in her deception, but at the last minute I decided that she should get away with her hands clean. For further adventures in gender fucking, stay tuned....

Dick

The first three days after a new haircut are the worst. It's three days of "Excuse me sir, this is the ladies' washroom" from women who think that I am both illiterate and unable to decipher the stick figure in a dress on the door. It's three days of "Dude, can I see your I.D." from twenty-year-old beer store employees. Three days of "Hey man, you dropped your tampon" from kids who think it's perfectly plausible that a sixteen-year-old boy is carrying around an O.B. After thirty-two years of having short hair I still can't figure out this phenomenon — it's not like on the fourth day the God of hair descends with ringlets in hand to turn me into a recognizable girl. And certainly these little gender confrontations continue throughout the weeks to follow, but I tell you, the first three days after a haircut are brutal. Today…is the first day.

I've just emerged from the washroom at the mall where I've left a wake of horrified onlookers. My girlfriend follows behind a minute later, laughing uproariously. "You're not going to believe this one," she says. "After you left a couple of twelve-year-old girls at the sink turned to each other and the one said, 'Like, oh my God. Did you see that? There was a guy in the washroom.' 'Totally,' said the other. 'It was a gay guy, but it was a guy anyway.'" I laugh. Some days you just have to laugh or you'd cry. But still, it's frustrating, and pretty soon I launch into my usual tirade of the injustice of it all. Oh, why, why can I not take a simple pee in peace?

My extremely pretty, never-ever-been-confused-for-a-boy girlfriend is quite unsympathetic. Normally she's absolutely wonderful about these things but today she's been unable to find the right pair of shoes and it's made her a bit cranky. "Oh, spare me the melodrama," she says. "You're not the only one who has shit to deal with. At least you don't have to worry about getting leered at and hit on constantly by men." I nod. She's right. I've seen the way straight men of all ages stare openly at her, catcall her, blatantly look her up and down. Frankly, I'll take the oh-my-God gawking of twelve-year-old girls any day over creepy guys staring at my tits. But you know, she's not entirely correct…some guys do check me out.

So it's Saturday afternoon and some cruel twist of fate has brought me to the Eaton Centre — epicentre of shopping hell. The place is crawling with loud tourists and suburban teenagers who have far too much disposable income taking up way too much space. I feel claustrophobic. I want desperately to leave. But alas, we're on a mission to find me a new pair of "business casual" trousers and by the looks of it we're not leaving any time soon. We've already done the gay-friendly stores (Banana Republic and Club Monaco) without any luck, and now we're in Roots, home of the all-Canadian sweatshirt. I'm poking around in a pile of cargo pants looking for something shapeless when my girlfriend comes over, turns up her nose at the pants and deems them "too dumpy." This makes me whiny: "But honey, I like them, they hide my fat ass. Am I looking fat today?" I ask, turning around to show her the evidence. She rolls her eyes. "You are SUCH a fag," she snorts and flounces off towards the baby Ts at Le Château. "Meet me in twenty minutes," she says over her shoulder.

I drag my ass over to the guys' khakis in the middle of the store. As I'm sorting through the rack I'm joined by a rather cute girl — a straight girl — kinda hip, kinda preppy and obviously looking for clothes for her shopping-impaired boyfriend, if the schlumpy knuckle dragger she's with is any indication. I move to stand beside her, and as I'm starting to check her out in my peripheral vision I hear a man's voice behind me ask: "Can I help you ladies with anything?" Obviously he's not talking to me, so I don't react, but the cutie pie beside me takes the schlump by the arm and moves on to the sweaters. I continue my search through the pants while casually scratching the back of my newly buzzed, very itchy head. The voice repeats, right behind me now: "Ma'am?" Now, strictly out of curiosity, you understand, I turn around to face a very sweet-looking, obviously gay, not-a-day-over-seventeen Roots employee, whose face suddenly collapses in shock upon looking me straight in the eye. "Oh my God, sir," he squeals, "I'm so sorry…"

It takes every ounce of strength I have not to burst out laughing. I bite my lip, tilt my head and study him — small-boned, blond spiky hair and beautiful blue eyes with no trace of facial hair. My first thought is "What a cute baby dyke he'd make," and I almost laugh to think how often he must be mistaken for a girl. He, however, is clearly horrified at his "mistake." He begins to blurt, "Sir I didn't, well, I just didn't…" and I raise a hand to stop his unnecessary apology. "It's okay sweetie…it happens all the time." And indeed it does, just not like this! I feel bad for him so I try to explain. "It must be the butt. I run a lot, you see, and so my butt is well, a little…beefy, kind of like a girl's, you know? Makes it hard to buy pants sometimes." His eyes nervously drift down to my hand, where I've grabbed the right cheek of my ass to prove my point. Clearly he likes what he sees, and I begin to see the wheels turn in his lovely young face. I know what he's thinking. He's picturing this beefy ass on top of him, or behind him, or wherever, and he's got a nice tight grip on it, and he's pulling it towards him and…Oh yes, I know what he's thinking. I read *Honcho*.

"Mmmmm," he murmurs, pretending to be concerned with my pants problem. "I understand your dilemma. So…how big are you? I mean, what's your size?" This is beginning to sound like the plot of a bad porno, and you know, I envy gay men the encyclopedia of smut scenarios that exists at the tip of their imaginations at all times. I swear, if a lesbian ever answered the "ding-dong" doorbell to find a hot pizza-delivery girl there she wouldn't know what the hell to do…gay men, they always know.

"Hmm…usually I take a thirty-one," I say. "But I better grab a thirty-two just to be safe."

He hands me the appropriate pairs and points me toward the change-rooms, deep, very deep in the back of the store. "If you need anything else," he says, "my name is Dick."

I giggle. I can't help it. "I'm sure it is…Dick. I'll let you know." I try on the first pair and sure enough, they're snug in the ass and big in the waist, just like a girl's. I open the door to find him there, waiting. Frankly, I'm surprised he's got this much time on his hands given that it's quite busy in the store, but hey, I'm not his boss so I lift my shirt to show him the looseness around the waist, revealing the men's gitch that I prefer to girly panties. He leans forward to peer down, and I catch him holding his gaze down there just a little too long. "Ahem." His head snaps up, face flushes. I raise a very amused eyebrow at him. "See something you like… Dick?" Apparently he's got quite an imagination as there's no bulge between me and my Calvins, but he seems to be conveniently ignoring this fact as he looks me right in the eye and smiles. "Yes, there is, as a matter of fact." *Oh boy*, I think. *Here we go.* And I wonder just how far I can carry this little game, suddenly worried that he'll expect me to whip out my ten-inch piece of throbbing man-meat, throw him up against the wall, yank his pants down and fuck him up against a pile of Sydney Olympic sweatshirts. And I'm thinking, *Who am I?* I'm usually like, Mr. Porno-Potty-Mouth, but I'm not sure how I'm going to talk my way out of this one.

I think quickly through my collection of fag mags, come up with a scenario, click into roll. I drop the smile, replaced with a steely-eyed glare. "Get in here," I sneer at him as I back into the changeroom. He looks around quickly to ensure we're alone and follows me in.

As soon as the door closes he reaches for my waistband. Cheeky little devil. I slap his hand away. Hard. Actually, a little harder than I had intended, but his eyes widen and glaze over as he pulls his hand back. I've seen that look before. "Sorry sir," he says demurely.

How old does this boy think I am — twenty? But I smile approvingly at him. "Good Dick. Very good," I say. "Now, why don't you be a nice boy and show me what you've got." I nod down toward his crotch. He's a bit shorter than me and very slight, and standing beside him now I feel positively burly. I sit down on the changeroom bench, widen my legs, fold my arms on my chest and frown at him, like the big tough guy he thinks I am. "Now Dick, I'm waiting." He quickly unbuttons his jeans and lets them fall to his knees, revealing tighty-whitey Fruit of the Looms. He reaches in with his right hand and pulls out the largest cock that I've, well...never seen.

I'm a little shocked at the size of the cock this little guy has but quite impressed and, frankly, a little envious — I have to pay $120 for something that big. I tell him to jerk off for me. And I tell him just how to do it. Faster, slower, right hand, left, make him stop for a while, tease him, make him beg to continue. And I make him talk to me, tell me what a bad boy he's being, how good this feels, how many times he's thought about doing this in the changeroom with some stranger. You know the script, you've seen the films. And then, just as quickly as it all started, his stroke becomes faster and harder, his breath quickens, his legs start to shake and... "Ask for it now, boy!"...

"May I come, sir?..."

"Go for it, Dick."

He comes, and while it's not exactly the streaming arc of jizz that I was hoping for, it's enough to make his legs buckle and he finishes on his knees down on the floor in front of me. When he finally collects himself and is breathing normally again he looks up at me.

"Can I see your cock now, sir? Please can I suck you off?"

I pause. "I don't think that would be a good idea, Dick," I say, quite honestly. "I don't want to scare you." I can only imagine what he is thinking…

"Besides," I say, checking my watch. "I think it's time you got back to work."

Everything happened so quickly that I didn't have time to examine the moral and ethical implications of just what the hell I was doing there. In retrospect, I think maybe I got caught up in the fun of it all, seeing how far I could take that little bit of deception without getting caught. Maybe, as my girlfriend often suggests, I really *am* a fag caught in a dyke's body. Maybe I was just horny and flat-out attracted to him, this boy who kind of reminded me of my very first girlfriend. And maybe, just maybe, it had to do with me being mistaken for a guy (a gay guy but a guy anyway) in a good way for once — a really good way rather than with all the usual scorn. Whatever the reason, there I was: Saturday afternoon at the mall, locked in a changeroom watching Dick — Roots' latest employee of the month, shoot his load for his Daddy-of-the-day.

↝ROBERTA BEST currently resides in the former apartment of another "reluctant pornographer," Bruce LaBruce. Clearly, there's something in the water.

☙ BARBARA BROWN

THE PLACE WAS CROWDED, noisy and almost smoke-free — remarkable for a bar on a Monday night. I squeezed my way between chatting groups and silent singles staking out their place for a glimpse of the stage. I found my own spot near the back, settling in to see what this Clit Lit thing was all about. I had known about the reading series for a long time, friends had read there, and yet it took me over a year to walk up the steep stairwell leading into the bar. The lights shifted. A woman in black with bright red lipstick stepped centre stage. The noise stopped, almost. The MC smiled at the crowd and told us what the evening would hold. There was a tense excitement in the room, a mix of longing and fear and pride.

I spent the first hour spellbound, in part from the quality of the writing, and in part from the courage of each person that walked onto the stage, wrestled with the mic and let their voice be heard. The line-up included first-time readers, published poets, some well-known crowd favourites and a few shy, self-deprecating readers who stumbled through their words and apologized for not being "real writers." I came to realize how much people put at risk when they read — their words, their dreams, themselves. I wanted to be one of them.

During the break, I took a deep breath and asked the organizer if I could read at the next event. She took my name and said she'd call to confirm. It was done, and I was petrified. That night I went home, picked two poems and began practicing. I read in my living room, in front of my bathroom mirror and in the kitchen while I cooked dinner. I fantasized my upcoming glory, the accolades that would be heaped upon me once the crowd heard my writing. I'd read publicly before, but those experiences didn't quell the rumblings in my belly or the shaking in my legs. The theme for the evening was "Genderfuck" and the bar was packed once again. The thrill of being in such close proximity to so many handsome, gorgeous queer women and men was heady enough. It felt like Pride in a confined space. When my turn came, I approached the mic to the sound of catcalls from friends. I stepped into the spotlight, its heat rising in my face. I felt my feet plant themselves on the stage, and let the pleasure of being seen ripple through me. As I scanned the room, I felt a shift of attention, the dimming of the crowd talk, and a growing anticipation. "What would come out of my mouth?" was as much my question as the crowd's. I began. I could hear my own voice, quiet and shaky, stretch out through the sound system. The echo returned to me through the faces of those who were listening. I heard myself say "cunt," then "woman," and knew this meant the poem was over. It also meant I could breathe again. The breathing happened as my friends cheered, and I shook off the nervousness. The second poem moved easier, louder. The whole read was over in less than five minutes. All that preparation for such a short time onstage, and it was worth it. The audience was howling. I stepped down and beetled back through the crowd to my friends.

Since my nervous first night of peeking into the Clit Lit world, I have gone on to successfully pursue wider publication of my writing — including one of the poems from that first night — been awarded an emerging writers' grant and come to believe more strongly in the value of my words. I have also become more playful with my pieces, less afraid to show them, less afraid of imperfection. Initially I read only polished works, poems and stories that I trusted and had substantially sweated over. That's changed. Now I bring materials to workshop, fragments of ideas, seeds I hope will germinate. I still get nervous as I walk up to the mic. I practice in my living room and with friends every time. I go even if I'm not reading. Listening to the work of other writers helps spark new ideas, and keeps me writing. But truthfully, what keeps me asking for a spot in the line-up, what keeps me walking up the steep stairwell into an oddly smokeless bar on a Monday night is that moment after the lights dim and the crowd quiets, after the attention shifts to the stage and the words have been read. It's the thrill of performing. And of being heard. It's the longing to be the one they're yelling for.

girls, boys

I'm a girl
I'm a girl
what does that mean
in this gender-fucked world
of girls are pink
  boys are blue
    girls do feelings
    boys do things, stuff
my soul feels rough and tumble
longing for gentle touch
of wise emotion
a woman's knowing

  gender stereotype
  you say
  woman's knowing is just
  too gender typical

  but there is something
  some space
  some, fuck! I don't know what
  that, if it isn't there
  I feel
  uneasy
  cramped
  needing to push myself in
  to try to be seen
  heard

to say
I see the world differently
fear
of cruel laughter
of being shut out
trickles up around my skull
into my jaw
through my normally strong legs
so I feel weak
inarticulate
dizzy with unknowing
stop being that way!
me, or them?

I feel stupid
when I know I am not
I feel unhonoured
dishonoured?
dishonourably discharged
from the fraternity of boys
of men
for having breasts
and feelings
for crying when I get hurt
and wanting to talk about experience
not just things, stuff

the door is closed
with scornful looks saying
you're weird
backs turned to my conversation
I want to be in the fraternity
to get to do their stuff
be one of them
one of the boys, but
I am not

BARBARA BROWN

aimless
unsure of what to do with myself
I stand
awkward

my belly says
go find a woman
a woman
with a cunt or a dick
go find a woman

My breasts
I love my breasts
they're beautiful
the perfect size
according to white western body myth

36B
round, firm
sweet areolae
pink on white
red on white
fading stretch marks
from fast, early growth
teased and groped
a place of pain
silky skin scarred in ways
your eyes can't see

remember
someone said to me
hands on my nipples
these seeds planted
will grow
they will be a sign of
your evilness
for all to see

remember
remember
but do not tell

years I lived looking down
seeing evil
years I lived learning to love
looking down
finally
finally
years I lived knowing
my breasts are beautiful

I thought I'd arrived
so why now
is this question pressing
pushing up from inside me

my mother asks for me
what craziness is this?

why risk bold scars
and loss of sensation?

what about babies
don't you want babies?

how will you breastfeed?
breastfeeding's important
for the child's development

I know.
I know.

then why?

BARBARA BROWN

momma,
I don't want them any more
they weigh heavy on my heart
and make flying more difficult
I don't need them

to be me
letting them go
is being me

will you help me fly
or ask me to be weighed down
by a body I don't want
not like this anyway

I love my breasts
they're beautiful
I will love my chest
I will be beautiful
still
don't take that away
when they take my breasts
I'd rather you rub my back
when the healing pains come
I'd rather you watch me fly
and laugh with pleasure at my freedom

come see me, momma
come see me
when they take my breasts
I'll be beautiful
I'll love my chest
I want to fly

BARBARA BROWN is a writer, artist and psycho-therapist. She lives in Toronto with her dog, Rita, and her unnamed but frequently accompanying computer. Barbara's writing has been published in the anthologies *ReCreations* (finalist for a 2001 Lambda Literary Award) and *Hot & Bothered 3*, and will appear in the upcoming anthologies *Girlplay* and *Intersex and Transfeminism*. She is also the initiator and editor of *My Breasts, My Choice*, a project exploring people's experience of breast and chest surgery.

221

THE YEAR CLIT LIT STARTED, I had attempted to unite some science fiction and horror authors to join me in a writers' group. I made really cool posters and put them up all over the university, bookstores and libraries. I had found five other writers to work with. At first the group went really well. It was about the writing, the rich stories that come from the science fiction and horror genres. Within about ten meetings, however, I began to notice that my writing was being critiqued for its queer content. I was told that my characters didn't *need* to be gay and that it wasn't necessary for the story. I heard the group's evaluations, but felt that they were censoring the content of my work more than simply critiquing it.

Among my frustrations was my sudden awareness that there really is no place for queers in horror and SF. My research concluded that yes, there are authors out there that are writing queer-themed work and yes, there are queer writers writing SF and horror. So where were they? For a member of any community, networking becomes natural, almost second nature. So where was my community? I heard through the grapevine that there was this interesting reading series called Clit Lit. Women were coming out and reading all sorts of stories without censoring themselves. It was also a very queer-positive space, as most of the regulars were lesbians. My other community.

I decided that I would share my SF and horror with Clit Lit on a night featuring transgendered work. I wrote "Cold Steel Utensil" originally as a novella, but saw how easily I could transform this piece into a nice short story by simply rewriting it in the first person. The main character is a dyke-tranny. I had no idea how the crowd was going to react. I had never heard *any* other SF stuff read on prior nights. And all the invites I had extended to my lesbian community had rewarded me with nothing. They never showed up. Why? Most never knew what science fiction was. They never knew it could be more than aliens living on other planets, or men in space suits. It is funny how often people tell me that my work is not

SF. What? You mean my futuristic hot and sexy cyborg story is general fiction? Nope. (I wear SF art. I write SF. I read SF. But I have never read a novel about a man in a space suit who is fighting a war against aliens who are from a far-off planet.) So I tell them, read the good stuff. SF is a lot more than the simple pulp novel. I can honestly say that reading my work at Clit Lit has been one of my most interesting experiences. Although I think my biggest reward for reading at Clit Lit is that I've converted a few literary snobs into SF fans (smile).

223

KATE CORKERY HUSTINS

Cold Steel Utensil

Cold steel metallic, my cock hard, polished with lube. WD-40 always does the trick. It's silver-plated, my bio-mechanical sex organ. I just can't help the fact that my copper-and-zinc-alloy prick drips a pee-and-oil mixture that stains the urinal. In a world full of gender fucks who's gonna care. Besides I always wear a condom to protect myself from rusting. It may not be the real thing, but at least it's mine. My name is Liam, Liam Mercer. I named myself after my father when I was eight. Almost twenty years later I'm a self-taught robotic engineer and, if I don't say so myself, a pretty hand-some guy. They used to say that there was nothing unusual about my sex life. Born a beautiful girl to a beautiful mama, I loved hopping on a nice fat prick just as much as sucking and fucking the juiciest pussy in town. How quickly times change.

You see, when I was twenty-one I was in a terrible accident that left me bottomless. Well, maybe bottomless is not the best description. During the war against the Canadians, my mother was a well-known rebel for the Republic of Newfoundland. It all started back in 1949 when Newfoundland joined Confederation with Canada. For the last one hundred years, Newfies have been the butt end of many stupid jokes. Downright racist, I suppose. Then again, once a Newfie, always a Newfie — and never a Canadian. I'd tell you a Canadian joke right now, but there's just nothing funny 'bout them damn mainlanders. Sure, I even dated one once. She foolishly thought her goldfish was pregnant. Can you believe that? Fish lay eggs. They don't get knocked up, silly mainlander.

I guess it was around fifty years ago when the treaty with Quebec Hydro ran out. We tried to leave with a ninety-eight percent vote for separation but Canada wouldn't let us go easy. They decided to fight for the lost island. The war began in 2031. Only ten years later, right around the time the Americans threatened to send in the Peace Corps, the big-bozo-brained found what they believed to be the rebels' hideout. My mother's hiding spot — our little home in Come-By-Chance, Newfoundland. They sent in assassins to destroy Mother, but all they got was me, because that was the day Mother went to town and hacked into CESUS, downing the RCMP's lines for weeks.

I tell ya, alone, I had no chance against the Canadians. They bombed our house while I was sitting in the outhouse taking a pee when come-a-flying right through the outhouse door was half the kitchen window, stained-glass figurines and all. Ripped me right apart, right at my very seams. Dead centre aim, smack right through my lap and, whack! Took half of me with 'em. Sure by' one of the fellas from down the road was inside the house fixing the plumbing. He was blown from here to Carboneer. God bless his soul. Now, I don't remember much to be honest, but when I awoke and was told of the Republic of Newfoundland's victory, it was not hard at all to fill in the pieces. Sure as the Pope's vow of abstinence, we Newfies kicked some serious Canuck ass.

Upon my awakening, dreaded pain enveloped my eyes, for what I saw were no feet, no legs, no thighs, not even a cunt left on me. My life has ever since changed. In a coma with no hope for survival it was the better part of eight months before my cure came 'round. You see, it was not just any coma I was inflicted with; I was in a deep depression where my physical body would just not wake up. One day I foggily remember waking to find this little redheaded nurse tending to my bottom half. "Jesus, Mary and Joseph!" I jumped right up. What I saw were shiny muscular legs! Shiny!? "Oh good, you're awake. The doctor told me to massage you 'til you woke. How do you feel?" I heard somewhat of a voice, sorta like Charlie Brown's teacher, just fading away. And that's all I remember until I finally woke for good.

The nurse's name was Lucy-Lynn Jones. I called her Lou-Lou. Standing at five-foot-ten, she was no ordinary nurse. She was a typically gorgeous Newfie. It wasn't just her short red joyful bounces of hair that made it love at first sight, but that sure helped. My sweetheart Lou-Lou was also a war amputee. She'd lost an arm, but ended up gaining one mean massaging machine. Which gets me to the story. Me, little Liam, the cutest tomboy in Come-By Chance, was now void of sex. Even if I really really wanted to jerk off, there was nothing for me to jerk at. Taking a few laps around me precious flaps was now totally impossible. According to the doctors, that would never change. I was to be sexless forever. They told me to consider different toys that might help rebuild desire.

"Some patients in your condition resort to different forms of marital aids to overcome their disability," one very ignorant doctor told me.

"A strap-on cock you mean? You moron! I already own every size, every style and every shape any cock has ever come in." I told them, I have no problem with desire, I just want to cum.

Time and time again, statistics show that Newfies have more sex than any other cultural group in North America. With Lou-Lou's insatiable sex drive and my longing to cum, it didn't take us long to come up with an idea. Of course! We would manufacture the perfect sex organ. The technology was there. After all, the doctor did give me back most of my bottom half. My legs are wired-on microscopic circuit boards with tiny little cables that are attached to my muscles, major nerves and spinal column. I can feel my steel, with automatic inner-heating devices to give me the notion that real blood flows in my fake veins. Also I'm fixed up with an electronic notifying device that causes my left palm to itch when they need oil. My legs are attached as well as any of yours are. Yet mine, mine are indestructible. And plus, my cold steel utensils appropriate no Barbie doll I've ever met, for they were moulded from my very own old ones.

As a young, er, girl, I was adept at creating my own friends. I think I was five when I first saw *Star Wars Episode One* — a brilliant classic from the past century. The young Skywalker was more than just an inspiration. I created three robotic pals that year alone. Mind you it helps when your mother is a super-genius hacking electronic engineer. I made my first gender-specific pal at twelve. It was a she-he. I named her Rei Toei, after Walter Gibson's virtual woman in his book *Idoru*. Boy did Mother ever have a lark about that. I still have the picture she kept of me and Rei, my face red in frustration when I got my hand caught amidst her very huge clunky breasts trying to shut down her off switch. I certainly learned never to place an off switch between two steel hooters again.

So on with my story. You see, once I get an idea there's no turning back. I needed a sex. A way to make myself cum. Yeah, I still had the two little tits God gave me. Mother did always tell me to count my blessings, but it just wasn't the same. Lou-Lou and I spent three months designing and perfecting my metal prick and another two more looking for parts. Sure, we even had to order parts in from St. John's, because the local corner store was all out of joints. And then came the day. Not just another dildo. No ordinary cock was mine. I wasn't about to be left with no limp piece of skin that needed pumping up like an old tire. I wanted a cock that was going to make me cum. I was asleep for the surgery. Lou-Lou was to follow exact instructions on how to plug me back in and wake me up…and sure enough, that morning I awoke sweating, feeling a small pressure in my bladder. Damn, I thought, I have to pee. My eyes lazily flowered open to find Lou-Lou's red head bobbing up and down between my legs. I tried to sit up. "Lou-Lou, I have to pee. Oh, let me see it, let me see my new cock!"

"You don't have to pee. Liam, relax, don't worry." She barely got her words out what with all that saliva dripping from her chin. She sure didn't waste another moment before going back down again. I flung all the pillows behind my back so I could admire Lou-Lou. Not just any woman, my Lou-Lou. She's a *real* cocksucker. She gobbled my cock and took it deep. She alternately licked and sucked, my body temperature rising past the boiling point. My nipples were so hard, the little things stood out like mountains in the Prairies. I tugged and squeezed them to remind myself I wasn't dreaming. I began to thrust and utter strange guttural sounds, totally involuntary, bending my body to reach her lips. My big fat climax was approaching. The urgency was too much, I grabbed her hair and shoved her head up and down hard. Her mouth, luscious pink stretched lips, encompassed my new metal organ completely. Suddenly my body was overwhelmed with tingles and every inch of my skin went bright red. KABOOM! KABOOM! KABOOM! — three complete body jerks, my face muscles still slack. I shot my load right in Lou-Lou. The immediate after-effects glowing, just sensational.

As my orgasm subsided I pulled her head off me. The condom filled with my juices, spurts of ejaculation inflated the rubber so it looked like a water balloon hanging off the end of me. It even splashed as it hit the floor. Exquisitely fucking excellent. Giggling, I muttered, "Thanks Lou-Lou!" For all I could do was lie there, mystified. It had actually worked. All riled up, my throbbing pulsating rod was not made of meat, but was as good as any natural-born. It was just wired properly, and attached to my insides adjoined to my old G-spot.

Smiling, Lou-Lou came up next to me and wrapped her arms around my neck. "I knew you didn't *really* have to pee," she whispered. "And Liam, what a nice cock you have." She nuzzled her freckle–bean face into mine and we kissed.

"Wait, now I really have to wizz." I jumped up and headed to the bathroom. My cock, now limp, swung from side to side. I nearly ran into the wall, I couldn't take my eyes off it. I lifted up the toilet seat and sat down. CLINK. My dick hit the bowl. Laughing hysterically, I stood up again and aimed. A new duty to my new sex. "I can pee standing." My twelve-year-old self was screaming congratulations. Clear yellow piss streamed from the metal piece of meat dangling between my legs.

"Liam! Don't forget to lube!" Lou-Lou called out to me.

"I know, I know. It'll rust without. I won't forget." Cock in hand I shook away the excess pee, took some toilet paper, wiped and filled up my reserve with WD-40. Oh, my cock, my cock, the perfect external sexual extremity. I could hardly wait to get back into bed and give the rest of Lou-Lou's holes a test drive.

BENT ON WRITING

⟜KATE CORKERY HUSTINS grew up in St. John's, Newfoundland. A proud Newfie, she left at seventeen to travel across Canada and for the next ten years lived in British Columbia, Alberta and Ontario, where she now lives with her life partner. Kate's work has been published in *The Muse*, *The Harrow* and *Xtra!* magazine. She is currently the senior editor of *Sol Rising — The Magazine of Speculation, Fantasy and Science Fiction*. She has performed at Clit Lit, Strange Sisters, Michigan Women's Music Festival, the Volcano Room and Buddies in Bad Times Theatre. While rumoured to be "hilariously funny," "gregarious" and "deadpan," Kate writes to entertain in the Irish tradition of storytelling. Recently the focus of her work has been queer/transgendered horror and futuristic tales of woe. She is now at work on a novel, *The Portrait*.

CAROL THAMES

IT WAS YET ANOTHER ONE of the readings that I participated in for Clit Lit. I had just recently ended a relationship and I was now dating this new woman. I found her so sexually exciting, alive, giving and open. My connection with her allowed me to step outside of the conventional box. I wanted to explore this non-conventional box with its many sides and angles, as well as its many hidden, secret corners. That night, when I was reading, I felt free, free to be the woman I had suppressed for so many years. I chose pieces to embark on this new and raunchy journey — a journey about exploring my sexual self as a very sexy, hot and horny lesbian femme. And I was enjoying every minute. Enjoying this new woman, the new sexual gift that my universe had granted me. She was wild and crazy and I wanted everything that she offered. This woman was everything I wanted and needed to fulfil my lustful nature.

She didn't care much for poetry and yet she came out that night to support me, and I wanted her even more for this sacrifice. She was hot. I was hot. I looked at her and my animal nature, the things that make me raw, were raised within. I could have fucked her wherever we were. At one point during the event we were standing along the back wall of the bar. She reached over and kissed me and then slipped her hand between my legs. She began stroking my clit and I became totally engrossed in ecstasy. I wanted her so badly. I wanted to do the nasty, and for her to do all the nasty things to my body that make me come alive and feel randy. She had the touch that freed my hidden talents. There were times throughout the evening when I looked at her and wanted to drag her to the bathroom, drop my drawers and have her fuck me.

The heat, the want, the hunger didn't allow us to stay for the entire series of readers. We left through the back door early in order to go off and indulge in each other. She was the reawakening that I needed to move from my state of repression to a non-repressed state of being. She was what I needed and wanted. She was the Bits and Bytes and I was the kid in the candy store.

Gay Divorcee

I am the Gay Divorcee.
Relationship ends
and Relationship begins.
And what is a Gay Divorcee Femme to do
but just begin the hunt?
So my first thought was, The Classifieds:

"Lover seeking Lover"
"Woman seeking Woman"
"Butch seeking Femme"
"Bitch seeking Bitch"
"Cunt seeking Cunt"

Ooooh
How I want my juices to flow
as I howl like the bitch
the bitch dog that I am.
Allow my eyes
to roll back — to that place
The unknown domain.

I am the Gay Divorcee
Newly released on a city of unsuspecting women.
Butches,
That is.
I am the vampire
Lost in my hunger and lust.
Seeking contact.

I read through the classified section and
Ads jump off the pages at me:
"Attractive Femme seeks Femme..."
This beats long nights of masturbation sessions.
"Slim Fit Stable..."
I wonder what this means
in a Lesbian context?

What I know is
I am a BSW — not a Bachelor Degree of Social Work
But a
Black. Single. Woman.
Seeking
Seeking lust — desire
Hunger — satisfaction
Lips interlocking in kisses
Passion because I am a passionate woman.

So I read on
with my fingers exploring
body
tits
cunt...
"Femme attractive, PRO-fess-ion-al..."
"Buxom Babe..."

Yes, I am the PRO-FESS-ION-AL
The BUXOM BABE
Seeking a Butch top
I can own.

↝ **CAROL THAMES** is a wild/crazy/reckless and eager woman who completed her training in Theatre Arts. Ms. Thames's training led to her becoming a writer/performance artist/poet/actor/director/radio host/member of the Toronto Women's Bathhouse Committee, and, as one of her daughters tells her, a "hot mama." This black, single, lesbian/queer femme is also a mother raising two magnificent future warrior women. Ms. Thames contributed to the Caribbean lesbian anthology *Tongues on Fire* (Women's Press). She co-hosts the radio show *Black Queer Voice* and has written and directed a lesbian play, *Ms. Walker.*

232

Until Death

It was early evening on the terrace of the Harbour Café. Homeward bound, traffic hummed along the nearby freeway, an undertone to the clink of glasses and the racket of conversation from the bar. Beyond the islands almost hidden by mist, lightning zigzagged through the clouds. "I think we are playing with fire," I said.

Tom looked away, across the still, grey lake, brushed a fly away from his face, smoothed back his hair. "I'm not sure what you mean." He swirled his beer.

"He could kill one of us, or both, if he found out."

"You worry too much. He wouldn't do that." He casually lit a cigarette, turning his chair to catch more of the slanting sun on his already evenly tanned face.

"Well, look at what he did before. He went over the top then."

"That was an impulse, he's probably got it more together now."

"I wouldn't bet on that," I said.

Tom blew a thin blue stream into the air, took off his wraparounds, then looked at me, his eyes narrowing. "It's getting late. You look drained. You need to get more sleep." He turned abruptly and called the waiter.

Tom's coolness aggravated me, as if nothing had ever happened. As if it didn't matter, us being seen together, kissing me on the street, choosing to sit on restaurant patios, always in full view. Flaunting us, inviting trouble. I wanted him to be as worried as I was.

One week later, in his bedroom, he removed his contact lenses. "And how is your friend the Lord Christopher today?"

"As ever — King of the World."

"Why then do you stay with the little bastard?" This was probably the fiftieth anniversary of the first time he'd asked me.

"We've talked about that before," I snapped.

"What's this week's version?"

"Same as last week's."

"The money?"

"The money."

Always the money. Christopher Tennant was rich — as in millions. When we met he said that he was a broker. Later he said that I seemed sincere about making a relationship so he told me the history of his English aristocratic family and the whole bag of assets. I disliked his belief that the rest of the world was inferior to him, but I was impressed by wealth and knew that if I tried really hard I could prove my undying love for him until death did us part — preferably his first. To give him credit, Chris wasn't one of those washed-out relatives of an aristocrat who fled to the colonies; he was the real thing: son of a lord, and son of a bitch.

"I won't harm myself the next time," he had assured me, his body shaking with rage. "The next time you fuck around on me I'll kill you, and whoever you're with." I didn't tell Tom all that Chris said. I was afraid I'd never see him again. Or maybe I was just too angry with his nonchalant attitude.

"Maybe, if you're so worried," Tom said, "we should kill *him* first." He sent a perfectly formed smoke ring to the ceiling. His shirt was off, skin damp as he lay on his bed, daylight fading through the slatted windows, the room filling with shadows, streetcars trundling by. I got up and closed the blinds. I needed something to do. It was the feeling I always get when bad news hits me — a kind of freeze on my mind.

"You're joking." I was certain that he wasn't.

"Like that old Barbara Stanwyck movie where they get rid of her husband to get the money, and each other."

"Only they didn't get the money, or each other, they got bullets," I reminded him.

"Poor planning. Things are different in real life. One can get away with more."

"He's got a gun, you know."

"He has?" I nodded. "Hmm," Tom continued. "He's just the type to have one. Insecure personality, probably practices blowing people away in front of a mirror, teaching the world a lesson. What kind is it?"

"A revolver — thirty-calibre."

"What I'd expect. A toy. Real men play with semi-automatics. Does he carry it?"

"No, it's in his desk drawer, usually locked."

"What a cliché!"

"Aren't we going a bit far?" I hardly recognized the stifled voice as my own.

"Don't worry. I'm not going to shoot him. Too noisy, too messy by far. I just don't want to be his sitting target. If we let things go the crazy bastard may pull some evil stunt. Besides, I'm in a killing mood," he continued, excitement driving his voice. "It's okay to kill a mad dog, n'est pas?" Then he added, putting his shades back on, "I told you before, you're too chicken to go for what you really want."

Once before, Tom had used the same words with me. We were leaving a club by the waterside late at night, the tepid air heavy with the smell of perfume and smoke, both slightly drunk and toked up. "What next partner?" he'd asked, pushing his hand down the back of my pants.

"Let's get a cab."

"Not yet," he slurred, "I want to pass a little time right here, and then we can get home and do the other thing." He stood on the dock looking out across the lake — into the dark, I thought. Then he turned to me and said, "You see that boat out there, doesn't it look interesting and expensive, and waiting for something to happen to it?"

"Let's get home before you cook up some mad plan," I pleaded.

"Yes, that's it, what about me going out there to make a night call on those good people? With a little luck I may find them abed. I can be a pirate tonight," he shouted, throwing his fist in the air.

"You're crazy. Don't even think of it, Tom. Just mug someone on the street — please." We walked slowly down to the end of the dock, where he again stared out at the boat. Then he quickly pulled his shirt and runners off and let his chinos slip to the ground. He was naked then and I only had a glimpse of his muscled body before he dove off and, with his well-timed crawl, moved through the black water as if in a straight line towards the boat. I was aware of nothing but the methodical sounds of his strokes and music in the distance. When he got back he had a watch on his wrist. "Congratulate me." There was triumph in his voice. "From their bedside table, and I didn't have to disturb my hosts." He kept chuckling as he put his clothes back on.

Back in his apartment I lit up a joint and lay beside him on the bed.

"Tom, I could never do that."

"You're too chicken to go for what you want," he said gruffly, but then softer, "that's the beauty of our relationship; you and I are so different. You drop back when I go forward, it's an energy between us, that complex interplay of your mind with mine, that movement to and fro." His voice dropped to a whisper. "I trust you but you don't trust me — do you?"

"I do," I lied. "But you scare me."

He began to stroke my arm, his fingers making a circular pattern on my skin, across my shoulder, down my belly. "Fear, contrary to what is usually believed, creates our heroism. Just trust me and what I feel for you, and the forces of life will bring us through." He laughed. "That's got a good sound to it, doesn't it? A touch of the philosophical." Then he slid on top of me and gazed at me with his brown glazed-over eyes. Afterwards he slipped from the bed, washed off and lay down beside me, lit a cigarette.

"That was really hot. I think the idea of killing Christopher Tennant gets me burning." Tom was like that. Just mention a killing, anything dangerous, and he got that flush of excitement and interest, asking questions, getting details. He even smelled differently, like his brain was manufacturing some chemical that seeped out through his skin.

"Sometimes I feel that I'm just a good fuck for you," I blurted.

He turned suddenly, his head on his hand, eyebrows raised, then started to laugh. "That might be better judged by me — but seriously, what exactly are you trying to say about this unique relationship?"

"I don't know what you want from me. It feels like events are just rolling over me without control. I feel so fucking submissive."

"I like you being submissive — like just now." He was smirking. I got up from the bed. I'd never tell him that I couldn't get enough of him, not just the sex, but of everything about him. Suddenly serious, he said, "You can't even begin to realize how much you mean to me. You won't believe me when I say this, but I desperately need you in my life." If I were ever to believe him, it would have been then. I said nothing. He stubbed his cigarette and pulled me to him once more, and I surrendered, not to Tom, but to my own endless desire and the emptiness of failure.

We'd first met at a party. He came over to me with that studied unshaven, scruffy street look, brushed his thigh up against mine and whispered into my ear. He smelled of smoke and booze and kept moving his tongue across his lower lip. "Hi, I'm Tom. Why are you here?"

"My partner, Chris," I shouted above the music, aroused by his come-on. "He knows the host."

"I suppose he fucked him, just like I did."

"Not that I know of course — but then I may not have been told about it."

He moved to my other side. "How long have you known this Chris?"

"About three years."

"A regular happily married couple — complete with infidelities."

"Not so happy all the time."

"A guy who looks like you should be made happy all night and every night and well into the next day." I could only stare at him. He stared back. I should have stopped there but he took me by the hand and drew me into the den. With a PC shooting images at us, he pushed me up against the door, undid my belt and felt for my uncoiling cock. He licked my neck slowly as if tasting me, and then bit me. "That one's for Chris," he murmured.

I can still bring back the smell of his sweat, and the starchy crackle of his shirt as he unbuttoned it. I was fascinated by his energy and by his calculated sexuality, and even before we were finished I was thinking only about how I could see him again. "It's unlikely I'll be able to see you again, " I told him as we pulled our clothes on.

"I want you. You're perfect. I'll get you."

We were lovers for nearly two months before Chris found out. He almost killed himself slitting his wrist in front of me, hitting an artery. Blood sprayed the wall. I could smell it as he stared at me with eyes like globes, as if amazed that he could do something so spectacular and dangerous. I was terrified by the violence of it. "I'll never see Tom again," I swore, and I really believed what I was saying at the time. A month later

I contacted Tom, at first just as friends, which lasted for a few meetings, and then we were into it all over again.

Tom told me that he had a plan and that it would be better if I knew nothing of it. "Ignorance of events guarantees a more genuine reaction on first getting the news. You'll be a suspect but I've set you up with a fool-proof alibi." He smiled, as he often did when he had some punchline ready. "It would only spoil the ending for you."

"I should leave you before this becomes a complete nightmare." I was sitting on the side of his bed. He was standing in front of me.

"Perhaps you should, but you know that you won't." He moved closer to me, put his hand around the back of my neck and pulled my head to him.

Chris was found naked and strangled in our apartment. Tom had timed it to coincide with one of my business trips to New York. I identified Chris at the city morgue when I saw the old scar on his wrist. I didn't look at his face. When I came out of the building Tom was standing across the street, smoking. He saw me, threw his cigarette into the gutter and strolled away. He had meticulously accounted for everything.

At the inquest it was noted that Chris had taken home an unidentified person. I testified, as directed by Tom, that we often used the leather belt as part of our sexual practice, and that I was aware that Chris took home strangers when I was away, and had frequently warned him of the dangers. The police said that one of the stolen credit cards had been used in Montreal a few days after the crime. Otherwise there were no leads. It was a routine gay murder.

When I phoned Tom a few days after the inquest he asked me to phone back as he was on another line. I did. I knew that at some point the police would come back to me. I also knew they would trace the relationship that I was having with Tom, and would question him on it. "I suppose this is the point where we shouldn't be seen together," I said.

"That's not a problem now," Tom said briskly. "I don't intend to become a character from some sordid movie, bent with guilt and remorse. He's dead. We're alive. It's our time now."

Two months later, on Tom's evidence, I was arrested and convicted on the charge of conspiracy to murder Christopher Tennant. Tom sat looking straight ahead in the overheated courtroom as he described our relationship in cold, well-worked phrases. "The accused formed an immediate addictive attachment to me. He told me on many occasions that he was passionately in love with me, and that if Christopher Tennant were dead we could have an exciting life together as he was the main beneficiary of the will. He knew a man who was willing to kill Christopher Tennant for one hundred thousand dollars and he said he would legally sign over half of the inheritance to me if I would testify that Christopher Tennant led a dissolute and dangerous lifestyle." It didn't take the jury long to reach a verdict.

Tom visited me a few months into my term. He was unshaven, hair uncombed, and his blue-striped shirt was open at the neck. Adjusting his shades and smoothing his hair behind his ears, his voice cool and level, he asked me how they were treating me here. "Does it matter now?" I instantly threw back.

"I suppose not." He waited a while, and then continued in what he probably considered his sincerest tone. "I'm sorry this had to happen to you. It was obvious that they would try to pin it on one or both of us, and that the first one they went to should make the first move. I could have contacted them to tell my story but, as you know, I prefer the thrill of chance. You had the same option if they went to you first, although I suspect you wouldn't do something like that to me." From the other side of the Plexiglas he flicked me a smile, paused as one would to assess the impact of a joke and then straightened in his chair. He took off his shades, gazed at them, seemed to hesitate, then lifted his eyes in one movement to meet mine. "If I could love anyone, I would love you."

I looked away from him, embarrassed by his awkward attempt to seek some kind of forgiveness. Dust quivered in sunrays streaming from the skylight. Someone was sobbing in a nearby cubicle. We were silent. I waited until he stood up to leave and then I pressed my fingertips against the barrier, feeling the coldness of prison printed on them. He leaned forward quickly, matched his fingers against mine. As he moved I saw his neck muscles tighten and his pulse move tautly below his oiled skin. I thought I smelled his cologne mixed with the dryness of the air. I wanted to be in his apartment again, the noise of the streetcars, the lights flickering across the room, the smell of him as we lay naked on the bed with his fingers trailing down my belly, holding me with his gaze. I wanted to feel him again, his damp skin, to look into his tea-coloured eyes, to hold the steely soft-skinned columns of his back as he curved his body, suddenly forcing himself into me.

➛ **STEVE NUGENT** was born in Ireland and now lives in Canada. He has contributed book reviews, essays and literary interviews to *fab* magazine and *Eye* magazine. Steve's short fiction has been published in *The Church-Wellesley Review*, *excalibur* and the collections *Quickies 2*, *Exhibitions*, *Buttmen* and *Afterwords*.

✒ TONY ESPOSITO

COMING FROM QUEBEC, this was my very first reading in English. My past readings, in French, were university-related, and therefore not charged with the audience contact found at Clit Lit. This reading made me feel part of the queer world of literature in Toronto. The reaction from the audience was comforting. I expressed my nervousness and my fear that my accent would be in the way of understanding my pieces. It seems everything was fine. That gave me the strength to accept other subsequent readings. That night I felt a welcoming door opened for me.

241

Leash

(for Andrew)

You made a noticeable entrance.

They saw your perfect muscular body. They saw your square jaw. They saw your shaved head. They saw the man. Covered with leather and iron. Underlining your masculine form. Perfect picture.

Your eyes are icy blue. In your hand, you held a leash restraining a man. He is nothing like you. The Prince and the Toad. A kinky moment in the life of two very different men. Or a long-time complicity. They'd never know.

All they saw was the perfect man, the black string, the lucky slave.

They did not see the invisible link. The lives connected. And the care that travels through a leather bond.

I saw you before.

I saw you. Realize the force in those three words. The position of power given to the "I." The dominated passivity of the "you." The only choices of the "you" are to confront or to hide. There is some accusing tone in this. Some invisible finger pointing. "I" simply sees. "You" must be doing something to be seen. Something worth being pointed at.

I saw *you*.

In the disorganized movements of the dance floor, our eyes met. A fraction of a fragment of time. I won't pretend that time froze for us and that the moment lasted an eternity. No, it was just a glimpse.

They saw your perfect muscular body. They saw your square jaw. They saw your shaved head. They saw the man.

I saw you, not your body. Well, I admit I have noticed it too. It is remarkable. But it is only a nice shell. No, what I saw was inside your blue eyes.

I saw tenderness. A lot of it. A loving strength. I saw care for the ones you love. All kinds of things forgotten. Forgiven hurts. Hopes and dreams.

I saw fear. And loneliness. And insecurity. All kinds of things impossible to believe. They don't match the shell.

In that glimpse, I had an open sky with your soul written in white letters...

...and then the lights of the dance floor came back, melting everything in a syncopated beat.

And now I create this leash between us, made of ink and paper. Bonding you tirelessly forever. In shape and in situation you didn't choose.

But they only see the words.

Paths

Nine o'clock is the best hour. Everyone has gone home. I was alone in the library, my fingers reading the Braille transcript of the intense verses of Angelo di Roberto.

One wish — let me in
The flower of your foreskin
And your lips of velvet.
We are flesh, blood and sweat.

I heard footsteps. Light but masculine footsteps coming closer. Chair legs kissing the floor. Search of things in a zipped bag. Something put on a table. A pencil rolled three centimetres. Money tinkled. Then the silence was re-established, except for the butterfly sound of pages turned.

If your love is sunrise
I want to sleep on your thighs
To wake up and see
The splendour of your manhood glory

Zip again. Chair again. Footsteps again. Coming closer. Passing me. Getting to the nearest bookshelves. And as he passed, the delicious smell of a peach invaded me.

Let my hand play the organ
Touching every inch of the man...

I couldn't concentrate. My mind was disturbed by the strength of that smell.

The footsteps. They stopped by my side. A hand — his hand — took mine. He gently drove it to his mouth. I followed the lines of his lips. Rose petals. He captured one of my fingers in his mouth. His saliva was sticky.

I smelled it again. Peach. He freed my finger and placed it on his bare hip. Thick drops of liquid. I kissed them.

I tasted it. Along the curves of his chest. I hope my tongue caught every drop of the sweet juice. It led me from the valley of his hip through the forest of his stomach, scaling the mountains of his nipples. And as my tongue, like a salmon, was fighting against the tasty current, I found his shoulder. The moon was there, surely shining over some cherry trees.

There was a crescent of peach on his shoulder.

245

TONY ESPOSITO

↝ TONY ESPOSITO was born in Paris, France. As a baby, he moved to Quebec, where he grew up. Tony is well-known in Quebec, where he has published more than twenty short stories in French. Two bands have included his songs as part of their repertoires. Tony has produced two plays, one in French and one in English, in Montreal. Since his move to Toronto he has published five English texts.

✒ HAMISH MᴬᶜDONALD

I WAS ASKED to co-curate a gay men's night in the reading series. I suggested the name "Spunky" and we ran with it. I blush every time I say "Clit Lit." The evening went well and I got a good response to this piece, which was fun to write.

Lighthearted

Greg shut down his computer, locked the filing cabinet in his desk and nearly vomited. His work for the week was finished, it was six o'clock on Friday and now he had no choice but to go out into the world. Tonight, in particular, that meant going to a party. A party full of gay men. Technically, the term applied to him too, but in practice he was a failure at gay. He took his jacket from the rack near the office door. A perfect example, he thought, this jacket is at least three years out of style. He had no style. His apartment was messy, he owned no cologne, used $2.99 gel in his hair to hold it to one side and was dismal at making conversation. And now he was going to a party — straight from work, no shower.

He slipped his passcard in the elevator panel and pressed "G." The old car bumped to the ground floor. As he walked out of the building, Greg turned back to look at it. This was one of his biggest joys, working in the Concourse Building. While his office inside was a plain honeycomb of cubicles with fluorescent lights, the exterior of the building always struck him as a marvel. Its dark grey Deco façade stretched up away from his eyes, deeply ridged with grooves and punctuated with diamond-shaped accents. The archway over the building's entrance held his imagination. The mosaic tiles portrayed symbols of Canadian industry — plough, air- plane, wheat, etc. — in basic colours over gold. It wasn't that the piece was all that stunning, but for Greg it represented a forward-looking hope.

He turned and walked along Adelaide Street. The summer evening was warm, temperature unchanged even though the sun was burning down to an ember on the horizon behind him. The hope of industry, he thought to himself, looking at the buildings on all sides. In the distance he saw a building that looked like a plug-in air freshener. Yuck. All this boxed-in life. He smiled to himself. I should talk, he thought. Everything he did was part of an attempt to stave off the messiness of the world:

247

HAMISH MACDONALD

work was messy, family was messy, people were messy. And now he was going to a party. He'd promised his co-worker Jean that he'd go. There would be lots of gay men there, she said. Great. Greg imagined what they said about him behind his back. "What a waste." And, "Nice-looking but so boring, so badly put together."

The sky overhead slowly turned a dark turquoise and the streetlights came on. What if he had it all wrong? What if he met someone tonight whom he really liked? His stomach lurched again. He stopped walking and considered not going to the party after all. He looked back down the street. And the streetlight went out the instant he looked at it. Greg laughed to himself. He'd seen that a couple of times in his life. It was just a coincidence, he knew, but still neat. The sight was enough to lift his mood.

At the party Jean immediately dragged him across the room to face another man. "Greg Stiver, this is Vince Arturo. He's an electrician. And you use electricity. See how much you have in common?" With that, she left them alone. The two men laughed at the awkward moment and Greg felt a sensation like a current flash through his chest as the other man looked into his eyes. Vince offered a handshake. Then he carried them easily off into conversation. Soon they fell away from the rest of the party, talking on the patio by themselves. Greg found himself thinking about all the people he knew who were getting married this summer. It was a thirty-something thing to do, he figured. But why couldn't he meet someone too? Maybe someone like Vince. Not that I can get married, he remembered with a twinge of resentment.

Vince had to go, he eventually announced. He stood up, stretched his legs and groaned. They'd been sitting on the metal chairs for hours. He had a contract to get to early in the morning. Greg stood too and reached into his back pocket, pulling out his very fat wallet (also not gay, he'd been told). He took out one of his business cards and offered it to Vince. "Here's my phone number and my e-mail address." Then he took the card back, pulled a pen out of his pocket and scribbled on the card. "Oh, and this is my home number." Greg paused expectantly. "Maybe we can get together some-time?" He pulled a slip of paper from his wallet and handed Vince the pen. "Great," said Vince. "Oh, right, I'll give you my number too. I have to be honest, though." Greg's stomach depressurized, waiting for whatever news was to follow. "I'm pretty busy. I don't have a lot of time with this latest condo contract." He smiled. "But, yeah, I'll give you a call." They shook hands once more and Vince left the party.

Greg quickly found himself in "polite time" — the time between realizing he wanted to leave and when he actually did. With a quick goodbye to Jean, he soon slipped out to walk home. The air was cool and he took a shortcut through the Annex, knowing that there was a street with lilacs on it whose smell he always enjoyed. He played with the paper with Vince's phone number in his pocket, and then he took it out. He was being stupid, he told himself, getting all excited over this guy. Just then, the streetlight ahead of him went out. He stopped and looked back. The light behind him flickered, then went dark, too. Greg put the paper back in his pocket and hurried home.

A few days later at work Greg pressed the "check mail" button on his computer again. The short, tinny ping told him there was no mail, just as it had when he'd come into the office on the weekend to check. Maybe Vince didn't have e-mail. But he probably did have a phone. Greg tapped a pen against his finger, then threw it down on his desk. He checked his home phone for messages, already knowing there were none. Exasperated, he left for lunch. Prime Time Donuts didn't make the fanciest lunch on the block, but that was just fine. One of their cellophane-wrapped sandwiches suited his appetite and his budget. Besides, the shop, stuck in the corner of the office building, was convenient, despite being about as attractive as a tennis visor on the Queen of England.

Greg felt deranged, thinking so much about this stranger, but no act of reason could unseat Vince from his mind. He snapped out of his reverie and checked his watch. Seven-thirty; it had stopped. He looked at the wall clock: one-twenty. Greg cursed himself for his distraction and hurried back to his desk. Again there were no messages. He checked his e-mail, only to receive a "cannot connect — network error" message.

"Jean," he called out. Jean's head appeared over his carpeted wall partition. "Are you having any problems with the network?"

"Nope. It's fine."

"I'm having a — " he began, but then the fluorescent light in his cubicle flickered and went out. "I'm having a problem with...with things."

Jean came around to sit on Greg's desk and he recounted his experiences of the past few days, being careful to acknowledge that the bizarre connections could all be in his head. "Streetlight interference effect," she said flatly, "or SLI. I've read about it. You're too old for it to be the poltergeist effect. Or it could be an alien implant. Have you ever had a sense of losing time?"

"Never mind," Greg said. "I'm just going to go home for the afternoon. I'm feeling a bit stressed."

Greg flipped his Metropass at the streetcar driver. The car lurched forward and he stumbled to a seat. After five blocks, the whirring streetcar engine made a thunk-thunk noise and the car slid to a halt. The driver left the car and tugged at the power cable. But Greg knew there was nothing wrong; he'd already left the car and started walking. Moments later, the streetcar drove by. As he passed the Canada Life tower, he stopped to look up at the light bulb–pyramid weather indicator at its peak. The temperature was holding steady, it showed. Then it blinked off.

Greg walked through the old entrance of the University Theatre. "Is Vince here?" he asked one of the men working on the condo development. The man pointed further into the concrete and drywall mess. Greg waved hi when he saw Vince, who looked confused at first, then smiled. "Sorry to bother you here at work," said Greg, "but I'm having a bit of an emergency." Vince led him out to a park behind the development and sat him on a big concrete slab that served as a bench. Greg outlined his problem, leaving out the part that implicated Vince. "So, in your professional opinion," he finally asked, "does any of this make sense?"

Vince shook his head. "No, none. That's impossible."

"Yes, it's all just coincidence," Greg agreed. "That's what I thought."

"I wouldn't worry about it." Vince stood. "I have to get back to work now but why don't we get together for dinner? Something touristy. I know, meet me at the CN Tower restaurant at eight." Greg agreed, forgetting about the implications of the choice.

The view of the city outside the tower changed slowly as the room revolved. "This place...has...a lot..." Greg collapsed on a chair in the restaurant. "A lot of stairs."

"Why didn't you take the — ?"

"It was broken," interrupted Greg. Now he knew he sounded like a kook so he might as well keep going. "Look, I'm going crazy," he said, still catching his breath. "I keep thinking about — " The tiny halogen light overhead made a *plink* sound and went dark. Greg, who was not surprised, continued on without a beat. "I keep thinking about you." Just then the lights around them made tinkling sounds and winked out. "I'm really," Greg stammered, "I'm really — " Corners of darkness unfolded in the restaurant like an origami box. Greg leaned across the table. "I'm really interested in you!" The bar sank into night. With a metallic groan, the restaurant shuddered to a standstill. Darkness spread like a ripple across the city below, snuffing out the lights in the buildings and along the streets. As his eyes adjusted to the faint moonlight, Greg could see Vince's astonished smile.

"Could you," Vince said slowly and carefully, "could you keep it like this for a minute?" Greg laughed, and Vince took his hand. "I feel the same way." The light over their heads popped back to life. Vince led Greg away from the table, out of the restaurant and into the dark city. Everything they passed came back to light.

251

HAMISH MACDONALD is the author of the 1999 novel *doublezero*, and has since written a second book, *The Willies*. Hamish lives in Edinburgh, Scotland.

BRENDA ZAVALA-ANTUNEZ

Untitled

El mundo no se acaba
El mundo no se ha acabado
tus ojos siguen comiendose los mios
y tu boca es la misma de hace 100 años
No me dejes morder tus labios que me los como
No me dejes respirar que te respiro.

The world is not done
the world has not finished
your eyes are still eating mine
and your mouth is the same from 100 years ago
don't let me bite your lips
I'd eat them
don't let me breathe
I'd inhale you.

BRENDA ZAVALA-ANTUNEZ started writing
poetry in her teens. Poetry is her way of shouting,
hating and loving. Spanish is her native language.
Brenda was born in Peru and moved to Canada in
1997.

✒ JENNIFER MORROW

WHENEVER I SEE A FIRST-TIME READER at the series, I remember reading my poems there for the first time. It seems like forever ago now, but the time I spent standing in front of the microphone felt interminable. Little did any of us know then that the series would grow into the runaway success that it has become. Over the years I have watched nervous writers read alongside published veterans, and smiled as the trembling in hands and voices invariably subsides. Clit Lit provides a major public service to new and young writers. An audience for their work eases those first fearful steps into the world of being heard — and being read. Clit Lit also brings writers together. Many months after my reading I heard the poems of another writer that spoke so vividly to my sense of beauty in language and nature. Oddly enough, she remembered my reading and we got talking. She subsequently invited me to read at another event. The friendship we now have is a direct result of the reading series.

253

JENNIFER MORROW

Rainy Season

You feel it long before you see it —
a shift in the forest canopy
a relaxing at the roots of your hair.
When the rain finally comes
it closes slowly over the hillside,
obscuring the landscape in waves.

Humbled beneath the pounding roof
language twists away from us
settles with a squawk in the rafters.
We let it go, words redundant in the gathering dim.
They would tumble into each other
the way the edge of trees blurs slowly into sky.

When do we turn to each other?
It is no longer clear which one of us is which.
This neck, this curve of hip
is it yours or mine?
Is this your tongue
that cries my words of love?

Treeline

In this country
no tree gives voice to the wind.
Where silence matters more than sound
only words carry on the breeze.

Science brought us here
when night relinquished its hold on summer
and snow rushed away in rivers.
In long boots we trudge across heaving tundra
counting blades of grass.
Each day we draw a smooth radius from camp
two miles to the salt marsh, two miles back.
If we look we see beyond the edge of sight —
a polar bear five miles away
the bleeding edge of trees
earth peeling back from sky.
But crouching over the minutiae of our work
it is easy to shrug off the weight of infinity.
For here under the pretext of numbers
we count only two.

You show me seaweed dry on willow boughs.
The sea a grey murmur at the horizon,
I can't imagine its tide turning at equinox,
Hudson Bay rushing over this land.

The sun changes the shape of the day
starting and ending in the same place

it makes an argument of time
bringing and bringing it back to the beginning.
In all the time we have to tell and not tell
we see each other in every light
complete each other's sentences
anticipate each thought.

Summer slows, stills, holds its breath.
Here in a moment
the time it takes to tell me
your heart waits behind the treeline,
the time it takes
for night to push in
on the edge of the day,
time to reappear.
We watch Northern Lights, tucked
deep in our parkas,
but I have remembered the future, and
summer sighs into fall.

Flying back to Churchill
we watch forest meet salt marsh
and already I miss you
the way trees yearn for tundra:
fixed in around each other
they become each other.
For those broad miles we call "treeline"
are no more a line than the time
between summer and winter,
high tide and low.

Now time has taken us over many treelines
and each landscape whispers a little of us both.
But in my mind we are on the salt marsh
as the Hudson Bay tide turns.
We pool around each other's ankles, waists,
rush into each other's lungs.

Love walks softly in the sea,
fills me before I can open my eyes.
When I dare to look,
my tears blend softly in the salt —
you surround me with the weight of years.

↝ JENNIFER MORROW is a community and
environmental activist and writer who now lives in
Bearskin Lake, Ontario, and is at work on a novel.

☛ KIRSTI WYNNE

I WAS TELLING MYSELF I wanted to be a writer. I'd been telling myself this for a while. It's not as if I hadn't written anything, it's just that nothing I'd written seemed to have a beginning, middle or end; at least nothing more than two paragraphs long. One night at Clit Lit I picked up the themes listed for the months to follow, and one topic jumped out: Genderfuck. I decide to sign myself up and then I'd *have* to write something. At home I sifted through all the self-considered crap that had been falling on my pages for the previous two years and I suddenly realized that I had a little jigsaw to play around with. In the end, I only wrote one totally new paragraph. Clit Lit has been one of the most generous gifts I've received in my four years of living in Canada. As nervous as I was that first time, I don't think I could have been in a more relaxed and encouraging environment. Any first-timers out there who feel like giving a public reading a shot: go for it. You won't regret it. Honest.

Small Hands

(Dedicated to my Dad)

One time last summer, I was sitting in Yorkville by that massive rock that had been chopped up and imported from France and then glued back together. I was having a last smoke before my shift started and some guy, finishing his hot dog, was sitting about fifteen feet from me. I didn't notice him until he called over. "Why do you want to look like a boy?" I was a bit perplexed. Eighteen months earlier, before I came out, I'd be asked that question all the time and it always made me angry 'cos I'd just be wearing jeans and a T-shirt and what the fuck's it got to do with you anyway? However, by this time, I was so convinced that I actually was a boy that it threw me a little.

"How d'you know I was a girl?"

"Well, I watched you walk over and sit down and I looked at your face and I couldn't decide so I looked at your hands."

"Oh?"

"They're female hands."

"Oh."

I used to hate my hands. They're small and my fingers are short. Not long before I came out a girl told me she liked my hands. I couldn't imagine why, but in her eyes I saw wisdoms that I had yet to discover. I joked around with her, told her I imagined lesbians to prefer much longer fingers than my little ones, and she laughed and then laughed harder when she saw how confused I appeared.

It seems that in England the inquisitive aren't so polite. Last time I was home I had a fifty-odd-year-old guy approach me in a bar to blatantly accuse me of wanting to be male. After being refused a dance with my friend, he looked me up and down, turned back to her and asked her if she was a lesbian. Then he told me, in no uncertain terms, that I wanted to be a bloke. "You wanna be a bloke." I told him I did not but I wasn't expecting him to believe me, which he didn't. I understand why it was a bit confusing but I answered him as straightforwardly as he accused me. He insisted that I did and his expression suggested that perhaps I was a bit deluded. "Nah yer do. You wanna be a bloke."

"No really, I don't."

"Nah seriously, you do. I can tell. If you wanna be a bloke, right, you've gotta 'ave yer man'ood." He slowly started to lift his shirt and I was thinking, *Ah fuck no, don't do it.* So it was almost a relief when he revealed his hairy and pasty-white beer belly, gave it a slap and proclaimed: "That's yer man'ood that is. Right there." (Another slap.) I was trying to suppress laughter so I came out with more of a smirk and he looked insulted by that, fixed his eyes on mine. "Nah right, that's my man'ood that. Let's see yours."

"Nah, yer all right."

"Ah tell you what else. To be a bloke right, yuv gotta 'ave a bloke's job."

"Like what?" I asked.

"I dunno, like, er, bricklaying? Can you lay bricks?"

"I dunno, it's a skilled profession."

"You've gotta have a bloke's job if you wanna be a bloke."

"I don't."

"Yeah yer do...or roofing or drivin' a truck. What d'you do like, for a livin'?" What did I do for a living? I worked at a furniture store. All my fellow employees were male, including my boy-dyke boss. Along with vacuuming and dusting and making pretty arrangements, I had to lug sofas from one side of the store to another and load customers' hatchbacks with heavy boxes under the watchful eye of pathetically unhelpful husbands, whose wives thanked me for being a very helpful young man, whilst wondering why I wasn't in school. I didn't correct them anymore 'cos they just wouldn't get it and I assumed this guy wouldn't either. What did I do for a living? I decided I'd go for the points.

"I make furniture."

"Oh right, well that's sort of a bloke's job." I wondered if that was sort of a compliment.

I seemed to have gone up in his estimation. A little further along the way to "man'ood," even if I wouldn't show 'im ma belly. At the close of our conversation I almost convinced him that I really didn't want to be a bloke and that, in fact, I'm very happy to be a woman.

"Seriously?" he asked.

"Yeah."

Then a shadow of doubt crossed over his face and his eyes quizzed me once again. "Nah" he said, shaking his head. "You wanna be a bloke."

Before I knew I was queer, I desperately wanted to be a boy. I remember the posters of teen idols on my walls. There'd been one teenage Hollywood actor with a multitude of eight-by-tens neatly positioned and equally spaced, and within two months there'd been another actor in place. I don't once recall masturbating over any of them. What I do remember is wanting their clothes and their haircuts and the freedom to be like them. I so desperately wanted to be a boy that way.

When I was seven years old my brother started high-school and I watched him trying on his new school uniform. He looked so cool in the black Doc Martens and the dark grey Farrah trousers with the little yellow tab sewn on the back pocket, and the blazer and tie, both with the school shields on. I anticipated that one day it would be my turn. Then the excitement turned to angst because, of course, this wasn't the uniform I'd be wearing. I turned to my mum and begged her to pretend that I was a boy when I started school. I knew she loved me enough to understand. I really thought she'd go for it. "No Kirsti," she said. "We won't be able to do that. They won't let you. Maybe in a few years you'll change your mind." But I didn't change my mind.

A few years later we stayed in a caravan in the Lake District and I overheard some boy my brother had befriended ask about me. He wanted to know why, if I really wanted to be a boy, I didn't just have a sex change? A sex change? All I needed was to just have a sex change! I ran all the way back from the lake to the caravan and breathlessly asked my mum if that Christmas, if it wasn't too expensive, could I just have a sex change? Maybe, in a few years, I'd change my mind, she repeated. But it was only two years later that my mum had to take me to one side and suggest that perhaps wearing trunks to go swimming wasn't such a good idea any more because the neighbourhood boys had started to gather around the pool-room window. It was also around this time that I began to realize there were going to be many times ahead when I'd have to accept the gender

261

KIRSTI WYNNE

I'd been assigned. Up until then I could still tell people I was a tomboy — but by then I knew that even this was starting to sound a little strange.

By the time I moved to Manchester, when I was fourteen, I'd all but stopped telling people that I was a boy, and at seventeen, nobody knew. I never considered being queer; I didn't think that was the issue. I thought I'd been given this shitty hand that I had to learn to deal with. I couldn't look at girls; they intimidated me. I didn't look like them. I couldn't look like them. It simply wasn't me.

Sitting at a bar with my dad, he wanted to know what it was that made me want to be like a boy. I told him I didn't want to be *like a boy*, I just wanted to be me. I asked him what he thought the differences between men and women were. He tried to argue that as far as he was concerned, the only differences were biological. So I suggested we play a game and I pointed to a fully dressed woman across the bar. "Okay, that person in the red coat — is that a man or a woman?" He said he didn't feel like playing that game any more. Instead we talked about male and female attributes, whether they were societally defined or not, and I pointed out that for as many ticks as I'd get on the female side, there were definitely more on the male side. Ultimately, I think he agreed because he said he'd like, at last, to be able to take his little lad to the football match. And then he told me of how he and Mum had recently been rifling through my childhood pictures when suddenly they both burst out laughing at the realization that they should have known all along. "Even the ones of you in girls' clothes; you look like you're in drag!"

I laughed. That's exactly how I felt. So I wonder why I didn't know earlier myself? I had to be told and cajoled before I considered sleeping with a girl. But then everything started to slowly fall into place. Within a matter of weeks I became more confident with my appearance. I didn't care when someone mistook me for a boy. I didn't get embarrassed on their behalf when they realized their mistake, profusely apologizing. Getting on and off the subway, buying a pint of milk, being I.D.'d in bars — it all just became so much easier.

I don't feel like a different person, just a real version of me. A version now learning how to appreciate the girl I never could be. Girls still intimidate me but I try not to look away when they strike me hard, with a glance. Wink at me. Smile. And let me touch them with my female hands, which I don't mind so much now.

KIRSTI WYNNE moved to Toronto from England four years ago and came out shortly after. She is currently writing about her personal experience of transition: English girl to Canadian boy.

263

KIRSTI WYNNE

●◦ SHLOMIT SEGAL

The Visit

Lee hides chocolate bars
is always reading
the principal says
she looks like a street urchin

I say what an asshole
you nod
you look tired
often you yell
where are my keys
where's my wallet
you're late for school

Dori sticks stars on her ceiling
wants me to hold her snake
while she looks in her knapsack
she cried
cause she isn't singing a solo
in the choir
the children of children of
flower children
don't have TV

practice reiki on their cat
scatter books all over the floor

Lee likes to go to therapy
she's getting very morose
    you say
    it's just like her father

when she was five
Dori said
I want to be a lesbian
like grandma
    she doesn't remember that now
then we put on old music
and reminisce
try not to squabble
I rub your shoulders
and look forward
to heading home

➸ SHLOMIT SEGAL's writing has appeared in Outrage: Dykes and Bis Resist Homophobia, Plural Desires: Writing Bisexual Women's Lives, Fireweed, She's Gonna Be and From Memory to Transformation: Jewish Women's Voices. Shlomit's visual work has appeared on the covers of Canadian Women's Studies, Women's Studies Quarterly and Fireweed. Her more than twenty years of activism include involvement in the labour movement, rape-crisis centres and the Jewish Women's Committee to end the Occupation. Shlomit works as a graphic designer for the City of Toronto's planning department.

☙ NANCY VIVA DAVIS HALIFAX

AS USUAL, I HADN'T HAD TIME TO EAT and was running late. It was Monday night, so the ex had my kids, and I was going out to a little bar in the village called the Red Spot. I'd been trying to get to Clit Lit to listen to other writers for a long time. After not getting there for a year, I finally saw the curator's contact information in a local magazine, and so I contacted her. Turned out my first visit to Clit Lit would also be my first public reading. Papers in hand, I tried not to think, but my body granted me hiccoughs, and those persistent, rhythmic interruptions wouldn't let me forget, or speak. Drink water from the far rim of a glass, I thought. Swallow a teaspoon of sugar. Hold your breath. Nothing helped.

None of my friends were there when I arrived and there were no tables left. I saw one chair, asked the girl next to it if I could sit at her table. She said, "No, I'm waiting for someone." An hour later she was still alone. Either she'd been stood up or she was a liar and either way I didn't care for her. My anxiety was getting the better of me and I wanted to stay cool and relaxed. I was surprised when I was called to read. Amnesia had instilled itself at some point earlier that evening. I walked toward the microphone. The lights shone in my eyes and glared off my page; I couldn't see who was out there. Did my friends finally show? The microphone was too high for me and I failed in my single attempt to adjust it. No techies came out to assert their expertise so I told myself to deal. I stood at an awkward angle to my page and began. I'd chosen two poems that were part of my Ph.D. research, *Another Form of Water*. I finished and walked away. It was all a bit anti-climactic.

Shortly after my reading, two of my best girlfriends walked in red-faced and embarrassed at having arrived late. They treated me to wine and pizza and I gently harassed them. At the break, another writer approached me and we chatted. She was much published already and said that I might want to think about approaching publishers too.

Words Can Not Contain This Body

I

Words that ache
old words like bones
fracture
syllables,
repeat silence.
Words can not contain this body.

II

At night words pool in the corner of your mouth
trickle out and
stain your pillow.
Fleshy words
tender meanings
fall from my mouth
in a soft
graphite
line.

NANCY VIVA DAVIS HALIFAX

III

Your thumb
pushes against my lips
pushes them apart and
lips flatten
distort
reveal brittle aged newsprint
upon which words
can no longer
be read.

Your words remind me of an interior
a touch
a final drawing.

↦ NANCY VIVA DAVIS HALIFAX is a writer and visual artist. She first read her work at Clit Lit. She has recently returned from a studio residency as a writer at Art Space, Big Tancook Island, Nova Scotia, where she was working on a manuscript entitled *Another Form of Water*. Nancy has had work published in *My Breasts, My Choice* (Sumach Press), *Feminist Art Therapy, American Journal of Art Therapy*, and the *Review of Feminist Approaches to Art Therapy*.

MIRHA-SOLEIL ROSS

I GOT A CALL FROM ELIZABETH Ruth asking if I'd be interested in putting together a transsexual program for the Clit Lit series. The fact that the series had been open not only to trans men but also to non-trans-sexual men is what prompted me to say yes and organize a mixed-gender event. We've had our share of gender bender/gender blender events: vague intentions, artistically pretentious and politically retarded attempts at romanticizing, glamorizing and capitalizing on queer Anglo-America's booming obsession with "gender" and all things in between. I suggested that we do something specific for once, something unprecedented: let's talk, write and perform about *sex*. Elizabeth liked the idea and so we called the night "Trans-Sex-Fictions" and invited everyone to a "steamy evening of porno-poetic projections, fantasy booth action, satirical soundscape, mouth-to-mouth story telling and other undiluted trans-SEX oral rampages."

It was in this context that I presented my own story about my invig-orating and always-evolving relationship with ghosts, spirits and Satan himself! It was the second time I'd presented this story in public. The audience's response was over the top. The story has its moments but I had to wonder: is it soooo funny? To the point of barfing your beers, corn chips, salsa and guacamole? I've been dealing with ghosts since I was a child and it is a strange feeling to be surrounded by people who have never experienced frightening spirits in the middle of the night or who have never had to stand up for themselves in other realms. I get a big sar-castic kick out of people laughing so much at what they think is the prod-uct of my own extravagant and fertile imagination.

I always thought I couldn't write, and then in 1998 it became clear that nobody was gonna knock at my door and say, "Oh Mirha-Soleil, you're so amazing, I want to help you out. Let me write your stories so you can perform them!" I had to severely kick myself in the ass, stop whining and just get to it. Even though I'm slow, I've been able to write about half a dozen short ten-to-twenty-minute performance texts since then, and I am working on my first seventy-five-minute fully-scripted one-woman performance art show. Events like Clit Lit are essential experimenting grounds for people like me, who don't come from the literary world, but who are committed to telling stories and making sure we don't put people to sleep while doing so.

Ghostly Affairs

I was visiting my great-aunt Rita — *ma tante* Rita — the oldest sister of my maternal grandmother, one day when I was five years old. I was very excited about visiting her, because she had just bought an automatic French-fry making machine, one that cut the potatoes in a zigzag shape. My old tante Rita had a reputation amongst both the adults and the kids on our street for serving the best French fries. She was a sick woman with bad arthritis, severe asthma and chronic eczema around her elbows and knees. She chain-smoked Mark Ten cigarettes, one after the other, package after package. She could smoke up to three, even four packages a day, so you can imagine the poetic soundscape that offered itself as a backdrop for our exquisite French-fry feasts...

I was eating one day when I suddenly became interested in a large picture hanging on her kitchen wall. The figure in the picture didn't look like a real person, and his activities didn't yet make sense to me. I was intrigued. I stopped eating, grabbed my glass of ice-cold Kik Cola, swallowed a mouthful of it and naïvely asked: "Who is the man in the picture?" Ma tante Rita gave me a long, penetrating, almost vicious look and answered: "It's the devil. His name is Satan and one day he's gonna come and shove his two-foot-long red hot burning pitchfork up your ass while you're sleeping!"

People sometimes ask why I'm so wacky. Well, that's because I grew up surrounded by wacky people and very impressive images. Until then I had never heard of a man popping out of nowhere to impale me like a marshmallow in the middle of the night. It was all very stunning to a five-year-old. I dropped my French fry, made a silent but stinky wet fart and looked at the picture again. I was now able to see what was going on more clearly: there was a man, a very unusual man — white, tall, skinny but muscular, with a long nose, an extended narrow tongue, large ram horns, crooked teeth, hooves, an extremely hairy ass and back and a short but very thick erect uncircumcised penis. Over a fire he was heating a pitchfork — the kind farmers use to pick up bundles of hay and cow dung. Behind him gathered a dozen men and women with their tongues hanging out wildly, trying to lick his ass. The picture was powerful. It terrified me, confused me, grossed me out and turned me on all at the same time.

Ma tante Rita's evil prophecy had an immediate and permanent impact. From that very night I started sleeping on my back, tucking my entire body — head, shoulders, arms, hips, legs, feet, toes and especially butt-cheeks — under the blankets. It was my best strategy. If I was well-tucked under my blankets and the devil came while I slept, he would first have to untuck me in order to get to me. This would wake me up, of course, and give me enough time to scream my lungs out and alert our three miniature chihuahuas, who were sleeping with me in the attic. In my childish mind I concluded that Coco, Coquette and Pompon's loud, piercing, fast-paced yapping, their sharp half-rotting teeth and abominable breath would scare any devil away. I also, from that very night, refused to go to bed if there wasn't a full one-hundred-watt light bulb shining over my bed. No little kiddie night light was gonna be powerful enough to help me repel Satan.

This fear of being impaled by the devil's pitchfork also meant that I was never again going to be able to have a deep sleep. I was always going to keep some tie to reality. It caused me to have, almost on a nightly basis, what some people call astral projections or out-of-body experiences. Over the last twenty-five years I've gone on a few trips that would rival many new-agers' search for shamanistic thrill. Most of my out-of-body time has been spent running away from demons, entities and other evil forces. Sometimes they are full-scale monsters who try to maim and sexually assault me. Try and take over my mind and body, to possess me. Sometimes I see only an arm floating in front of me, trying to choke me, or a pair of eyes trying to intimidate me. But last year a shift occurred.

One morning I was resting in my bed when I suddenly felt a foul energy surrounding me, filling the whole bedroom. I tried to concentrate and gather my strength in order to face whatever was there when I heard this evil voice telling me something I didn't clearly understand. It threatened my cats. I screamed, "Fuck off!" in the direction of the voice. It took about a second and my attic bedroom was again peaceful. This was the beginning of a new era in my relationship with spirits, ghosts and yes, the devil himself, because I confronted them and won. They were no longer going to be in charge. Whenever I see spirits or ghosts now, they appear to be inoffensive, sometimes goofy and often lonely, sad, sexually repressed and frustrated.

I am a prostitute and giving people affection, a few good licks in the right places and a piece of my ass is, for me, a humanitarian vocation. So, over time, I have done what comes naturally and started to have sex with the spirits. I had to be a little bit persuasive at first, I would even say aggressive, but once they really took notice of my irresistible features, they didn't need a workshop to figure out where and how to eat and suck and lick... They liked the look, they liked the taste, they liked the smell, they like it all!

I love big burly round men with healthy bellies and big asses and one of my otherworldly regulars, Bartholomé, fits that type exactly. He is a round orange giant half-pumpkin/half-human spirit. And he knows exactly how to get me off. I don't have to explain to him that my penis doesn't function like a guy's penis. He looks me right in the eyes and says: "Baby, no need to talk. I know where your juicy pussy is." And then he proceeds to slurp his big pumpkin-human spirit tongue left and right under my balls, up and down, in and out of my ass. OUF!

Another of my favourite ghost lovers is one I call Sylvester because he has a lisp. He claims to be the spirit of a forty-eight-year-old New York City bachelor and celibate post-office worker who was electrocuted and died in the late 1980s. Sylvester explained to me that when it happened he was having a bath, got overly excited listening to Olivia Newton-John's hit "Physical" and started to do jumping jacks horizontally in his tub, accidentally knocking his music box into the water. He was still a virgin when he died. Now he has a thing for boobies and had been dreaming about them for decades. I am very grateful to Sylvester because all he does is suck on my nipples and massage my breasts, which helps prevent encapsulation around my implants.

Until now, I haven't told many people about ma tante Rita, her threat, or about my sexual interactions with demons and spirits. I've wanted to avoid ending up on the front page of some self-professed "modern-primitive" porno zine under the heading, "Shemale Ho Jacks Off and Gives Head to Dirty Old Ghosts." Or maybe on the cover of a transgendered magazine beside the caption, "Woman of Transsexual Experience and Survivor of the Sex Industry Becomes a Spirit Sexual Healer." I, of course, stopped a long time ago buying into the socio-cultural Christian construct of the devil. But I also know that there is a split between what I stand for politically and what I believe when I begin to fall asleep.

So instead of identifying myself as someone who was traumatized as a child and who is now dissociating and in need of feminist therapy at $75–150 an hour (sliding scale), I accept living and experimenting with contradictions in my life. I still anticipate that Satan himself will pay me a visit one day, either when I'm sleeping or when I'm having one of my out-of-body excursions. But I've got big plans for him now: if he does come around, *he'd* better be prepared to follow orders. He'd better be ready to bend on his knees and shove his long muscular tongue real deep up my red hot burning French ass!

→ **MIRHA-SOLEIL ROSS** is a transsexual performer, videomaker, sex worker and community/cultural activist who grew up amongst mountains of scrap, sewer rats and bottles of gin in Notre-Dame du Sacré Coeur, one of the poorest districts on the south shore of Montreal. With Xanthra Mackay she edited and published *Gendertrash*, a political magazine for transsexual and transgendered people. Her many videos have been screened at festivals across Canada, the U.S. and Europe. Mirha-Soleil founded and curated Counting Past 2 — Canada's first annual transsexual and transgendered multi-disciplinary art festival. She also developed MEAL-TRANS — the first funded multi-service, peer-run program for low-income and street-active transsexual and transgendered people in Toronto. Her work appears in the upcoming Sumach Press book *My Breasts, My Choice*. Mirha-Soleil was awarded a Canada Council for the Arts grant in 2001 to create a one-woman performance show based on her ten years of experience and political struggle as a transsexual prostitute.

REGAN McCLURE

I HAVE ALWAYS WANTED TO BE a writer. I have never wanted to be a performer. Prior to Clit Lit, I was in no danger of being asked to perform since there aren't many chances for someone who's never read her work to stand up on stage. I might blow it. I might mumble for twenty minutes. Anything could happen, so naturally there aren't many producers willing to take these risks. Aside from these invitation-only readings, a writer can always take a chance by volunteering at a fundraiser event or open-mic night. Unfortunately, novice ramblings often have to compete with comedy, music and other, livelier acts, usually in a bar, often to a rowdy and impatient crowd. Not that any of this bothered me. Because I never wanted to perform, remember? I went to Clit Lit because I suffer from the other problem — rarely having a chance to hear new writers do their thing.

At the end of the evening Elizabeth Ruth asked me if I wanted to read at next month's event. She knew I wrote science fiction and short stories, and so she asked. Cajoled, even. I must have been drunk, because somehow I agreed. Okay, I wasn't actually drunk, but I knew I should agree on the spot because if I thought about it even for a minute I might run away. Unlike extroverts who get up onstage and think, "Cool, finally everyone's looking at ME!" I can't imagine standing in front of a crowd and still being able to squeak out my words. So, in the spirit of making a commitment to face my fears at a much later date, I agreed. I had faith that these things get easier with time, and if there was ever a gentle and patient crowd, I knew it was definitely the hundred or so people who gathered at Clit Lit.

Anyway, I said yes and then spent the next month forgetting about it. After a blissful span of days, I found the horrifying words "reading @ Mon. 7 p.m." hiding in the pages of my datebook. I had three days to prepare. This launched a flurry of deciding what to read, rewriting it and practicing in front of a mirror holding a light bulb up in front of my face. Here is the sum total of what I learned from this experience:

275

REGAN McCLURE

I. Reading your writing out loud really improves it. Really, really, really.

II. Don't ever try to read from normal twelve-point type. Try twenty-point, double-spaced, or else the paper will compete with the light-bulb for parking space in front of your nose.

III. Close the bathroom door when you do this, or face the ridicule and/or angst of your roommates as you read the same thing over and over and over…

IV. Let them in to use the bathroom every so often.

V. The curator probably doesn't really care that you've timed yourself at 15.5 minutes when she's allotted you fifteen, and you don't really need to call her five times to discuss it.

So I did step into that gentle light and read in public. Sorry, I can't give you details. I don't actually remember much about it. I can only piece together a few facts from the dizzying high that accompanied my 15.5 minutes of fame:

I. I wave my hands a lot when I talk. If I do this onstage, things get knocked over.

II. I might as well lick the microphone and get it over with. I really need to cram my face into that thing for it to pick up my voice.

III. I shouldn't look directly at the lights unless I want to blink my way through the rest of the reading with little blue sun spots in my eyes.

IV. I am, in fact, capable of reading a lesbian erotic piece when Elizabeth Ruth's mother is in the audience.

Since that night, I've been onstage four other times at Clit Lit. Okay, so it *does* get easier. I'm not sure if my performance is getting any better, but my writing sure is. The piece I read that night was subsequently published in an anthology from Alyson Books. I received a Canada Council grant to help me write my novel, and was invited to read at another literary shindig where I met other writers with whom I now exchange work. Reading out loud gave me a better sense of pacing and dialogue. Reading in public meant direct feedback about whether I'd captured the audience with my story, or whether they paid more attention to playing with their swizzle sticks. I learned to adapt the rules of grammar to more colloquial rhythms, and that's made my writing more natural, more direct. All this helps my story come alive in the world. And I have always wanted to be a storyteller.

Presents

My mother has sent me a birthday present in the mail. I can tell it's from her as soon as I see it; no one wraps presents like my mother. It isn't just wrapped, it's hermetically sealed. I need sharp scissors to cut the twine wrapped three times around the box. This is the twine that you see in stores and think, "Who buys that stuff?" My mother buys it, all of it. Of all the Celtic knot magics, I think the double granny knot is the most powerful. I know from experience that human fingers cannot undo the binding on these packages, that cold steel is needed to sever it a safe distance down the twine.

There are two layers of brown wrapping paper, each hospital-corner fold also sealed from end to end with fibre-reinforced packing tape. My name is on the paper, underneath the knot that guides you to it. My name is also on the box, in case the twine and paper come off in the mysterious Canada Post sorting machines. My name is also on the bottom of the box, in case the naked box is found upside down and no one thinks to turn it over. The box itself is made of corrugated cardboard, with an edge crush resistance to thirty-two pounds per square inch, and a maximum capacity of sixty-five pounds. Its current weight is light as a feather, however, so I know that the box is there to prevent punctures and slashings, not because the present itself strains the capacity. I cut away the tape and reveal a plastic bag in case the box is immersed in water. This makes sense to my mother; I do live in the Great Lakes region after all.

Inside the plastic, I find some padding — fourteen double-ply paper towels and six sheets of bubble wrap nestle the present lovingly. I take out the brightly coloured gift paper. This is where the real present begins. The tape on the gift wrap is not fibre reinforced. That would be vulgar. It is invisible tape, almost wanton in its scanty application. It surrenders to my flying fingers in a few seconds to reveal the gift laid bare before me. It's a pillow. I don't know why, but for some reason I thought it might be something breakable. The pillow is hand-embroidered by my mother, perhaps an extension of that Celtic knot magic mentioned previously. The pillow has a zipper, so I can wash the embroidered cover. Washing instructions are not inside, that too would be vulgar. These instructions will be conveyed verbally in a follow-up phone call.

Had her hair not turned grey at the age of twenty from worry, the box would probably have been traditionally stuffed with trimmings saved over a decade or so towards this single goal. Instead, there is modern foam filling. I haven't checked, but I'm certain it is hypoallergenic foam. She worries, my mother does. She worries in a way that makes me look like a reckless fool in the way I arrange to meet friends for dinner. Hiro's Sushi — eight o'clock, I might say. As I talk, the universe slips sideways into an evil plot to thwart those words as soon as they leave my mouth. Foolishly, I rarely make a plan B. What if the TTC breaks down? What if I get lost? If I get lost, I could leave a message on her machine indicating an alternate location known to both of us. Unless, of course, she gets lost as well, in which case I could perhaps include a description of the neighbourhood landmarks so she can find her way out of wherever she is and get to the Plan B location. Perhaps to forestall the whole problem I will provide my dinner date with a detailed map of the neighbourhood right from the start. I should also make sure she has taxi money on her. Taxis can get you out of anywhere. You should never leave the house without some money to get you home.

I rest my hand on the beautiful pillow. It's skilfully embroidered with rabbits playfully rendered in the medieval style of William de Morgan, a nineteenth-century potter. I know this because my mother enclosed the historical references of her artistic inspiration with the pillow for me to study. Knowing the history of a present is essential to fully appreciating it. In the midst of the one-woman environmental disaster that now covers my bedroom floor, I am aware of how my mother's presence fills the room. I reflect on how different I am from her: I reuse wrapping paper when I wrap my presents. It seems like a huge waste of paper to use it only once. I dutifully sort through the paper, box and padding and start packing them away.

I don't mean to be critical. I have learned a great deal from opening my mother's presents over the years. I still love the moments of anticipation.

I savour them, in fact. I prefer the beginning of a race to the finish line, the night before a holiday to the day itself and the taste of unspoken-words just before they emerge from my mouth. In these moments, when anything is possible, I feel the future stretch brightly ahead of me like the last ribbon of gift wrap just before the present is revealed — perfect and untouched. I also appreciate ritual, the announcement that the object has a greater meaning than its bare presence might imply. Ritual dresses up a moment; lets you take a long look at it arriving and departing. I still have this vague sensation that nothing is truly significant if it happens too quickly.

When I was a child I would tear at presents wildly with my fingers and never minded getting paper cuts. My mother once said that *I* was a gift she gave to herself. I was adopted by her and my father — a status I have enjoyed throughout my life. I was *chosen*, not born, into the family, she told me. Selected like a gift, not thrust upon my parents by the accident of biology.

My mother has a fondness for double-sided gift wrap, so that the brilliant colours can be seen from the outside and also as the present is laid bare — still perfect in its nest of wrapping paper, where it can be admired for a fleeting, satisfied moment. With all that this wrapping is meant to commu-nicate, I wonder what it has been like for my mother to watch me, over the years, tear it apart before her eyes. I have liberated toys, clothes, books and pillows from their peaceful, beautiful bondage and exposed them to the dusty world of ragged edges that catch and tear most everything that passes. It's hard to find this kind of paper these days, and shipping my presents across a continent has necessitated some further changes in how my mother wraps things. Still, she continues to send me presents, and I still struggle with unwrapping them.

↝ REGAN McCLURE is a tortured writer who keeps avoiding her writing while being employed as a Web site designer for non-profit organizations. She is currently taking a year off so she can focus on avoiding the writing full-time.

☛ KAREN WOODMAN

I WENT TO THE FIRST CLIT LIT. There were friends from my writing workshop in the audience. I read a story about waiting for my laundry to dry in Vancouver. It wasn't very sexy. A few years later, I found myself back after I had moved away from the city. It cured my off-kilter, homesick feelings.

Coal

smoke ring tilted silence
lips slow curl
ice cube tinkle
criss-cross rain
over slick black windows

lip to lip
thumb to palm spelling
heartbeat lullaby
sound to song
chant curses
change names
mark bodies like sheets of poetry

who knew you had so much to say
spitting diamonds
infra-red
between streetcars
along the rails
flames so quiet
dangerous like held breath
cut on every corner.

281

KAREN WOODMAN

Alberta

Chefs chop and coffee grinds churn a rhythm,
repetitive like the blues but with the face of a woman
who collects dead things.
She grieves, measuring herself against centuries
of women just trying to utter their own names
with hands neatly folded or scarred and torn,
moving, in conversation, or slowly inside herself,
playing hooky
her surface, diamond etched
the lines around her mouth and eyes
tracing other loves.

A river gushing trickles into crevices along the way,
curling along inside itself
until whirlpools collide along a shifting surface
A scientist wants to know what lies below this surface,
forever shifting form. What concept do faint outlines suggest?
How will the river become the scientist's idea?
Where do rivers flow inside the mind of a scientist?

There is nature wherever tears fall.
In some neighbourhoods we weep in fresh air.

Surfaces reveal themselves without even trying
a scent, a stare, a frozen silence.

The path on this hill has been made
from centuries of water falling.

paths often lead toward water
tonight, where my foot falls becomes my path
and every time the wind hits my face
I am reminded of infinite direction.
It will become an outline,
a picture of a place I visited.

Tonight, lovers are meeting on lines
strung through continents,
beneath oceans, reflecting off satellites.

Outside the temperature is dropping
and no one is certain how long it will take to get home.
A woman writes at her desk. She is working late.
Her pen drifts off the page and she draws the head of a dog
on a book of matches. Snow is falling.
The blizzard may shut down the city.

She wants to change into something soft and a little used,
something that reminds her of a war.
elegant, that feels expensive but is really very cheap.
something that has been worn before.

She remembers a woman wearing printed flowers whispering,
"I always come up smellin' like a rose,"

Northern Alberta open fields where she imagined she could see forever.
Mustard coloured canola, popcorn clouds and a horizon,
where, if she stared long enough she sensed a curve on either side,
as if the planet were showing its contours.
"I miss you," she heard.

Distance,
an arduous journey, or something else
romantic, for no reason. A gasp or the flickering wink of recognition
from someone you hoped to see.

Romantic nonsense words in unfamiliar languages
an absurd arrangement without country, roots or etymology
sounds that are just passing through, delighted with conversation.

KAREN WOODMAN is a visual artist and writer.
Her work appears in *Queen Street Quarterly*, *The
Church–Wellesley Review*, *Pottersfield Portfolio*, *She's
Gonna Be, Hot & Bothered 2 & 3* (Arsenal Pulp
Press) and *Queer View Mirror 2* (Arsenal Pulp Press).
Karen has lived in Vancouver and Toronto and now
makes her home in Ottawa.

☛ ROEWAN CROWE

WRITING HASN'T COME EASY to me. Divining words to then craft into poems or stories has come slow. After getting my first poem published in 1994, I hid for several years, terrified to be so public. I'm finally at the point where I can say I want to be able to belt out the stories that are still wrapped up tight in silence. I grew up in a house without books, a house where much remained unspoken. There were lots of stories though, the most intriguing being the ones that I knew were there but hadn't yet heard in words, the ones that shaped my life, that I could only hear hints of as I snuck out of bed into the hallway and listened to my parents' whispers late into the night. Reclaiming my wild imagination and finding written and visual languages to express these stories has been a vital resuscitation. I'm drawn to tell the forbidden stories, the hard ones, the stories you find when you root around. Stories people really don't want to hear. Stories folks say aren't any of your business. Stories that sound like an old-style country song.

Now writing is a way for me to connect my present queer femme self to my university-educated self to my working-class self. I am estranged from my birth family; I was booted out for being queer, and I think, for betraying them by going to school and learning things my folks didn't care to understand. I miss them something terrible, so now I like to write about people like them, to get closer. I also lost connection with my working-class sensibilities when I travelled through the university. Somehow I was convinced that if I was formally educated (that's Dr. Crowe), I was no longer working class. Thank goodness for writers and professors who never drew those distinctions. What remains true is that most of what I have worked hard to claim — to write, make art, think about the unspoken things, express my queer femme self — has taken me further and further away from my family and my roots — working-class, prairie, rural, small town.

Clit Lit was the first place I read my stories; it was the first public space where I felt able to take all of myself. Queer. Working-class. Angry.

Grieving. Formally educated. Thoughtful. Political. Bold. Full of feeling. It was tremendously powerful to enter a cultural space where I didn't have to check certain kinds of experiences at the door. The first time I read at Clit Lit I was absolutely terrified. It was exhilarating. I felt energized. I knew there was an audience that was willing to listen to my work, to be with the rough edges, and to find, hopefully, some part of themselves in my writing. It was there that I claimed my complicated history and began to say out loud: I write. It wasn't until I was onstage, reading my work, that I started to feel like I might actually *be* a writer.

The poem entitled "Johnny & Cher, I Cut my Hair" explores the complicated relationships between my queer femme self and my working-class self, particularly in relation to my Dad. The prose piece "Empty Pies and Stones" is taken from the novel I'm presently working on. It's the story of Fox and her search for justice on the prairies. Fox is an artist, obsessed with Hollywood westerns and old-style country music. Fox has been blown around in her life like a tumbleweed, and the wind has finally blown her up against a story from her past. One day while roaming the streets of Toronto the wind whispers to her, "GO west." She travels west from Toronto to small-town Saskatchewan, unravelling (and deconstructing) stories of the west as she travels, until she encounters Grace, and a story from rural Saskatchewan. The story that is developing is one of love, racism, terror and redemption. It's a celebration of rural working-class culture — truck drivers, cowgirls, trailer courts, rural landscapes and small towns. It is also a critique of it, uncovering messages of judgement and hatred. I'm writing myself a place, telling the stories that I long to hear. Clit Lit was where it all started.

Empty Pies and Stones

I broke Jimmy's heart when I wouldn't leave with him to Regina. Truth is it broke mine too. Not that I ever had a soft, open heart. After all, our beating hearts are tough muscles and that's a good thing, the way we kick 'em around like rocks on the side of the road. My heart? It's been a stone boulder for as long as I can remember. About the size of a large man's fist clenched tight. Smooth and grey on the outside. An ordinary stone. Somehow Jimmy found his way inside my boulder heart. And when he left, when I sent him away, I raised a sledge hammer to my stone heart and broke it into a hundred jagged little pieces. Like a white plate shattering as it falls to the floor when the diner gets busy and I've got my mind on too many things. But as far as I'm concerned, hearts don't get broke by accident. Sometimes when I'm outside, working hard, digging up the toughened earth I call my garden or hauling out the storm windows in preparation for fall, I can feel the edges of those sharp stones pressing up against my lungs. Those gravelly edges threaten to puncture a hole straight through my chest. Makes it hard for me to breathe, my heart hurting like that, sharp and constant, Jimmy with me all the time. Guess you could say he took my breath away.

Jimmy came to this small town with a dream of owning land. He wanted to try his hand at growing things. Maybe try soybeans, a few of his favourite vegetables, cabbage, bok choy, snow peas. He thought the diner might earn him enough money to do that. But the Tumbleweed Grill didn't take off here like other Chinese-food restaurants had in small towns. Oh, there were a few regulars, most of them potash miners, who'd stop in before or after they'd been underground. And on Sundays, every now and again, Jimmy's flapjacks lured families inside after a morning in church. The booths would fill up with starched white shirts and proper skirts. Everyone looking restrained and uncomfortable until pancakes smothered with butter and maple syrup touched their tongues. Pretty soon collars unbuttoned, sleeves rolled up, gloves and hats were off, resting beside one another on the table. Kids ran about, leaving behind them a trail of sticky fingerprints.

But there weren't enough Sundays when folks felt charitable enough to do any more than pay the bills and feed ourselves. Jimmy said it was bad luck, but we both knew different. Most people from around here wouldn't eat at the Tumbleweed Grill. We each shouldered the blame, and never spoke of it. I told Jimmy if he wanted to make a go of it, he would have to live a careful life, and shacking up with me was reckless, given the life I'd lived and the mistakes I'd made. I certainly wasn't the respectable White woman that would help Jimmy in his business. There was a catch. No woman who worked with Jimmy at the diner could possibly be respectable. Most folks from these parts hold on tight to their beliefs like they were the last days of summer, and they thought White women shouldn't work in a Chinese-run business, not even a woman like me. I wish Jimmy and I would have talked about all that. Guess that's spilled milk.

So one day when Jimmy came home from his monthly trip to the city, his social trip — a little bit of gambling and visiting with his friends — it came as no surprise that he wanted us to close down the diner and move to Regina. One of the partners at the Lucky Dragon was leaving and they'd be happy to have Jimmy join them. Maybe then we would earn enough money to get the land Jimmy dreamed of night and day. But how could I leave this small town with my big secret?

I first met Jimmy just days after my girl died. I was looking for a place to stay. I never told him what happened. Shame and fear sealed me up tight. Made me afraid to leave these few buildings we call a town. He let me stay with him at the restaurant. For the first while I slept in Jimmy's room at the back of the diner and he slept on a cot in the kitchen. I earned my keep. I was a hard worker, just like Jimmy, and I offered him my labour. I peeled potatoes, served food and coffee, wiped tables, baked pies. Jimmy, he did everything. Cooked and cleaned, chopped and baked, peeled and scrubbed. Things I'd never seen a man do before. I hadn't ever seen a man so competent and at home in a kitchen. Heck, I'd never seen a man in the kitchen before 'cept if he was filling his face and making a mess! The first time I ever felt at ease with another person was when the two of us were busy there. I figure that's why I decided to stay with Jimmy, because of how I felt inside when we stood together, working. And the food Jimmy cooked. Best food I ever ate. Sometimes when I'm lying awake in the middle of the night or playing a game of solitaire, I'll have a craving so strong for my favourite dish. Jimmy used to make it special for me — garlic crab and egg baked in the oven. Jimmy never made fun of me or pointed out that every time he put the live crabs into the steaming hot stainless-steel pot on the stove I'd disappear. I'd head into the main part of the diner, looking for my smokes or busying myself with something. He knew when to leave well enough alone. He was kind that way, though sometimes I curse him for that, wish he would have pushed me to talk. I can't blame him though. Each time he'd leave for Regina I'd say, "Who'd look after the diner if we both went? We can't afford to close our doors for me to go off gallivanting with you and your friends." I'd be at the sink, doing dishes, he'd chuckle, come around the back of me and slide his hands around my waist. Hold me, just like that, quiet. I can still feel his hands lingering 'round my waist, taste crab on my tongue. Sure am blessed he was in my life. Not much left from those days, except Jimmy's ghost hands and this gravel-pit heart of mine. When the tears won't stop falling or when my body's held tight by rage I bake pies. Just like my Mom taught me. Ask anyone from around here and they'll tell you I make the best pies. No contest. So, when I'm a wreck with feelings like that I bake empty pies. I punch the pastry dough down 'til my knuckles are red and raw. Lord I make a mess, the kitchen floor and cupboards covered in flour. I roll the pastry hard into the table, slam down the bread pin, roll it over and over again. When it feels right, I slap the shells into pie plates. I hastily slice the edges off, and then pinch them real hard. Throw them in the oven 'til they're baked. Empty without any filling. I pull them out of the oven with my bare hands, just like my mother and my grandmother used to do. At first it hurt like hell but after a while I got used to it and now I don't feel a thing. My kitchen fills up with toughened, empty pies. I throw them away when they start getting dusty. Not too long ago Jimmy had a heart attack, struck him down dead right out front of the Lucky Dragon. The day I got the news, from one of Jimmy's close friends, I went into town to the co-op store and bought up all the flour they had. Nothing strange about it. No one ever said anything about my empty pies for all those years, so when I walked into the co-op with my eyes red from crying, all shaky from being up all night, no one said a word. Except Lloyd, his voice reaching me from over the counter. "Baking pies today, Grace? Let me help you with that flour." We slung those bags of flour over our shoulders and carried them out to Lloyd's truck like we were carrying babies. Lloyd and I rode in silence and he left me with all those bags of flour in my kitchen. I must have baked a hundred empty pies. I stayed up for two days straight until the time when I knew they'd be laying Jimmy's body into the ground. That's when I baked Jimmy's favourite. Sour cream and raisin.

Some might say I'm still punishing myself for what happened to my babygirl. Don't you feel sorry for me, I allow myself small pleasures. I bake my pies, play solitaire, and in the summer there's gardening to fill my time. Not all my pies are empty. I still make pies for folks around here, especially when someone's getting married or for a family reunion. And I sell single pies at the co-op store. See here? I've got a picture of Jimmy facing east to open fields so he can watch the sunrise and spring arrive. Sometimes I take him right outside with me. Set him down on a pile of well-worked dirt so he can be near me while I'm down on my knees, thinning carrots, picking weeds and piling stones around me.

Johnny & Cher, I Cut My Hair

She was young when she learned to say, "Hi, I'm Johnny Cash,"
then she'd hum from the deep of her throat,
swing her imaginary guitar around from the back of her.
Play *some grief, some joy, memories are made of this*
rock her guitar back around and take a bow.
She'd be dressed in black. Just like Johnny on the TV.

Johnny had been through hard times.
Years of hard times.
Even though he never did time,
he knew what the inside of a jail looked like.
He knew about the jails we construct for ourselves, hard and unforgiving.
He fought for freedom from steel bars around our hearts.

Late at night, while she was painting her nails candy apple red,
like the pickup truck of her dreams,
Johnny sang to the working-class girl in her,
to the trailer-court farm girl, riding horses skidoos and motorcycles.
She's driving into the night, driving real hard,
daring to tame the wild and angry with her fine femme smile.

Johnny sang to this femme dressed in black,
sang to her when she'd be hanging around construction sites in the city,
watching gravel trucks and front end loaders,
through wired windows,
straining to hear the voice of her dad.

She'd catch a few words, and
suddenly she'd be feeling a little more at ease in this big city,
a slight pang for her prairie home takes her back —

— Back to riding in her dad's pickup truck on a Friday afternoon.
Happily father and daughter bumpity bump bump
down washboard gravel roads,
dust dancing behind them, windows cranked up tight.
There's a new highway taking form beside them as they drive along,
a hum of big equipment plowing through their small town.

She loved the earth movers most of all.
They were the biggest thing she'd ever seen.
Huge and impressive. Yellow like the cat her dad operated.
Sometimes when she'd visit him on a job site,
he'd let her shift the gears.
He read her quiet mind, and said,
"You know you could drive one of those earth movers if you wanted to."
She smiled at his belief in her.
Wrapped it around her heart and held it there,
as she slammed shut the green door. Watched his Ford drive away.

Paper bag in one hand, filled with pjs and a change of clothes.
She waved good-bye with the other.
Soon she's sitting with her best friend, mesmerized by Cher.
Each with hairbrush in hand,
gently stroking their locks,
waiting for their hair to grow long.
Just like Cher on the TV,
a scamp, a tramp, and a bit of a vamp, she was a v-a-m-p. Vamp.
They giggled. Pressed polished fingers into backs,
showing how long their hair had grown since the last week.

Years later, her hair nearly long as Cher's
she watches it fall to the floor, clipped and swept away.
Whispered words of a butch lover linger,

dykes don't have long hair.
So here she is now, dressed in black,
wrestling the diesel femme in her back.
Wishing her hair was as long as Cher's
now she's singing a new song by Johnny Cash.

I'm gonna break,
I'm gonna break,
I'm gonna break my rusty cage
and run.

↝ ROEWAN CROWE recently moved from Toronto
to Winnipeg for love and art. She's currently crafting
her first novel — unravelling tales of the Wild West
to reveal a prairie story. She dreams about Gillian
Welch beltin' out an old-style working-class country
tune to Grace, one of the main characters in her
book. Roewan writes, makes art and teaches women's
studies at the University of Manitoba.

●◆ ANNA CAMILLERI

I HAD JUST FINISHED WRITING a first draft of "Girls Run Circles" hours before I read it at Clit Lit. I had prepared other material for the night, but I set that aside. "Girls Run Circles" was a departure for me — I had never been so successful at just letting the tide of images and sounds pull into the writing, rather than being led by my dreaded editor self — a word-eating monster who disregards all that is magical. Writing "Girls Run Circles" was pure ecstasy — the ecstatic being both deeply pleasurable *and* painful. I couldn't type fast enough, and I couldn't stop vibrating.

This is how I began when I stepped onto the twelve-inch riser-stage, still vibrating. I pride myself on being prepared, being polished, and I let all of this go. I told the audience that I had just finished writing the piece I was going to read, but it wasn't meant as a disclaimer. It was an invitation to workshop. I wanted to know whether my feeling about this poem was personal (and not necessarily relevant to others) or if the audience would really connect. By the time I had finished reading I had my answer. The audience was visibly moved. Later, I went on to collaborate with Lynn Phillips: her musical composition and arrangement and my vocal stylings and direction created a performance that had voice, form and heart. "Girls Run Circles" then became part of a full-length show called *Too Close To Fire*, which Taste This — a decidedly queer interdisciplinary performance troupe — toured to eleven cities in Canada and the U.S.

Girls Run Circles

Two girls run circles around the metal bus stop.
The taller girl, the one with rows of neat braids tied with ribbon,
is making chomping, chewing sounds — intermittent growls.
The other girl, flushed cheeks candy apple red,
squeals high pitch at the horror of being bitten.

Delighting, sparking, spinning
in the exhilaration of this high speed chase,
cutting through the wind like silver fish.
Round and round.
Summer vacation, full-sun-sidewalk merry go round.

They swim in each other's girl,
In each other's laughter,

In the high stakes — this is all that matters game — of predator, prey.
They are complete and reckless
and there is nothing else but the belly of their joy.

I want to take them by their small, sweaty hands,
sit on a stoop
littered with bubble gum wrappers and cigarette butts.
Tell them what I know
and hope my words may offer some protection.

Give them a story that is confounding, contradictory
and truer than the stories they will hear.

Sugar and spice and everything nice
A diamond is a girl's best friend
The world is your oyster.

Give them a story that is more true,
Most true
True blue.

I would say — you will lose yourselves.
Life is about finding much of who we once were.
And there are lots of lost girls who eventually
find something of themselves again.

I would tell them
you are precious and special and beautiful,
Not because you are girls, good girls, pretty girls
— just because you are.

See girls — I would say,
You will be celebrated for being pretty,
the rest of you will remain unseen.
This will be expected of you on your saddest days.
You will be picked apart and berated and judged
for not being the right kind of girl
By the time you are eleven jenny craig will be your role model,
and you will feel you are the only remiss, lonely girl,
The only lonely girl in the world

You will writhe in the unbearable tightness of your skin.
Yet, you will want the eyes of strangers on you.
You will learn to hold their gaze and
drop your eyes to the ground when you feel consumed.
You will revel and repulse in those words
"You are a pretty girl,
a good girl."

Those words, a capital investment
in building a legion of broken girls
will send you into a snowstorm at midnight to a seven eleven
where you will buy chips, pop, chocolate bars and licorice
curl in front of the television set.
Tell yourself you ain't worth shit,
tell yourself you are unlovable
because your father ignores you
your mother left
and kindnesses are far and few between.

You will try to wash all the dirt and angst and pain away
with anything that offers some relief —
Haze of toilet bowl blow
Tequila shooters, diets
Food to wash it all down
Sex with someone — anyone
Sex for love, sex for affirmation.

You will learn to trade everything you have and are
for a little bit of peace.
You will try to be what people want you to be.
A nice girl.
A pleasant, polite, unobtrusive, non-threatening girl.
A girl who says "no thank you" and "yes sir" without hesitation
A modest girl with no obvious sexual or self expression.

You will try to be what they want,
Scouring through the hallways of pop culture for tips.
And discover it is never enough.
Discover there is a false bottom.

I would ask them
To remember the day in the blazing sun,
the day they played catch around the pole.
Remember the heat in your body,

the grit on your hands,
the sweat trickling down the back of your neck,
the sticky orange around your mouth from the freezie you slurped back?

Your laughter filled the streets — your streets.
Remember the quarter you found
In the sidewalk crack you stepped on but were trying to jump over
Playing hop scotch all the way to the corner store
and the jaw breaker you bought and passed back and forth,
sticky mouth to sticky mouth
until it was just a little bump of sweet?
Remember strangers looking at you disapprovingly for your recklessness
and how you just didn't care what anyone thought?
Remember.

And if they were to tell me they had forgotten everything,
I would say, make it up girls.
Give yourself a story that you need —
even if it's confounding, contradictory.
Imagine a love that is so fierce, it brings thunder to its knees.
Imagine that love for yourself
and trust yourself to share it as you see fit.

I will tell them life is about finding who we once were.
And the other half,
is about making it up as we go along —
from bits of dream, longing and the imagination of a child.
from bits of dream, longing and the imagination of a child.
from bits of dream, longing and the imagination of a child.

➥ **ANNA CAMILLERI** is a Toronto-based award-winning writer, performer, curator, and producer. She co-founded the interdisciplinary performance troup Taste This, with whom she has toured Canada and the U.S. extensively. Taste This published *Boys Like her: Transfictions* (Press Gang) to critical and popular acclaim. Anna is currently writing her first novel, *Red Herring in the Ring*, and her first play, *Red Luna*, and she is co-creator and co-editor of *Brazen Femme: Queering Femininity*, an anthology to be published by Arsenal Pulp Press in Fall 2002. Anna can be contacted at redeye@interlog.com

●◁ CAITLIN FISHER

I CHOSE THIS PIECE for my first reading at Clit Lit. What I remember best about that night was that the room was absolutely packed. People were sitting in a wide semi-circle on the floor in front of the stage and there were lots of cross-legged men in the front row. The audience was terrific, really attentive, leaning in a little bit…I could hear a few beer bottles rattling in the back but the room was mostly quiet. I paused for a second after the line "I am a quarry girl, a motherless girl, an English girl, a kissing girl" and when I started the next line, "The boy we are chasing is tearing away on foot," all those guys in front started laughing so hard. I loved that. At some levels this is an uncomfortable piece, I think, but there are still lots of places to laugh and the idea that the chase was understood as humorous really worked with and against what happens next to that boy. I've read this piece in public before, but sadly, no one ever laughed at that line or helped me to set up the ending quite so well as did that Clit Lit audience.

I later made this piece the central tale in a hypermedia novella. Actually, two or three other pieces I read for the first time in public at Clit Lit are also included in the work. The novella, *These Waves of Girls*, won the 2001 International Fiction Prize for electronic literature in New York.

Vanessa

Vanessa. Here she is at three, up ahead in the laneway, thin hair shining down that back and I'm chasing her, in a line of children all trailing toys. The Fisher-Price phone slows me down. But I was always faster than Vanessa and I could always always catch her.

At six she had an attractive, wandering hazel eye. I would brush the hair off her face, her earnest hands trying to stop me.

With Vanessa things happened. All sorts of lessons that left metal tastes in my mouth. In our mouths as we kissed. She was born in Canada, England on her lips, her accent strong against my tongue. We went to different schools. Her friends were not my friends. And there was need, in her hunting pack, to keep pace.

Vanessa had always roamed shopping malls alone; quarries. Secretly I harboured large fears in her adultless world…though not in my own sweet terrain where I could run faster, confidently, could wrestle and hold and there was no child who could beat me, not older, not younger, not even my brother's friends, boys in their teens whom I would set upon like a feral child and they would hold back because I was a child — and because they were weak.

At Vanessa's house our roles reversed and often I held back. I just didn't get her mother sleeping in the bathroom, door shut (years later I would spot Evelyn in a London department store, recognizing that hand I saw between the hall and the bathroom: she is a dream, she has an English accent, and she sleeps and sleeps because she is tired and smart. She forgets to make up good games for children to play at parties — my mother always makes up good games — instead Evelyn makes us all pull those toys around and around the house and even at three I think — "This stinks!" But there is Vanessa up front with that hair. And she's my friend. And her mother is crying).

So. At ten. With Vanessa. I am a quarry girl, a motherless girl, an English girl, a kissing girl.

The boy we are chasing is tearing away on foot but we have bicycles and soon we've blocked the exit to the quarry. He retreats to his bike. Wary. Two...Three...He's off. I watch him...his thin calf, the back of that flying bicycle, his eye, scared, as he turns. I feel all of our girl eyes looking in that one direction, giddy, in pursuit. We girls are a line of warmth and when we see the flutter and swallow in that boy's face, the left foot slipping from the pedal, his skidding, the unforced errors, we are a burst of electricity. We hold back, not wanting to catch him just yet. We move with our bikes, with his fear. And the weird thing is, we're silent. I think back and the only sounds I hear are tires on gravel and a thin wheeze up front.

Boys don't frighten any of us. I know this though I don't know any of the other girls' names...I've never seen these girls before but I do know that at all our different schools the girls are smarter and bigger and choose gangs and friends first and grab boys and kiss them and keep them corralled for the whole of recess. It's always been like this.

At ten we press our girl bodies against them and our tongues into them. And yes, we scratch — why not? We scratch and pull hair because all's fair and even if the boys turn, catch us in their small hands, and running, push us, momentum, not them, sending us to the ground, they can't hold us. And other boys might come running to see but never never in time because boys don't have weight, don't have the substance to keep us on the gravel, and by the time a crowd arrives our hands like hammers have forced the boys to release our legs strong thick-kneed dangerous have twisted them underneath us, and sometimes they are crying out by the time other defeated boys arrive. This is what I learn as I ride...we girls, we're reading each other's minds.

When I kiss Vanessa later, I wonder if those other girls taste me on their lips.

Where was I? Ten. Summer. With Vanessa, with her friends whose names I don't know. We find this boy. Pursue. Slowly, in unison, not speaking, we circle and stop him. And make him take down his pants, because he doesn't want to. And we pull away his bicycle. And this sandpit is huge and there are no adults anywhere in the world and one girl kicks sand. And then we are all kicking, kicking wild like every time we've been told not to kick sand has been stored up tight in our bodies waiting for this frenzy and yes, the sand does get in our eyes and I can't even remember seeing us doing it, just breathing and tearing. As the sand clears he's crumbling and sobbing and we seem so much bigger than he is, there, like a shell-less thing, his penis coated with gravel. And he wasn't supposed to be that small.

He's turned his head and pressed his face right into the dirt, lets out a scream. Muffled. Crazy.

two

three

four

five.

Then we're running scattered, scared too, and I taste blood in my mouth as I get back on my bike, like one of the other girls has bitten her cheek. We're off like bees, but not before our hands dip and clutch knowingly, return to our bodies holding his clothes. I'm sorry, we say, silent, it's only to slow you down.

I never see those girls again. Heading back to Vanessa's, I worry what her mother will say to us so flushed, so tingling, panting into the garage, clutching a small boy's shirt. But Evelyn is sleeping — again — and Vanessa and I go upstairs, take off our own shirts. It seems hours since I spoke. Vanessa pulls the bottom drawer right out of her dresser and in duet I place the shirt to the very back. She closes the door and I read her mind some more and put my fingers on her warm chest and slow her heart and she presses her lips against mine, sealing secrets. Her body is warm, beauty-marked, her hair thin across that lazy olive eye. I swallow hard and I am sorry, I would say something spell-breaking…but I can't feel what running boys feel, only this wave of girls.

◦ **CAITLIN FISHER**'s most recent publication, *These Waves of Girls*, a hypermedia novella exploring memory, girlhoods, cruelty, childhood play and sexuality, won the Electronic Literature Organization's 2001 International Award for Fiction. You can read it online at www.yorku.ca/caitlin/waves. Caitlin is founding editor of *j_spot: The Journal of Social and Political Thought*, a member of the Public Access art collective and an Assistant Professor of Fine Arts and Cultural Studies at York University, Toronto. She is a member of the Stern Writing Mistresses.

✒ ZOE WHITTALL

IN SOME WAYS I THINK OF CLIT LIT as a very dyke event: I've cruised, schmoozed, made out in the bathroom, left early to avoid ex-girlfriends, got drunk and said inappropriate things, showed off and shied away. In some ways, I think of the series as primarily a literary event — one with a kind and engaged audience. Clit Lit allowed me to meet and network with other writers I might not have otherwise met. I've written pieces with the express purpose of reading on that stage. I've tried out experiments, received some laughs, gained confidence in my writing. I've been transfixed by my fellow readers and inspired to write again after months of writer's block.

305

ZOE WHITTALL

The Money Shot

for Alan Kaufman

I would not have liked to kiss
Jack Kerouac
I don't care that
Jimmy Dean *the human ashtray*
Wrote a poem called
"Ode to a Tijuana Toilet"

these are not my outlaw heroes

I can't be shocked by the
typed word *cunt*
descriptions of drunk nights
slapping poet dicks
down on the bar

Cause I have seen a thousand money shots
And it takes more every time

Jack Kerouac
Spent most of his life
drunk on his mother's couch

not on the road
to my literary revolution

ZOE WHITTALL has published a book of poetry, *The Best 10 Minutes of Your Life* (McGilligan, 2001), and has prose featured in *Ribsauce*, a collection of women writers from Montreal (Véhicule Press). Interviews with Whittall appear in *Impure: Reinventing the Word* (Conundrum, 2001). She has work forthcoming in *Brazen* (Arsenal Pulp Press).

BENT ON WRITING

GRAFFITTI PAGES